North to Canada

North to Canada

Men and Women Against the Vietnam War

&

James Dickerson

PRAEGER

Westport, Connecticut
London

Library of Congress Cataloging-in-Publication Data

Dickerson, James.
    North to Canada : men and women against the Vietnam War / James
Dickerson.
        p.   cm.
    Includes bibliographical references and index.
    ISBN 0–275–96211–3 (alk. paper)
    1. Vietnamese Conflict, 1961–1975—Protest movements—United
States.   2. Americans—Canada.   3. Vietnamese Conflict, 1961–1975—
Conscientious objectors.   4. Vietnamese Conflict, 1961–1975—Draft
resisters—United States.   5. Canada—Emigration and immigration.
6. United States—Emigration and immigration.   I. Title.
DS559.62.U6D53   1999
959.704′31—dc21   98–23568

British Library Cataloguing in Publication Data is available.

Library of Congress Catalog Card Number: 98–23568
ISBN: 0–275–96211–3

First published in 1999

Praeger Publishers, 88 Post Road West, Westport, CT 06881
An imprint of Greenwood Publishing Group, Inc.

Printed in the United States of America

The paper used in this book complies with the
Permanent Paper Standard issued by the National
Information Standards Organization (Z39.48–1984).

10 9 8 7 6 5 4 3 2

**To Ina,
with thanks**

Contents

Acknowledgments

I would like to thank the following for their help with this project: Michael Wolfson, Andrew Collins, Charles Sudduth, Diane Francis, Oliver Drerup, Jim Thomas, Patrick Grady, Richard Deaton, Rick Abraham, my editor Heather Ruland Staines, and Whitman Strong; Ed Frank and Cathy Evans at the Mississippi Valley Collection, University of Memphis; the Jean and Alexander Heard Library at Vanderbilt University; the Memphis and Shelby County Public Library; Mike Parrish at the Lyndon Johnson Library and Museum; the editors at the *Ottawa Citizen*; special thanks to David Rice and Debra Laframboise; Ross Fenemore, Reg Barrett, Eleanor Wolfson, Andrea Wolfson, Lynne Wolfson, my mother; and last, but not least, the warm-hearted and generous people of Canada.

Introduction

Vietnam. For those of my generation, the word hangs in our consciousness like the heavy, velvet backdrops that adorned the stages of our high school auditoriums. Over the years, dramas have come and gone in our lives, parading before the backdrop with pathos, bravado, and occasional good humor, but always the curtain was there, looming in the background, an ominous reminder of something dark and forbidding.

March 29, 1998, marked the twenty-fifth anniversary of the withdrawal of American troops from Vietnam. It hardly seems possible that it has been over thirty years since the Vietnam War was at its zenith. At the time, if you had asked those who fought against the war—and those who fought in the war—if the day would ever come when it would cease to matter, you would have been greeted with derisive laughter. The Vietnam War, whether you were for it or against it, *is* our generation: It is who we are.

The fact that Vietnam had fallen out of the popular vocabulary by the late 1990s, the fact that war resisters and veterans alike have been not only forgotten but ignominiously ignored, is not surprising when you consider that most Americans who are today in their twenties and thirties have no memory of that era, even if it was one of the most traumatic periods in American history. Those who do have clear memories are now in their late forties and fifties, a sizable segment of the population, but hardly one that fits the *sell, sell, sell* demographics of today's youth-oriented news and entertainment media.

Only a small percentage of the Americans who were eligible for the draft in the 1960s and early 1970s were targeted by the Selective Service System for induction into the armed forces. Of the nearly sixty million men and women who were of draft age, more than half were exempted because of their gender (no women allowed). Of the twenty-seven million men of draft age, nearly nine million enlisted, according to Professor Loren Baritz, author of the Vietnam War history *Backfire*, leaving a pool of eighteen million men, mostly teenagers, eligible for the draft.

Of that eighteen million, only 2,215,000 were actually drafted. Approximately fifteen million men avoided the draft—and the risk of combat in Vietnam—by seeking educational and employment deferments, health exemptions, and assignments to cushy positions in the National Guard. The most famous "dodger" to take the latter route was former Vice President Dan Quayle of Indiana. The most famous "dodger" to receive an educational exemption is probably President Bill Clinton. Actually it is that group that most logically qualifies for the "dodger" label, since of the three groups facing the draft—those who resisted and went to Canada, those who entered the armed forces, and those who received deferments and exemptions—only the latter group "dodged" the issue by seeking refuge in legal technicalities. There are important distinctions even within this group. Quayle and Clinton were both "dodgers," at least technically, but their motivations for avoiding the draft were at polar opposites. Before seeking refuge in the national guard, Quayle never expressed public opposition to the Vietnam War. In fact, in later years, he said he had supported the war. Clinton, by contrast, was very much opposed to the war and expressed that opposition at every opportunity.

Approximately 700,000 men were drafted and refused service or submitted to induction only to later desert. The maximum penalty for refusing or evading induction was a fine of ten thousand dollars and five years in a federal penitentiary. The maximum fine was seldom imposed, since most offenders were teenagers just out of high school or in their early twenties and just out of college (and had no money), but federal judges were not so shy about imposing the maximum prison sentence. According to figures compiled by the Justice Department and the Defense Department and presented to the House of Representatives Judiciary Committee during its March 1974 hearings on amnesty, here is the breakdown for the years between 1963 and 1974:

- 206,775 men were referred to United States Attorneys for prosecution (with 9,167 men actually arrested and convicted of draft law violations).
- more than 500,000 men and women were classified as deserters (with nearly 4,000 actually captured and prosecuted for desertion).
- 28,661 deserters were still at large when the figures were compiled in 1974.

Not included in these figures are statistics on the men and women who went to Canada or Sweden in opposition to the war in Vietnam. The exact number will probably never be known, since neither the United States nor Canada compiled statistics on war resisters. Since the United States government consistently provided figures throughout the Vietnam War that were later proved to be inflated or deflated, which ever was advantageous to the government's political goals, the figures on resisters provided to the House of Representatives should probably be considered minimal figures on those who resisted the war effort. The actual figures are probably much higher.

Nonetheless, it is possible to arrive at a reasonably accurate approximation. Canadian government figures compiled by Immigration Statistics Canada show that 191,522 American men and women emigrated to Canada between 1965 and the end of 1973. Those are the "legal" immigrants who applied for landed immigrant status, which provided them with work permits, health care, and other benefits. Not included are the thousands of war exiles, particularly the deserters, who went to Canada and lived normal lives without ever making their presence known to the government. In the 1960s and 1970s, it was possible to go to Canada and live and work for years as a tourist or visitor without ever having that status challenged by Canadian authorities.

With over 200,000 draft evasion referrals to United States Attorneys, an official immigration of approximately the same number of Americans to Canada, and approximately 500,000 desertions, a safe estimate for the number of men and women who went to Canada during the Vietnam War would probably be 500,000, with women comprising about half that total. That would make it one of the largest mass exoduses in history of Americans emigrating from their homeland, with the migration to Canada of an estimated 100,000 Americans loyal to Great Britain during the American Revolution qualifying for a distant second place.

North to Canada is the story of those estimated half million men and women who went to Canada in opposition to the war in Vietnam. The focus of this book is on six male draft resisters and one female draft resister who went to Canada and did not return to the United States, and one man who went and later returned. To a lessor extent, the stories of dozens of other war resisters are included throughout the text.

North to Canada also includes a history of the Vietnam War and of the progression of domestic politics that accompanied the war—all as seen through the eyes of the war resisters. What that means, with a few notable exceptions, is that the history of the Vietnam War offered in this book is presented as it was being written at the time American men and women were making decisions about supporting or opposing the war. A case can be made that the best way to understand those decisions is to see and hear what the resisters were seeing and hearing as events transpired.

The primary news sources used in this book were obtained from the publications that supplied that information to the resisters at the time the news was actually being made—*Newsweek, Time, Life, Look, Maclean's, Amex-Canada*, the *Toronto Star, Associated Press*, the *New York Times*, the *Los Angeles Times*, the *Washington Post*, the *Globe and Mail*, and the *New Republic* (the unofficial "bible" for war resisters in the early years). I have used no news sources that were later proved to be incorrect or erroneous.

Almost all of the statistics used in this book were obtained from U.S. and Canadian government sources and from recognized polling organizations. Throughout the war years, war resisters frequently questioned the accuracy of government figures, and in many instances, they were correct to do so, especially as they related to body counts in the war. Nonetheless, I have used official government figures throughout the book, since they provide the only consistent source of statistical data available to researchers.

Since American scholars and academics were writing extensively about the war as it was being fought, I have drawn heavily upon their research and insights as published during the years in question. For academic sources, I have relied most heavily on the works of Bernard Fall (Howard University), Hans J. Morgenthau (University of Chicago), and Loren Baritz (University of Massachusetts). Some of my secondary historical sources opposed the war; others supported the war. I have presented conflicting viewpoints whenever it seemed useful to understand a particular conflict or event. On a few occasions, I have drawn upon research undertaken in the years since the war ended, but that was done primarily to correct errors of reporting or scholarly analysis published during the war years.

Accordingly, the history of the war that appears in this book should not be viewed as revisionist or based on contemporary hindsight. Nor should the historical facts used in this book be viewed as skewed in favor of the resisters. I have used the most historically accurate information available. As a journalist with some thirty years experience, I view facts as sacrosanct and existing beyond the perimeters of viewpoint, and I have made a painstaking effort to verify the accuracy of all the facts presented in this book.

The interpretation of the facts presented in this book is another matter: Clearly, the purpose of the book is to allow Vietnam War resisters to have their say about the war and its aftermath. Some Americans won't like that, especially those of the World War II and Korean War generations, and I would be the first to say they are entitled to their opinions. Some of them will be angered that I have classified Vietnam veterans and war resisters together as joint victims of the war.

What I have learned in the twenty-five years since the war ended is that it is the veterans and the resisters who have the most in common, who have the most respect for each other's positions, and who have had the most intelligent dialogue over the years on the subject of the war. It is those individuals who were too old to be affected by the war, or those who received deferments or exemptions from the draft, who seem to have been taken out of the loop with the passage of time. Ironically, it is individuals in those two groups, those who had nothing personally at stake, who today seem to have the most intractable opinions about the war. That is the way it is now. That is the way it was then.

Some readers will be surprised that this book begins with the story of a female war resister. If you ever have occasion to speak to the woman in question, Diane Francis, you will understand why. All these years after the war has ended, she is still passionate about the cause and still proud to call herself a resister. There is a lingering misconception that opposition to the war, insofar as it lead to exile in Canada, was a male-only phenomenon.

Nothing could be further from the truth. Although they were not themselves subject to induction into the armed forces, women played a significant role in the draft resistance movement. They were equal partners in every sense of the word. Very few male draft resisters went to Canada without a woman at their side. Most of the women were every bit as dedicated to the cause as were the men they accompanied. Actually, some of the women who went to Canada went alone and did so because of their opposition to the war. They wanted to find a new life. There are even a few instances in which female soldiers deserted from the armed forces and went to Canada and Sweden because of their opposition to the war.

As I was writing this book, I received a letter from a woman in Canada who responded to a letter to the editor I had published in an Ontario newspaper. "I was most intrigued by your interest and request, and needless to say, experienced a flood of memories about our own experience," she wrote. "I use the term 'our' because it was a journey for my husband and me, through conflict, turmoil, shattered relationships,

soul searching, and sacrifice in order to live according to our conscience." Another woman wrote to take me to task for not mentioning
the contributions of women in a letter to the editor I had sent to an Ottawa newspaper: "Your book, which sounds very interesting, is ne-
glecting a portion of Americans or ex-Americans who are also here
because of the war in Vietnam—the women." She encouraged me to include women in the book.

That is a refrain I heard often while researching *North to Canada*, and
it is the reason why women have been included as equal partners in this
story of American resistance to the war in Vietnam. If that concept of-
fends war-resistance purists, or right-wing ideologues who have
painted a different picture of the anti-war movement, then so be it.

For twenty-five years, America has walked on tiptoes around the
subject of Vietnam. Those who were against the war and those who supported the war have been able to put aside their differences by agreeing
on catch-phrases to describe what happened in Vietnam. Everyone has
more or less agreed to call it a "mistake" and to refer to the "lessons" of
Vietnam—and then to move on to other things.

That was probably a good idea in the beginning. Passions were too
intense to allow for an intelligent discussion of the war. Everyone
needed time to heal. Everyone needed a good long rest. For most
Americans, especially those who were never asked to give their lives for
their country, that solution has worked fairly well. Today, they think
more about e-mail technology and stock market investments than they
do about Vietnam or its significance.

For two groups—the war exiles and those who served in Vietnam—the moratorium on discussing the war has been a disservice. It
has resulted in fewer medical and financial benefits to the vets than they
deserve, and for the exiles, it has resulted in a lack of closure. The fact
that Vietnam is still a living, breathing issue was confirmed by three dis-
turbing news stories in 1997 and 1998.

The first dealt with the arrest of forty-eight-year-old grandfather and
deserter Randall J. Caudill, who was apprehended in September 1997
during a routine border crossing in Washington State. Since deserting
from the Marine Corps in 1968, Caudill had lived in Winnipeg, Manitoba. That September, he had re-entered the United States after visiting
his daughter on Vancouver Island and was on his way back to Winnipeg
when he was apprehended. He was taken to Camp Pendleton, California, where he appeared before a court-martial judge, who asked him
why he had ever enlisted.

"At the time, to serve my country and go to Vietnam," he answered.

"So, why did you go to Canada," asked the judge.

"I was nineteen and not very pleased with the situation."

Caudill could have been sentenced to up to three years in prison. He pleaded guilty to desertion, but he did not receive a prison sentence. Instead, he was given a bad conduct discharge, making him just another one of the 500,000 or so to receive such discharges. Then he was allowed to return to his home in Canada.

The second story was an Associated Press dispatch with a Hanoi dateline that reported that new information obtained in 1997 indicated that more than three million Vietnamese had been killed in the war. That means that one out of two households lost at least one family member in the fighting. Said the Vietnam News Agency: "The findings show the losses in life are great and cause long aftermath."

The nearly sixty thousand[1] Americans who died in Vietnam is small compared to the three million Vietnamese who died, but the American losses came at a greater cost, for they came not in defense of a homeland, as occurred with the Vietnamese, but in defense of an ill-conceived government policy that allowed the American armaments industry to pocket, on average, $3,200,000 for every American solider killed in the war.

As Americans were dying in Vietnam—and others were being forced into exile in Canada and Sweden—a handful of Americans were using the political process to become wealthy at their expense. Defense profits are not the only issue of the war—it may not even be the major issue of the war—but, until that complex and elusive story is told, the critical "lessons" of Vietnam will remain unlearned.

Had that "lesson" been properly examined after Vietnam, there would have been no congressional debates and Justice Department investigations in recent years on campaign finance reform, for Congress would have felt compelled to enact laws to prohibit those associated with defense industries from influencing foreign policy with campaign contributions. The fact that lawmakers are still struggling with the issue is proof enough that they are nowhere near resolving it. Campaign finance reform would come quickly enough if the American public knew the truth about Vietnam.

The prospect of telling the fathers and mothers of the men who died in Vietnam that American businesses profited from those deaths, to the tune of about $160 billion, obviously appeals to no one. Today there are vets with mangled arms and legs who need work but can't get it, not even from the defense industries that profited from their sacrifices on the battlefield. To those who still believe that the war in Vietnam was about patriotism or defending the national interest or keeping the Chinese Communists out of Southeast Asia, that trade-off may be an acceptable cost of doing business.

To those who resisted the war, those who believed it was more about profits for the defense industry, racism, and abuse of power, it is not an acceptable trade-off. The irony of it is that twenty-five years after the war ended, the Chinese Communists today stand accused of trying to buy their way into the American political process with campaign contributions, adopting the same game plan used by the defense industries that once profited from Cold War opposition to their interests. Who can blame them? If that is the way Americans want to play the game, the Chinese would be foolish to not play by the rules. Sadly, those who would like to learn the "lessons" of Vietnam need look no further than the dictum "follow the money." The trail is still hot and well traveled.

In 1974, in testimony before a congressional subcommittee in support of her bill to provide unconditional amnesty to war resisters, Representative Bella Abzug of New York came close to addressing the issue when she referred to the corruption of the war effort. "I am angered and I am sickened when I consider all the tragedies of the war, but I do not direct my anger at those who refused to fight, who were themselves victimized," she said. "I direct my anger at the responsible parties—the warmakers in our government. They are the ones who dishonored our soldiers by using them and wasting them in a corrupt enterprise. If the government had listened to the draft resister, the demonstrator, and the deserter long ago, many lives would have been saved and much suffering averted."

North to Canada is dedicated to the belief that it is not too late to learn from the Vietnam experience.

NOTE

1. In 1974, one year after the last American troops were withdrawn from Vietnam, Congress set the number of American soldiers killed in action at 45,900. That number rose over the years to nearly 60,000 as Missing in Action figures and other deaths due to battlefield injuries were reconciled with the original figures. Readers will see escalating figures used in this book to reflect the numbers reported in the years in question.

1

1968

Diane Francis: Women Against the War

By the late 1990s, the Vietnam War resister with the highest profile in Canada was never drafted, was never even eligible for the draft, yet despite what would appear to be a technical disqualification, was in the first wave of Americans to seek asylum in Canada because of opposition to the war. Her name is Diane Francis. Her trek north began shortly after graduation from a Chicago-area high school in 1964. She had enrolled in the pre-med program at the University of Illinois and, at the age of eighteen, was preparing to pursue the American Dream when fate intervened in the form of a handsome twenty-one-year-old Englishman named Frank Francis.

Diane and Frank met during the summer of 1964. He was a graphic designer who had come to the United States the year before to find work after becoming disillusioned with the politics of his native England. He was granted a "green card," which allowed him to accept employment as an alien, but there was a condition attached—he was required to register for the U.S. draft. Since the draft board in Queens, New York, was closest to his point of entry into the United States, he registered there, not really giving much thought to it at the time.

Diane and Frank dated throughout the summer and into fall. By the end of the year, they realized they wanted to make a life together, but Frank's uncertain draft status hung over them like a dark cloud. At that time, Selective Service regulations specified that married registrants could be given a deferment, so in the spring of 1965, Diane withdrew from school and married Frank.

That April, student activists organized the first anti-war march on Washington to protest the Vietnam War. Hans Morgenthau, a leading political science academician at that time—his textbook, *Politics Among Nations*, was used in political science college courses across the country—wrote an article for the *New York Times Magazine* that was highly critical of American involvement in Vietnam.

No sooner did Diane and Frank get married than it was announced that the only married registrants who would get deferments would be those with children. Diane and Frank considered that option, but at ages twenty-two and nineteen, they decided they were much too young to have children. Since they were both opposed to the war in Vietnam, and Frank had decided that going into the American armed forces was out of the question, they investigated all their options.

"We tried the reserves, but there were long waiting lists," said Diane. "We realized we had to get out of the country." Frank did not want to live in Britain again, so they obtained information from the Australian consulate; but Australia's extradition laws for draft-related offenses were vague and uncertain, and they quickly abandoned that idea.

Only two countries, Canada and Sweden, had laws that did not permit the extradition of immigrants for prosecution of draft-related offenses. Most of the war resisters who chose Sweden were deserters who had been stationed at bases in West Germany. However, some deserters, such as Ray Jones III—the first deserter to apply for a residence permit—fled to Sweden in 1967 after service in Vietnam. By 1970, approximately five hundred deserters and draft resisters had applied for residency in Sweden, including twenty-five Vietnam veterans.

Swedish Prime Minister Olaf Palme told *U.S. News and World Report* in June 1970 that the Swedish government did not encourage anyone to desert from the armed forces and had no official position toward war resisters. Officially, Palme's comments were accurate, but unofficially, the Swedish government determined that war resisters were entitled to a wide range of generous benefits, including a living allowance, free language school, and job training.

Canada was the logical destination for most war resisters, not just because it was the most accessible—United States and Canada share the longest undefended border in the world (2,500 miles)—but because Canadians, for the most part, were sympathetic to their cause. That tradition of welcoming dissenters began with the United Empire Loyalists, who were loyal to England during the American Revolution, and extended through the Civil War with the admission of runaway slaves.

Canada did not have a fugitive slave law and followed the common law doctrine that a slave became free upon touching free soil. In Canada, conscription was a hot political issue during both world wars. It was not imposed during World War I until 1917, and when it was initially imposed during World War II, it was done so with an understanding that draftees could be used only for home defense (Canadian draftees were not sent overseas until 1944). The draft was terminated at the end of the war and was never reinstated, thus Canada had no draft laws during the Vietnam War years and refused to extradite residents who were alleged to have broken laws that did not exist in Canada.

Diane and Frank spent a year weighing their options.

Canada seemed the logical place for them to go, so they drove north on a fact-finding tour, visiting Toronto, Montreal, and Ottawa before returning to Chicago. They decided that if they had to leave the country Toronto would be their destination. Most war resisters made the same choice, primarily because Toronto, with its sprawling suburbs and tree-lined neighborhoods, was the Canadian city that most resembled American cities of years gone by. With a population of over two million, it was large enough to get lost in and small enough to allow for the type of cultural navigation necessary for assimilation.

The day after April Fools' Day, 1966, Frank received a notice from the draft board in Queens ordering him to report for his pre-induction physical. He called them and told them he had decided to emigrate to Canada. "No problem," they said. "You can report to the board in Buffalo." Today, Diane laughs when she thinks about it: "They just weren't going to take no for an answer."

Diane and Frank knew then that time had run out. On April 4 ("Immigrants never forget the date they arrive," said Diane) they loaded up all their pots and pans and clothing into the used car they recently had purchased, and they drove across the border into Canada and headed toward Toronto. They had fifteen hundred dollars in cash and absolutely no idea what lay ahead. Diane was nineteen and Frank was twenty-one. They were young and fearless and utterly convinced they were doing the right thing.

Toronto was brimming with American expatriates in 1966. Canadian immigration figures show that between the start of 1963 and the end of 1966, 56,958 American citizens entered Canada and applied for permanent residency. Diane was among 17,514 Americans to do so in 1966. Anyone could visit Canada—the borders were and still are open to everyone—but in order to stay and work in Canada, there was a requirement that individuals obtain landed immigrant status.

There were two ways to do that: Application could be made at a Canadian consulate before entering Canada, and, if the applicant scored enough points on a rating scale, he or she would be entitled to take up residency, or application could be made after arriving in the country on a visit. Most war resisters chose the latter, since consulate officials had considerable discretion with the point system and if an individual was rejected there was no provision for appeal.

The first thing Diane and Frank did upon arriving in Toronto was to move into a rooming house and start looking for work. They had left Diane's mother's address as a forwarding address. "The city was filled with draft dodgers—rooming houses were filled with them," said Diane. "There was a lot of anti-war activity. There were protests on Canadian campuses to stop the war. A lot of the professors were Americans."

Four months after they arrived, Diane's mother forwarded them a letter from the draft board in Queens. Frank had failed to report for his physical as ordered, and the letter was sent to notify him that the penalty was five years in prison and a fine of ten thousand dollars. "We thought, 'Oh, God, now this is a problem,' " said Diane. "We knew we could not go back, maybe ever. It was a big bridge to burn. Frank sat down and drafted a long, handwritten letter to the draft board in Queens and told them that he had pursued the American Dream to Canada—and that was why he didn't show up for the physical. I was very upset. It was a tough time for a lot of people. We figured we'd just have to be miserable."

Finally, Frank received a response from the draft board.

"I was at work and he was at home when the letter arrived," said Diane. "He called me and said he was too nervous to open it. I said, 'Pour yourself a Bud, light a cigarette, and read it to me over the phone.' So he opened it up and the letter said he had been reclassified as a departed alien."

Diane and Frank were ecstatic. They were off the hook with the American government and free to come and go as they pleased—or so they thought. But their freedom had come at a high cost. No longer could Frank indulge his idealistic concept of the American Dream, and no longer could Diane feel that her homeland was the land of the free and the home of the brave.

The Vietnam War did not happen overnight. By the time Diane and Frank crossed the border into Canada, there were over 300,000 American troops in Vietnam, with over five thousand already relegated to body-bag status. American soldiers had been in South Vietnam since 1954, the year the eight-year-old Indochina War between Vietnamese nationalists and the French ended with a negotiated settlement at a conference in Geneva, Switzerland.

The conference was attended by Britain, the Soviet Union, France, the United States, China, Cambodia, Laos, representatives of the

French-sponsored forces based in the south, and representatives of the Vietnamese nationalists, whose government was named the Democratic Republic of Vietnam and based in the north. Under the terms of the agreement, Vietnam was partitioned at the 17th parallel pending reunification in a general election scheduled for July 1956.

In the years between 1954 and 1956, President Dwight D. Eisenhower sent advisors to South Vietnam to train the army organized by President Ngo Dinh Diem, the newly elected leader of South Vietnam. Under pressure from right-wing political leaders who feared the expansion of Communist China into the region, a coalition of corporations made up of businesses that had an interest in the region's abundant natural resources, and national defense contractors that had grown accustomed to substantial contracts during World War II, Eisenhower decided it was in America's best interests that American troops replace the defeated French troops. Said Eisenhower: "If Indochina goes, several things happen right away. The peninsula . . . would be scarcely defensible. The tin and tungsten that we so greatly value from that area would cease coming."

In the months leading up to July 1956, when the elections were scheduled to take place, the International Control Commission, which had been put in place by the participants of the Geneva conference to oversee the transition, reported that the North Vietnamese had fulfilled its obligations under the agreement. Fearful of a North Vietnamese victory, President Eisenhower pressured President Diem into canceling the elections, thus ensuring the resumption of hostilities.

Fighting against President Diem's American-trained army was a force of South Vietnamese nationalists called the Viet Cong. The first injuries to American troops came in 1957, but not until 1961 were additional troops in substantial numbers sent to Vietnam by newly elected President John F. Kennedy. The Hanoi government, which had pretty much stayed out of the fighting until 1960, matched the American escalation with men and supplies.

In 1963, South Vietnamese military leaders, unhappy with the way the war was going, asked American officials if they would support a military coup. When American officials, knowing full well that a coup meant the murder of Diem, responded in what military leaders considered a wishy-washy manner, they dropped the idea. Meanwhile, Diem launched a vicious attack against protesting Buddhist monks with special forces financed by the CIA, according to documents published in the *Pentagon Papers*, alienating the CIA, which had wanted the special forces used only for covert operations, and South Vietnamese military leaders, who feared the creation of yet another battleground in the south.

Upon further reflection, American officials encouraged the South Vietnamese military leaders to proceed with the coup, according to Professor Loren Boritz. Documents published in the *Pentagon Papers* later revealed that President Kennedy advised South Vietnamese Ambassador Henry Cabot Lodge that he had decided to give the coup his "full support." Kennedy promised to help in any way possible to "conclude this operation successfully." As a result, President Diem and his brother were shot and stabbed to death in November 1963, putting the presidency firmly in the hands of the military. Three weeks later, President Kennedy was assassinated.

By 1964, President Lyndon B. Johnson had bolstered the American presence in Vietnam to 25,000 troops. In August, an American destroyer, the *Maddox*, was sent on a secret mission in support of South Vietnamese commando raids against two North Vietnamese islands in the Gulf of Tonkin. During the raid, the *Maddox* attracted fire from several North Vietnamese torpedo boats that apparently thought the destroyer was under the South Vietnamese flag. That information was relayed to President Johnson, who, according to Bartiz, ordered another destroyer to join the *Maddox*. The incident created a dilemma for Johnson, who wanted to keep the mission secret.

The following day, Johnson received word that both destroyers had been attacked by the North Vietnamese. It was not true, according to admissions made in later years by Defense Secretary Robert McNamara, but since news of the incident had been leaked to the press by military officials, it provided the administration with an excuse to ask Congress for increased authorization to expand the war.

Faced with news stories about the alleged "attack" and reports from the president that they had, in fact, occurred, Congress approved a bill, called the Gulf of Tonkin Resolution, that gave Johnson the authority he requested. He used that authority to order bombing raids into North Vietnam, the first of the war. Only later did the American public discover that the second attack—the one that was used as an excuse for the Gulf of Tonkin Resolution—never took place. The Gulf of Tonkin incident was the first big lie of the war, but not the last.

The war escalated rapidly with Johnson in office. By 1966, American pilots were bombing targets in the Hanoi-Haiphong area, and opposition to the war was rising in the United States. Fifteen students at the University of Michigan demonstrated against the war at a local draft board and lost their student deferments. The Georgia legislature refused to seat black activist Julian Bond because of his opposition to the war. A high school history teacher in Massachusetts was denied tenure because he criticized the administration's Vietnam policy. The FBI announced it was going to investigate all organizations that had spoken out against the war.

By 1967, the American government had spun out of control in its efforts to control dissent, and the military, fearful of an uprising, had assigned personnel to domestic surveillance. The U.S. Army set up over 350 secret record centers and assigned more than 1,500 plainclothes agents to gather information on Americans who were opposed to the war. Targeted were elected officials who spoke out against the war, protesters attending peace rallies, and business executives who contributed money to antiwar organizations. The secret agents carried fake IDs and sometimes posed as news reporters. They attended meetings and took down names. Often, posing as newspaper reporters, they took photographs to place in the secret files for future reference.

By the end of the decade, the army's counter-intelligence agents had compiled secret dossiers on over 100,000 American citizens. Using code names such as Steep Hill, Rose Bush, and Lantern Spike, the agents operated independently of the government and were not accountable to anyone in government. In addition to the files compiled by its own secret agents, the army assembled additional files using Defense Department security clearance information, criminal files obtained from local police departments, and files received from the FBI. All together, the army gathered files on eighteen million American citizens, which were kept in computerized data banks called "scores."

Of particular interest to agents of all branches of the services were off-post coffeehouses operated by civilian groups and underground newspapers. "The primary means of obtaining information on both the coffeehouses and the underground newspapers was to penetrate them with either a military intelligence agent or a military informant, who would report back on the group's activities. These reports were typically shared with the FBI and local law enforcement agencies," concluded the Select Committee to Study Governmental Operations, which investigated the army's activities in 1976 at the request of the U.S. Senate. The Senate committee also found that the Internal Revenue Service used nearly 3,000 agents to gather information on citizens opposed to the war and concluded that the IRS activity "led to serious and illegal abuse of IRS investigative powers and to a compromise of the privacy and integrity of the tax return."

Not to the outdone by the military and the IRS, the FBI escalated a counter-intelligence mission entitled Cointelpro that had been created in 1956 to counteract Supreme Court rulings that limited the government's power to undermine lawful dissident groups. FBI agents broke into homes and offices to steal and copy letters and documents and to install secret listening devices, all without search warrants or court authority. The operation was terminated in 1971 when antiwar activists broke into an FBI office in Media, Pennsylvania, and confiscated Cointelpro documents and distributed them to the news media. Calling the FBI's activities a "sophisticated vigilante operation aimed squarely at preventing the exercise of First Amendment rights of speech and association," the Senate committee said such techniques were "intolerable in a democratic society" and demonstrated the consequences of the government "to take the law into its own hands for the 'greater good' of the country."

In March 1967, *Time* magazine published a story that attempted to address rumors that President Johnson's advisors were deeply divided over the bombing of North Vietnam. According to the rumors, Defense Secretary Robert McNamara was on one side (against) and the president, Secretary of State Dean Rusk, and the Pentagon were on the other side (for). Unknown to *Time*, Johnson's chief advisor on Vietnam—at least on the major decisions that had political ramifications—was neither McNamara nor Rusk, but his old friend Supreme Court Justice Abe Fortas, who met secretly with Johnson on a regular basis to advise him on his war policy, according to author Bruce Allen Murphy in *Fortas: The Rise and Ruin of a Supreme Court Justice*. Said Murphy: "No issue better illustrated [Fortas's] position in the constellation of advisers and subordinates surrounding the president than the war in Vietnam."

Johnson kept his association with Fortas a secret, since it was a breach of the constitutional separation of powers. Eventually Fortas was forced to resign in disgrace after press reports that he had accepted money from a defense contractor led to a full-scale FBI investigation of his activities.

McNamara and Rusk both denied they had a difference of opinion on war policy, but *Time* reporters obtained transcripts of McNarmara's testimony before closed hearings of the Senate Armed Services and Appropriations Committees that indicated otherwise. Said McNamara to the senators: "I don't believe that the bombing up to the present has significantly reduced, nor any bombing that I could contemplate in the future would significantly reduce, the actual flow of men and material to the South."

Later in the year, McNamara went to Guam to meet with General William Westmoreland, who was in charge of American forces in Vietnam. Westmoreland wanted more troops. McNamara was looking for a justification to send more troops. By the summer of 1967, there were

463,000 American troops in Vietnam, with another 15,000 scheduled for assignment before the end of the year. Pentagon sources told reporters that they thought it would take about 600,000 men to win the war.

Shortly after McNamara's' return, President Johnson told reporters, "Suffice it for me to say that we are generally pleased with the progress we have made militarily. We are very sure that we are on the right track." François Sully, writing for the *New Republic*, said, "American officers must choose between pacification and large-scale mobile operations against Viet Cong regiments and battalions. There will never be enough Americans to accomplish both missions concurrently." Westmoreland got the additional troops he wanted, but that meant higher draft calls and stepped up public resistance.

In October, civil rights leader Martin Luther King held a press conference in Washington at which he said that if the government would not shut down the war, the government would have to be shut down by the people. If significant progress was not made on ending the war, he said, he would return to Washington to lead massive demonstrations against the government. King left Washington to report to the Birmingham jail to serve a five-day sentence for defying a court order against racial demonstrations. When he was released, he announced plans to return to Washington to camp out in tents in front of the White House. Said King, "We must let it be known that we will stay until our problem is solved."

David Halberstam, writing in *Harper's*, said a visit to Vietnam had left him convinced that neither the South Vietnamese nor the Americans could win the war: "I have a sense that we are once again coming to a dead end in Indochina."

By then, Johnson felt besieged. He told his advisors, "We've almost lost the war in the last two months in the court of public opinion. These demonstrators . . . are trying to show that we need somebody else to take over the country." He was right. Before the year was out, Senator Eugene McCarthy had announced that he would challenge Johnson for the Democratic nomination for president.

"I think a lot of people were sleepwalking through it," said Diane Francis. "The strategy among the boys I went to high school with was that if you were smart enough to go to university, then you did that to get the deferment. If you couldn't go to university, you did a Dan Quayle's or a Bill Clinton. You got someone to pull strings for you. That's what most people were thinking about. Frank was no one from nowhere—a working poor immigrant. We didn't have daddies like Dan Quayle, so it became an issue we had to deal with. I hated the damn war, and it wasn't even Frank's country. But everyone had their own reasons.

Basically they were just kids. They wanted to get laid. To get a job. They didn't want to think about the domino theory or the Evil Empire—they just wanted to live their lives. History offered us a crossroads and we took the path less traveled—and it's made all the difference in the world."

Toronto was a vibrant city in 1967. The streets were safe. The economy was growing. The subway was clean and efficient. The people were friendly and helpful; a painful reminder to American war resisters of how Americans were once perceived by outsiders. Living in Toronto—once known as "Toronto the Good" because of its Sunday ban on movies, sports and alcoholic beverages—was like entering a time warp in which the men were all honest and straightforward like Jimmy Stewart and the women were all beautiful and headstrong like Katherine Hepburn.

There was a sense of well-being among the Americans living in Toronto. It was a city that bristled with energy and expectation and goodwill. Even the artifices of government seemed geared to the future. Toronto's new city hall resembled a flying saucer nestled between two ultra-modern high-rises. Americans had been emigrating to Toronto for years, sometimes for cultural reasons, but also because of lucrative teaching opportunities at colleges and universities and because a number of American international corporations, such as Exxon, had headquarters there and offered career advancement to American employees interested in relocating.

Interestingly, American immigrants did not seek each other out, as immigrants to America had done over the generations. There were no American enclaves or neighborhoods in Canada—with the exception of a couple of small communities in British Columbia in which the residents still wear bell-bottom jeans and live the lifestyles made famous by the hippies of the 1960s—and that is primarily because the new immigrants were more interested in forming associations with native Canadians.

The Vietnam-era war resisters were no different. Most were like Diane and Frank, who wanted to learn everything they could about their new country. "We didn't hang out with draft dodgers," said Diane. "We were people who thought we had won the first prize in life because we had been born in the United States. We were taught it was the best and biggest country in the world. My father said to me and Frank, 'But they don't have two-car garages in Canada.' Americans just don't travel, so you have a lot of ignorance. Frank had been to Paris and London, so he knew how nice other countries could be."

Most Canadians looked and talked—except for an occasional "eh" at the end of a sentence—like their neighbors to the south; the biggest difference between the two countries was not in the people, but in the governments. The Canadian government was people friendly. It actively looked for ways to make sure everyone had access to health care and employment opportunities. It intruded into the lives of its citizens only when it was necessary to protect lives and property. It did not order its citizens to travel to distant lands to kill strangers, nor did it imprison citizens who criticized the government.

The differences between the two countries were highlighted with regal clarity in the summer of 1967 when Queen Elizabeth of England and her husband Prince Philip visited the Canadian capital of Ottawa to help celebrate Canada's centennial. By virtue of Canada's Commonwealth status, Elizabeth was the Queen of Canada, a distinction that had immensely more to do with tradition than it did the with reality of modern government. Elizabeth was greeted by large crowds and received a thunderous reception. When she addressed the Canadian Parliament, she acknowledged the nation's "increasing power and authority" in world affairs. American war resisters followed the queen's visit with a curious blend of cultural detachment and newfound pride.

The only negative contact war resisters had with the Canadian government occurred shortly after their arrival when they were visited by officers of the Royal Canadian Mounted Police (the RCMP or "Mounties" as they are popularly known) at the request of the American government. The Mounties would invariably explain that they were intruding only to verify that the war resisters were indeed new residents of Canada. They asked no intrusive questions, nor did they suggest or imply that the new residents were not welcome in Canada. On the contrary, the friendly officers usually apologized for making the visits and offered hearty handshakes before departing.

No matter how pleasant Canada was to the new arrivals, they always had to look over their shoulders. "There were a couple of incidents that scared us—FBI agents who came across the border and arrested people," recalled Diane. "But there were diplomatic exchanges and that nonsense stopped."

Once Diane went by the American consulate to get her passport renewed. While taking care of the paperwork with the consulate official, she looked down at her file and—reading the upside-down lettering—saw the names of her uncles and their employers. "That upset me," she said. "One of my uncles was a defense contractor and I couldn't help but think, 'Geez, I wonder if it has affected his career.' "

By 1967, the aid centers for war resisters were at full strength, and there was a vast network of support groups across Canada. The Toronto Anti-Draft Programme published a 105-page book entitled *Manual for Draft-Age Immigrants to Canada* and distributed it to over 5,000 would-be exiles in waiting. The book was published by House of Anansi, a small, underground press that had built a national reputation with new fiction and non-fiction that focused on the "how to" aspect of adapting to Canadian laws.

The *Manual* offered background information on Canadian law and history and explained the immigration procedure for obtaining landed immigrant status in Canada. "Immigration is not the best choice for everyone and this pamphlet does not take sides," read the introduction. "Four other alternatives are open to draft-age Americans: deferment, conscientious objector status, jail or the armed forces . . . the toughest problem a draft resister faces is not how to immigrate but whether he really wants to. And only you can answer that for yourself. That's what Nuremberg was all about."

For most war resisters in 1967, immigration to Canada was looking better all the time. When the anti-war movement first began, there was a feeling among many dissenters that the most effective option was to go to jail in an effort to clog the court system. However, by 1967, it had become obvious that the court system was too vast to be clogged, and with most war resisters receiving the maximum sentence of five years, the prison alternative had lost much of its ideological luster.

One of the opponents for the war who went to prison was Captain Dale Noyd, a fighter pilot and Air Force Academy instructor in psychology. When it became obvious that he was going to be asked to use his skills in Vietnam, he asked the Air Force to allow him to resign or to assign him to duties unrelated to combat. He was opposed to the war, and he refused to fly training missions with student pilots. The Air Force responded by court martialing him and giving him a two-year prison sentence. Noyd served his time, but when he got out of prison he discovered that Air Force bombers were still destroying Vietnam villages on a daily basis. Other veterans and protesters got the message. The best way to slow the war machine was to go to Canada, not to prison.

The year 1968 was probably one of the most convulsive, violent, and bewildering in American history since the Civil War; most people who lived through it would be hard-pressed to name a more virulent year. It began with Martin Luther King's efforts to merge the civil rights movement with the antiwar movement. Said King: "If our nonviolent campaign doesn't generate some progress, people are just going to engage in more violent activity and the discussion of guerrilla warfare will be more extensive." The "flash point" of black rage is "close at hand," he said.

King's support of the antiwar movement sent shock waves into the White House, although officials publicly denied it at the time. White students were protesting the war on campuses, and black civil rights activists were taking their rage to the streets. The cities were burning, and the stock market was tumbling. The Gallup polling organization reported in February that President Johnson's popularity had dropped four points since the previous month—when he ordered the induction of 10,000 additional young men and for the first time talked about calling up the reserves—giving him an approval rating of only thirty-five percent.

Despite the entry of peace candidate Senator Eugene McCarthy into the presidential race, not many pundits thought President Johnson was in any danger of losing the nomination. The liberal *New Republic* said McCarthy had no hope of ousting the president, and the magazine reminded readers that McCarthy had said that Johnson, despite his shortcomings, was preferable to any of the Republican candidates, especially front-runner Richard Nixon. Surprisingly, McCarthy showed strong support in the initial small-state primaries.

Buoyed by McCarthy's success, Robert Kennedy announced in mid-March that he was entering the race. He reissued a book published the previous year, *To Seek a Newer World*, in which he apologized for his earlier support of the Vietnam War. Said Kennedy: "I am willing to bear my share of the responsibility, before history and before my fellow-citizens. But past error is no excuse for its own perpetuation."

On March 31, President Johnson went on television to announce a halt in the bombing of North Vietnam. He said he was doing it as a peace gesture. Then, in a move that was as unexpected as it was shocking, Johnson spoke the words that stunned the nation: "I shall not seek and I will not accept the nomination of my party for president of the United States." He was withdrawing from the race, he said, so that he could spend all his time working for peace. "I have concluded that I should not permit the presidency to become involved in partisan divisions that are developing this year."

The leadership hierarchy of the Democratic Party scurried to find a candidate to carry the Johnson mantle. The natural choice was Vice-President Hubert Humphrey. He was hawkish on the war but liberal on social issues. Early polling data after Johnson's announcement showed that Kennedy was the front-runner, with Humphrey second, and

McCarthy third. Humphrey's strategy was to stay out of the primaries, allowing Kennedy and McCarthy to slug it out, then to capture the nomination from the delegates by wheeling and dealing at the convention.

Four days before Johnson withdrew from the race, Martin Luther King went to Memphis, Tennessee, to lead a protest march in support of striking sanitation workers. The march turned into a riot, and 3,000 members of the National Guard were called out to restore order. Over 300 demonstrators were arrested. A black man was shot to death, and three others were wounded.

King returned to Atlanta to regroup. He was concerned about the violence in Memphis, especially since he knew it would be used by authorities as an excuse to curtail the massive peace demonstrations he had planned for Washington, D.C. It was while he was evaluating his options that President Johnson announced he would not run for re-election. It was while the political dust from that announcement was settling that King returned to Memphis on April 3 to re-exert his authority as a proponent of nonviolence. The following day King was shot to death on the balcony of a Memphis motel.

In the week following King's assassination, riots broke out in 172 cities. Forty-three people were killed and over 3,000 were injured. Police made more than 27,000 arrests as the president called out 20,000 federal troops and 30,000 national guardsmen. Soldiers with bayonets patrolled every major city in America. Armored tanks and personnel carriers were a common sight.

Oddly, the assassination boosted President Johnson's popularity. On April 5, the day after the assassination, White House aide Fred Panzer informed Johnson that results from the Harris Survey showed that his approval rating had reversed. Before the assassination, fifty-seven percent of those polled said they disapproved of the way the president was doing his job, said Panzer in a memorandum now on file in the LBJ Library. After the assassination, fifty-seven percent said they approved of his performance.

As the nation mourned the death of Dr. King and focused on the rioting and chaos taking place in the streets, Johnson stepped up military operations in Vietnam, even as he sought to use the bombing cessation as an incentive for peace talks. Johnson mobilized 25,000 reservists and directed that 10,000 new troops be sent to Vietnam, bringing the total U.S. troop strength up to 550,000.

Talking about peace was not good enough for opponents of the war. They wanted action. During the first fifteen weeks of 1968, more than 5,000 American soldiers were killed in Vietnam. When Johnson announced in May that Hanoi had agreed to participate in peace talks in Paris, there was little enthusiasm from war opponents. Everyone knew that peace talks would be long and laborious. Losing 15,000 soldiers every fifteen weeks was unacceptable to the peace movement.

For months, the Democratic primary in California, scheduled for June 6, had been shaping up as a decisive battleground over leadership of the peace wing of the party. When the votes were counted, Kennedy was declared the winner, taking forty-six percent to McCarthy's forty-two percent. It was immediately after his victory speech in the ballroom of the Ambassador Hotel that Kennedy was gunned down by an assassin.

Again, the nation was thrown into turmoil. Two major assassinations within two months created a wave of despair, fear and loathing, all of which ultimately came to be focused on the election. Each time an antiwar spokesman won the support of the public, he was gunned down, causing antiwar demonstrators to doubt the government's "lone gunman" explanations. McCarthy's supporters understandably feared for his life. Of the three men who had spoken out vociferously against the war, only McCarthy was still alive.

In August, at a convention held in Miami, the Republicans chose Richard Nixon as its nominee for president and Spiro Agnew for vice-president. Also in August, Democrats went to Chicago for a convention that later would be called "The Battle of Chicago." Nearly 10,000 antiwar activists descended upon the city to show support for McCarthy.

To greet them, Chicago Mayor Richard Daley called out a veritable army of heavily armed police officers and national guardsmen. The results were predictable: 700 civilians and 83 police officers were injured in hand-to-hand fighting on the streets of Chicago, and 653 demonstrators, many of them McCarthy supporters, were arrested and jailed. Two of the nation's most prominent Democrats—Lyndon Johnson and Edward Kennedy—did not even bother to attend the convention.

Later, the president's Commission on the Causes and Prevention of Violence issued a report faulting the police for using violence against the demonstrators. The commission called it a "police riot." It was the bloodiest political convention in American history. Hubert Humphrey emerged from the convention as the Democratic nominee, but few analysts gave him and his running mate, Edmund Muskie, much hope of overcoming the lead that Nixon had assumed in the public opinion polls. Humphrey surprised them all. Seven weeks from the election, Nixon had only an eight-point lead in the polls.

In early October, the National Mobilization to End the War, one of the "coffeehouse" organization under surveillance by secret army agents, held a "U.S. Military Week," during which servicemen were invited into the homes of antiwar activists for family dinners. The organization, unaware that it had been targeted by secret agents, also flooded airports and train terminals with antiwar leaflets and held a series of massive rallies.

Also in October, the Los Angeles Police Department sent two officers to the Marine facilities at Camp Pendleton for rifle training as snipers. When asked why by reporters, they said they thought the training would be beneficial during ghetto rioting.

By election day, Nixon and Humphrey were running neck to neck in the polls. As the returns started coming in, the victories were so balanced that there was a fear that neither would receive a majority, thus throwing the election into the House of Representatives. Nixon won the election, but only by the smallest of margins. Interviewed after the election, President Johnson told reporters that he thought the outcome of the election had been decided by the war and by the belief that McCarthy supporters had thrown the Democratic Party off balance.

When he took office, Nixon said he had a secret plan to end the war in Vietnam. Americans wanted to believe him, for to disbelieve him would be to relinquish all hope—and so believe him they did, everyone, that is, except the war protesters. Even the usually cynical editors at *New Republic* were optimistic, predicting Nixon would end the war in quick order: "Anyone can see that the country hates the war that destroyed Lyndon Johnson."

As the year ended, *Newsweek* ran a cover story on the Vietnam War, asking, "Can South Vietnam Stand Alone?" Commenting on the Paris peace talks, the magazine said the American delegation was "in a state of uncertainty." Not helping in the arena of public opinion were comments from ascot-wearing South Vietnamese leader Nguyen Ky, who came under criticism from Congress after a subcommittee discovered documents indicating that the South Vietnamese president had used a CIA-sponsored sabotage operation to smuggle opium from Laos to Saigon.

Ky added to his problems when he told reporters that his "only hero" was Adolf Hitler. Not many American eighteen year olds wanted to die for a man who worshipped Hitler, no matter what their flag-waving parents said, so they continued to flee to Canada in large numbers, according to data compiled by Immigration Statistics Canada, with a "legal" migration in 1968 of over 20,000 Americans.

Canada and the United States have a great deal in common economically and culturally, but when it comes to government and the news media, the two countries are radically different. Canada is governed by a prime minister and a Parliament, based on the British system. The prime minister is elected by the Parliament and can be discharged at its pleasure. When Parliament is in session, the prime minister is expected to be there on a regular basis to answer questions from the lawmakers. Sometimes the questions are blunt and charged with emotion.

When American war resisters first began seeking sanctuary in Canada in the mid-1960s, Lester Pearson was the prime minister. There were three major political parties at that time: the Conservative Party, the Liberal Party, and the New Democratic Party. Initially, many war resisters were confused by the names of the parties.

The Conservatives were not conservative in the sense that they followed a middle-of-the-road course; rather they leaned somewhat to the right. The Liberals were not liberal by American standards, in that they did not rely on the support of minorities and labor; they tended to stick to a middle-of-the-road agenda. The actual liberal members of Parliament, in the traditional sense familiar to Americans, usually belonged to the New Democratic Party, an unlikely coalition of labor, farmers, and left-wing ideologues.

Pearson was leader of the Liberal Party, which had opposed American intervention in Vietnam since the mid-1950s. Pearson was an affable, scholarly leader who had a quiet manner about him. He didn't make a big deal about allowing American war resisters in Canada anymore than he made a big deal about American involvement in the war. Both issues were handled quietly and diplomatically.

All that changed in the spring of 1968—as did the overall tone of government—with the election of Pierre Elliott Trudeau as prime minister. He was a young, flamboyant, handsome lawyer who had made waves as Lester Pearson's attorney general. One of his major projects as attorney general was the reform of the country's outmoded criminal code. He completely rewrote the laws on divorce and homosexuality and then, when the time was right, assumed the leadership of the Liberal Party in a hotly contested race.

Trudeau made it clear early on that his government would welcome American war resisters to Canada. In an interview with the *United Church Observer*, he said that a man's ultimate guide had to be his conscience and that if the law of the land went against his conscience, the man had an obligation to disobey the law. "Those who make the conscientious judgment that they must not participate in this war and who become draft dodgers have my complete sympathy, and indeed our political approach has been to give them access to Canada whether they are draft dodgers, or even more serious, deserters from the ranks of the armed forces."

One of the major differences between the news media of Canada and the United States during the 1960s and 1970s was that American journalists—at least those outside the South—tended to lean toward the liberal end of the political spectrum. Canadian journalists leaned toward the conservative end. There was very little opposition to the war resisters in Canada, but when it occurred it almost always originated with journalists. They did not interview Canadians who were opposed to the war resisters. They wrote opinion pieces that reflected their own viewpoints.

Oliver Clausen, a reporter with the Toronto *Globe and Mail*, wrote an unsympathetic piece on war resisters for the *New York Times Magazine* entitled "Boys Without a Country." Gail Cameron wrote an article for the *Ladies' Home Journal* in which she noted the "novelty of American boys abandoning their country in time of war."

Writing in the Canadian news magazine *Saturday Night*, Robert Fulford called the war resisters Canada's "newest minority." He told the story of a Texan who moved into a boarding house, only to discover two hours after moving in that a war resister was living just down the hall. They went for a walk and discovered three men a couple of houses away working on a motorcycle. They stopped to talk and discovered that all three were war resisters. And so it went. Fulford concluded that "Canadians who expect [war resisters] to be heroic are disappointed. They aren't even proud. . . . Anyone who dodges any draft knows that somewhere somebody thinks of him as a coward, pure and simple."

One reason for the philosophical differences among journalists of the two countries probably can be found in their perception of government. American journalists know that their government has a long history of citizen abuse: Americans of Japanese descent were interred in prison camps during World War II; African Americans were subjected to medical experiments during the 1950s and 1960s and prevented from voting in many states; native Americans, when they weren't being chased by soldiers, were forced to live in squalor on reservations; and, finally, citizens who opposed the government's war policy in Vietnam were imprisoned if they refused to take up arms. Added to that is a long history of graft and political corruption. America probably has more elected officials go to jail than any other democratic country.

American journalists, the best of them anyway, enter the profession because they feel an obligation to take on bad government. Canadian journalists have no such history. Their experience with government has essentially been positive. Throughout its history, Canadian government has seldom deviated from a middle-of-the-road political course; it has, for the most part, governed throughout the twentieth century with honor and compassion and dignity. For that reason, Canadian journalists did not have the same history of activism expressed by American journalists in the 1960s and 1970s, and they sometimes had a difficult time comprehending why American journalists and war resisters would place themselves in positions of opposition to the government.

All that changed with the election of Pierre Trudeau and with the arrival of American war resisters. For the first time, the Canadian press zeroed in on the new prime minister, not so much for his proposed legislation as for his lifestyle and views on social issues such as the Vietnam War. Trudeau was a bachelor, and he dated a series of young women who were usually blonde and glamorous. One of his romances was with American singer Barbra Streisand, who, according to press reports, spent at least one week-end at the prime minister's residence in Ottawa. Ironically, the more the media needled Trudeau for his lifestyle and views on war resisters, the more the public seemed to embrace him.

It took forever for the Canadian media to get a handle on Trudeau, but once they looked into his background, the essential Pierre became more understandable. His mother, Grace Elliot, was a descendant of a United Empire Loyalist family that fled the United States during the American Revolution. She married a French-Canadian named Charles-Emile, who made a fortune from an organization named the Automobile Owners' Association. Pierre grew up in a family of wealth and privilege at a time when French-Canadians were always on the outside of Canadian politics.

Old enough to fight during World War II, Trudeau refused, reflecting a common French-Canadian sentiment that the English should fight their own wars, even when it effected the future of France. He received a law degree from the University of Montreal and for a time worked for a prestigious Montreal law firm. Unhappy with life as a lawyer, he entered the London School of Economics. Before writing his dissertation, he left on a fact-finding tour on a motorcycle. He never returned to the London School of Economics, but he did manage, as a result of his tour, to land on U.S. Senator Joseph McCarthy's blacklist.

Trudeau did not attack the right-wing elements of the media head-on, but he made it clear that his private life was just that, and he governed with a moral compass that seldom sent him off course. Once when asked by a reporter about his refusal to serve in World War II, he shrugged, "Like most Quebeckers, I had been taught to keep away from imperialistic wars." The attitudes of the Canadian news media eventually changed, both toward Trudeau and toward the war resisters. By the early 1970s, newspapers were hiring war resisters as reporters and commentators. The conservative *Recorder & Times*, a daily located in Brockville, Ontario, allowed a war resister to write editorials on American politics. The editorials were unsigned and presented the resisters' opinions as the opinions of the newspapers.

As the years went by, the Canadian news media was altered in a more fundamental way by war resisters as they sought new careers in journalism. With them they brought their American concept of the role of the news media, particularly insofar as government was concerned. Diane Francis was among the war resisters who gravitated toward a career in journalism. "I was largely self-taught," she said. "I wanted to make a difference. I was a good writer in high school. I combined that talent with my interest in changing the world for the better."

Diane landed a job as a reporter with the *Financial Post*, Canada's leading business journal (it has been called the *Wall Street Journal* of Canada). "It is not surprising that a lot of draft dodgers have become extremely influential in some areas, especially journalism and publishing. We were very liberal people, and we thought the war was the dumbest thing that had ever happened and we didn't swallow the bullshit that came from [Lyndon Johnson] about the war."

Diane was watching television the night Robert Kennedy was assassinated and it had a profound effect on her. "I thought, my country is falling apart. What the hell is going on? We've got this war no one wants, people getting bumped off." She was watching when violence erupted at the Democratic Convention in 1968 in her hometown of Chicago. "I thought, 'America, you should be ashamed of yourself.' That was my hometown, and the cops were beating peoples' heads in. I thought, 'Thank God, I found another way to live.' "

In 1991, Diane was named editor of the *Financial Post*, a position she held until 1998, when the newspaper merged with a new national publication, the National Podt. Shr now serves at editor at large at the new newspaper. She also has regular slots as a radio broadcaster and a television commentator. She serves on several boards, including the Canadian foundation for AIDS Research and the Advisory Committee of the Clarke Institute of Psychiatry.

In her spare time, she has written six best-selling books, including *Controlling Interest—Who Owns Canada*, which reveals that thirty-two families and five conglomerates own one-third of Canada's corporate assets; *Contrepreneurs*, an exposé on stock market swindles; and *Underground Nation*, a look at the dangers Canada faces going into the twenty-first century.

In 1992, she was chosen *Chatelaine Magazine*'s "Woman of the Year." Today, she is one of the most influential women—and "draft dodgers"—in Canada. Technically, of course, Diane is not a draft dodger, but don't try telling her that, for evading the draft for the Vietnam War is the reason she went to Canada, and she considers herself as much of a draft dodger as any of the men who went to Canada—and she wears the badge with honor. Her marriage to Frank did not survive—they were divorced in 1994—but her commitment to the idealism that propelled them into Canada has continued unabated.

When Robert McNamara, former U.S. secretary of defense, published a book on the Vietnam War in 1995, Diane reviewed it for the *Financial Post*. "This man writes about this monstrous tragedy as though it was another lengthy Pentagon memorandum," she wrote. "There's no remorse. There is no guilt. And yet to me Vietnam represents America's Holocaust." She went on to say that McNamara's book was "an affront to my generation, whose lives were changed by Vietnam . . . the Pentagon fought this war with poor boys against poor people. Meanwhile, the Dan Quayles had a rich daddy and Bill Clinton got out of serving." The former secretary of defense had the "insights and soul of a gnat" and was unable to "see much beyond his own darkness."

Talking about McNamara's book in 1997, Diane said she felt "very bitter" about his view of history—and about the entire Vietnam War experience. "I didn't want to leave my country. It turned out great—Canada is a marvelous country—but I am very embittered. We went through hell. It was not easy going to a country where you don't know anyone, and your parents are thinking you are stupid, and they are worrying about you, and you are thinking that maybe you are stupid."

It was not until the mid-1980s that she was able to talk openly about her feelings. There were several reasons for that. "In the mid-1980s, Canada stopped being anti-American and elected a prime minister who was pro-American. Up until then there was an element of anti-Americanism. I'm not anti-American. I'm antiracism and anti-Vietnam War. At the same time that elements of anti-Americanism were going away, Americans started to deal with the fiasco [of the war]. There was a series of heart-rending movies. America was beginning to admit that it was wrong. My talking about my reasons for coming to Canada was a convergence of both of those things."

"As a group, American draft dodgers have assimilated," she said. "I'll be interviewing a business man here, and I'll say, 'You're a Yank, aren't you?'

"He'll say, 'Yeah.' "

"I'll say, 'When you'd come?' "

"He'll say, '1968.' "

"I'll say, 'Oh, a dodger!' "

"I recently gave a speech to 1,500 mayors in Toronto, and I talked about the United States. People want to know why I'm here in Canada. I say, 'Oh, I married a draft dodger.' Usually, I hear, 'Good for you'."

2

1969

Andrew Collins: Flight from the Home of the Blues

Andrew Collins was on the Dalmatia Coast of Yugoslavia when he received the bad news. He had been there only a short while, working under a Smithsonian Institution grant as the archeological supervisor of the excavation of the only retirement palace of the Roman empire. He was twenty-four. The bad news had arrived by telephone from his mother in Memphis, Tennessee. He had been drafted. Although he had not lived in Memphis since enrolling in Vanderbilt University in Nashville at the age of eighteen, the draft board had sent the notice to his mother's address, as was customary at that time.

Andrew's mother asked him to comply. He had bad vision, and it was unlikely he would be sent to Vietnam. Besides he came from a good family, and it was incomprehensible to his mother that he would not go into the army as ordered. Good families in the South always do what is expected of them.

Andrew had been born in Memphis at Baptist Hospital, then the largest privately owned hospital in the United States. At one time, the hospital had been owned by his grandfather, Espie Jennings, a Mississippi Delta planter—and a strict Baptist—who had rescued it from insolvency. Eventually, he turned the hospital back over to the church, but for years, Jennings maintained a penthouse apartment atop the hospital, surely making him the only American to live so close to life's gateway to birth and death. When he died, the hospital installed a plaque to commemorate his contributions to the community. Andrew was five at the time and remembers attending the unveiling.

Andrew had a privileged upbringing. He had two brothers, one who was older and one who was younger. He spent his childhood in an exclusive suburban neighborhood and attended East High School, one of the top-ranked secondary schools in the country. It was a public school and still one hundred percent segregated while Andrew was a student; today the enrollment is almost exclusively African American. Growing up, Andrew was isolated from poverty, politics, and racial strife. His parents belonged to the Chickasaw Country Club, where Memphis's elite gathered to play and plan the city's future.

Andrew's childhood was pretty uneventful until he was ten, at which time his father died. But even the trauma of that event was not enough to derail his close-knit family. Having two brothers helped. He spent his summers playing tennis at the country club and swimming. One of his childhood friends was Jesse Winchester, who as an adult had changed his name from Jimmy and enjoyed a successful career as a songwriter and recording artist. Andrew's mother and Jesse's mother often got together to play bridge.

Like Andrew's grandfather, Espie Jennings, the Winchesters had played an important role in Memphis history. Jimmy was named after his father, James R. Winchester, an Air Force captain whose forebearers had invented the famous Winchester rifle and had co-founded the city of Memphis. The Winchesters were very much a part of the city's heritage. They had fought the Yankees and the yellow fever epidemic and the flooding Mississippi River, and they had shown leadership in civic affairs. When blues founder W. C. Handy died in 1958, Jesse's grandfather delivered the funeral oration. The family's contributions were such that one of the city's main thoroughfares, Winchester Avenue, bears its name.

When Jesse's father came back from serving in the South Pacific during World War II, he shocked his family by declaring that he had become a pacifist. War was no way to solve problems. Instead of going to law school and then joining the family firm, he moved out of Memphis and became a farmer. Subsequently, he did return to Memphis and pursue a law career, which he worked at until his death in 1962, but not before imprinting into his young son the antiwar values he had acquired while serving in the South Pacific. Years later, Jesse described his father as one of the country's first hippies.

Andrew and Jesse both came of age during a time when Memphis was the musical center of the universe. It was the birthplace of the blues and the home of rock 'n' roll founder Elvis Presley. In the early to mid-1960s, Presley was very much a presence in the city, as was Stax Records, the Memphis-owned label that reshaped the musical landscape with artists such as Otis Redding ("Dock of the Bay") and Sam and Dave ("Soul Man").

Most of the music was being made by youths in their teens and high school bands that flourished during that time. Jesse was no exception. He played in groups named the Church Keys and the Midnighters. When time came to go to college, he broke with tradition and went to Williams College in Massachusetts, where he received a bachelor of arts degree in German. Before returning home to Memphis, he took some time off to travel in Europe.

But the clock was ticking, and he knew it. Shortly after returning to Memphis in 1967, he was working as a piano player in a local nightclub when he received his draft notice. Jesse's mother told him to follow his conscience. That path was clear: He was opposed to the war in Vietnam and did not see how he could in good conscience support it. Standing in the way, however, was his grandfather, who was still living. Jesse respected him more than any man living, and it pained him to even consider doing something that would cause his grandfather pain. But times had changed in Memphis—and across the South.

The Selective Service System, which decided who received draft notices, did not have a reputation for fairness. In the early years of the Vietnam War, many local boards targeted African Americans. Generally speaking, white southerners went into service only if they wanted to pursue a career in the service or if they were of a mind to travel and seek adventure. Selective Service board members were all appointed by the president of the United States upon recommendation of local politicians and businessmen. For the pasty fifty years, the Memphis Selective Service appointments had been controlled by E. H. "Boss" Crump and his successors, a politically based cartel that derived a significant percentage of its income from the defense industry.

In 1967, Jesse did the only thing he could do to be true to his conscience and his Southern heritage: He went to Montreal, Canada and refused to report to induction. Later, he told a reporter for the Toronto *Globe and Mail* about the day he left. "I didn't dare talk to anybody in Memphis because I was terrified," he said. "When I got to the airport, I was almost afraid to tell the ticket clerk I wanted a ticket to Montreal in case he put two and two together and called the police." It was the dead of winter when he arrived in Canada. "I had no idea it would be so cold. The airs in my nose froze as I inhaled and thawed as I exhaled."

Jesse was one of the first mid-Southerners to take a stand against the war insofar as the draft was concerned, but the war was very much an issue on college campuses. Andrew was attending Vanderbilt University when his opposition to the war solidified. "I was a typical teenager," he recalled of that time. "I had no affection for the military, for the political powers that be."

The assassination of President John F. Kennedy in 1963 had a profound effect on Andrew, as it did on many of the war resisters who went to Canada, for it was the murder, above all else, that convinced them that the political process had gone amuck and was no longer to be trusted. Andrew was a freshman at Vanderbilt on Friday, November 22, when the news services announced that the president had been slain in Dallas.

That weekend, Andrew and his girlfriend had made plans to attend a debutante's ball in Baltimore. Although the nation was in shock, the debutante ball took place as planned; afterward Andrew and his girlfriend stayed over and went into Washington on Monday for the funeral. "I remember perfectly seeing the horse with one boot and Jackie dressed in black," said Andrew. "I climbed into a tree to watch. I was very moved. I was a fan of the Kennedys. It wasn't anything like a turning point in my life. I just thought it was another example of a fucked up country."

After graduation from Vanderbilt, Andrew enrolled in the postgraduate program at the University of Minnesota. He earned a master's degree in English literature, then went on to receive a second master's degree in art history. He immediately enrolled in the University of Minnesota's doctoral program; his job in Yugoslavia was work that he intended to apply toward his Ph.D. By the time he received his induction notice, he already had decided what his response would be. Jesse had paved the way two years earlier and the assassination of Martin Luther King in Memphis in 1968 had only added fuel to the fire. "By then, I was so divorced from Memphis," he said. "I thought the assassination was typical of Memphis."

Andrew told his mother he was going to protest the war by not responding to the induction notice. That decision would make him a fugitive, but he felt he had no other choice. "I had a visceral distaste for Richard Nixon, and I was overwhelmingly opposed to American involvement in the war. I was not a political animal, but there was not even a flicker of doubt in my mind about the wrongness of the war. I thought the White House was full of crooks—and it was. I thought the Vietnam War was a quagmire—and it was."

As 1968 drew to a close, South Vietnamese Vice President Nguyen Cao Ky invited an American camera crew over the holidays into his rented house in a fashionable suburb of Paris, where peace talks were continuing, though not at an encouraging pace. The exclusive interview was for CBS television's "Face the Nation," a weekly interview and discussion show.

Speaking in uncertain English, the elegantly dressed Ky dropped a bombshell. "We must look at all realities and try to solve them. We never accept—and we will never accept—[National Liberation] Front as an entity, but it is a reality. We are ready to hear them, to meet with them to talk with them, discuss their problems." The news media were stunned. The South Vietnamese government, to date, had refused to acknowledge the existence of the Viet Cong. Now Ky was talking about the "realities" of South Vietnamese politics. Did his comments amount to a breakthrough in the peace talks?

Before reporters in Paris could question him further about his comments, he and his wife returned to Saigon. He was met at the airport by reporters who asked him if his "entity" comment meant the government was going to recognize the Viet Cong. Ky smiled broadly, obviously enjoying the attention. Not at all, he explained. A man may go out with a woman, he said, and that is a reality, but if the woman is not his wife, then she is not an "entity." The reporters scratched their heads in confusion, but Ky was not talking babble. The Viet Cong was fighting against government troops because it did not recognize the legitimacy of the South Vietnamese government. Ky was sending a message to the Viet Cong that he would recognize it if it recognized him. Ky knew that would never happen. It was just a propaganda ploy.

In reality, the South Vietnamese government was focusing it efforts, not on the peace talks, but on the battleground, where two programs—the Accelerated Pacification Campaign (APC) and Phung Hoang, known to the Americans as Phoenix—were underway to take control of the hamlets. Under the rules of APC, South Vietnamese troops in overwhelming numbers descended upon small hamlets with populations of 500 or less. Once the perimeter was secure, South Vietnamese and American intelligence agents were sent into the village to interrogate the residents. If the leaders were found to be sympathetic to the Viet Cong, they were removed from the village.

One favorite method used by the Americans, according to the Viet Cong, was to take the leaders up in helicopters and drop them from a high altitude. New leaders were chosen by the Americans for the hamlet, and the troops moved on to the next hamlet.

The operation known as Phoenix was similar to APC but did not involve the initial deployment of troops. Instead, South Vietnamese and American intelligence agents interrogated suspected Viet Cong sympathizers, working from a "black list" of names obtained in previous operations.

In the United States, the transfer of power followed a different route. In January 1969, Richard Nixon was sworn in as president of the United States on the steps of the Capitol as Lyndon Johnson and Hubert Humphrey looked on. "We cannot learn from one another until we stop shouting at one another," Nixon said in his inaugural speech. He said he had been embarrassed by war protesters during the campaign, and he pledged a lower voice on his part and an effort to bind "black and white together, as one nation." His inaugural parade was met with roving groups of Yippies, some wearing dour Nixon masks. The new, "lowered voice" Nixon did not fool the demonstrators for one moment, and they did not understand why the rest of America did not see the obvious.

Throughout his campaign, Nixon promised to bring an "honorable end" to the war in Vietnam. He won the election because most voters wanted to believe him, especially older voters to whom it was incomprehensible that their government would ever deceive them. Contrary to his public statements about the war and about lowering his voice, Nixon took steps behind the scenes to intensify the war, and on the home front, he added a new weapon to the government's intelligence-gathering arsenal—the Internal Revenue Service. He ordered the agency to form a special team to monitor the activities of political activists.

By the end of 1969, the secret IRS team had accumulated files on nearly 50,000 individuals who were opposed to the president's policies. Between July 1969 and September 1970, the secret team reviewed the tax returns of over 1,000 antiwar organizations and over 4,000 individuals who had expressed antiwar sentiments, according to internal IRS memos published in the *Washington Post*. Following the lead set by the IRS, both the FBI and army intelligence units stepped up their efforts to compile dossiers on Americans considered politically unfriendly to the president.

Three months into office, it became increasingly clear that Nixon had no secret plan to end the war. The Viet Cong launched a new offensive that caught American forces off guard, and it became clear that the level of combat was increasing, not decreasing, as Nixon claimed. *Newsweek* did an analysis entitled "The War: Nixon's Big Test." The article called into question Nixon's war strategy and concluded that "the suspicion persists among some critics that his only real policy is, in effect, more of the same."

Senator George McGovern denounced Nixon's war policy on the floor of the Senate to a nearly empty chamber. He said Nixon lacked the "strength and courage to reverse our course in Vietnam." Senator Edward Kennedy said he thought McGovern's stinging speech was premature, that Nixon should be given more time. Senate Majority Leader Mike Mansfield agreed but warned that Congress's patience was "growing thin."

By March 1969, the Vietnam War had claimed the lives of 33,063 American soldiers and wounded 207,583 others, according to *Newsweek*. That number was only 600 short of the total number of soldiers killed in the Korean War, but the number of wounded in Vietnam was more than twice the number for the Korean War. The number of dead was approaching the total number of American deaths in World War I (53,513) and already exceeded the number of wounded.

In February, *The Commercial Appeal*, Memphis's morning newspaper, sent one of its best reporters, Bill Thomas, to Canada with a Memphis man, Donald Dean Kugler, who had decided to defy the draft. Earlier, the newspaper had sent Thomas to Vietnam, and he had won the Ernie Pyle Award for his reporting on the war. Thomas's series of articles, entitled "Journey into Exile," were published on the front page with a disclaimer that the newspaper was telling a story and not advocating that draft-age men refuse to go into service. Thomas, who had served in the Army in the 1940s in the 82nd Airborne Division, made it clear that he was in favor of the war.

Thomas described Kugler as an "American tragedy." At age twenty-two, he was on the fast track of a teaching career. He was a graduate student at Memphis State University (it has since been renamed University of Memphis), where he taught two courses in freshman English composition. His supervisor, Harry C. Cothan, director of graduate teaching assistants, described him as an "unusually perceptive, intelligent" student. Dr. J. Lasley Dameron, an associate professor of English, described Kugler as one of the brightest students he had ever encountered.

Kugler told Thomas he just couldn't bring himself to support the war. "What are we doing over there?" he asked. "They don't really want us. I mean if we aren't wanted then what are we doing there?" He applied for a teaching deferment, but it was turned down because he was only teaching part time. When he received his induction notice, he called his father, an ordained minister who had served in Italy during World War II, and told him he would not be coming home for Christmas. He had decided to flee to Canada. His father told him that he understood. He told his son that his great-grandfather had come to America to escape the draft in Germany, adding that "maybe it runs in the family."

The night before he left Memphis, Kugler took his girlfriend to dinner at the Four Flames, the city's most historic and elegant restaurant. The next morning, with Thomas sitting at his side, he boarded a Greyhound bus and headed north to Canada. Thomas's stories were overdramatic at times and sometimes reflected his bias, but he was an honest reporter and did his best to tell the story straight. Kugler was not a native Southerner—he was born in Nebraska—but his story, which amounted to a "how to" manual on emigrating to Canada, struck a chord with the public and was symptomatic of changing attitudes about the war in the South.

At this point, the draft was claiming about 33,000 men a month. In an editorial, the *New Republic* said that concerns that the draft would decimate the nation's graduate schools were unfounded—only a fraction of those drafted would be graduate students. The war was "abominable," said the magazine, and graduate students should be encouraged to participate in "massive, selective conscientious objection" to the war effort. "Until there is no draft, men of conscience will have the option when called of refusing to serve, at their peril," said the editorial. "It is a nasty choice to force anyone to make, but it is a choice."

Once Andrew Collins decided his conscience would not allow him to serve in Vietnam, he notified the draft board in Memphis of his decision and the director of his study program at the Smithsonian Institution, who promptly informed him that the institute would have to terminate his funding. "We're going to want your return ticket back," she told him. "You are essentially wanted now that you have said no."

Andrew did not blame her for asking for the ticket; he knew she had a job to do and he knew his sponsors could not support him in his antiwar efforts, at least not officially. "She was a very nice woman, and she was sympathetic," he said. "She said, 'Why don't you just disappear?' "

Working with Andrew was a photographer who had been sent to Yugoslavia to document Andrew's research efforts at the palace. They were about the same age, but the photographer had not yet received his draft notice. Andrew told him of his decision. "Well, hell," said the photographer, who realized his work at the palace would be limited, "This is boring—I'm going with you." By 1990s standards, that seems like a rash decision, but in the 1960s it was not so unusual. There was an "us against them" atmosphere, and most Americans under thirty felt an intense solidarity.

Luckily, Andrew and the photographer had met two girls who worked for the Yugoslavian airline; the girls were agreeable to rewriting the tickets in Croatian. "We smoozed the girls and got our tickets rerouted all over the world," Andrew said. Their first stop was Athens, where they stayed until the weather turned bad and their money started running out.

Andrew stayed in contact with his mother and learned during one of his telephone conversations with her that the FBI had stopped by to visit her. The situation seemed to be deteriorating, so they used their tickets to work their way to Paris, where Andrew knew the American Friends Service Committee had an office. American Friends told them they could go to Sweden or to Canada, but if they wanted subsidies they had to go to Sweden. They talked about it, but neither wanted to go to Sweden. They stayed in Paris for a few weeks, going over their options, then decided to head back to the States. They still had plenty of travel options, thanks to the Yugoslavian girls who had rewritten their tickets.

Taking a circuitous route, they made their way to the Bahamas. Shuttle flights from Florida arrived in Nassau and departed every thirty minutes, carrying gamblers back and forth to the casinos. Andrew and the photographer donned flashy Hawaiian-style shirts and bought tickets to Fort Lauderdale, where Andrew's grandfather lived. They blended in perfectly with the casino crowd and were never asked for identification papers or passports. Andrew's mother flew down to Fort Lauderdale and tried to persuade him to give himself up to authorities.

Andrew was not interested. Instead, he decided to return to Minnesota. That was the place he considered home now, not Memphis. He and the photographer decided to go their separate ways. The photographer wanted to return to his home, where he planned to pursue a career in ceramics. However, before parting they switched identities, or at least Andrew switched identities. The two men were the same age and about the same height. The photographer gave Andrew his passport, Social Security card, and driver's license—and wished him well.

Andrew was a new man. He returned to Minneapolis and rented an apartment that was located just down the street from the university. He retrieved his belongings from the storage site that he had stashed them in before going to Yugoslavia. Using his new name, he got a job as a bartender and settled into his new underground life as a fugitive from the FBI. He re-established contact with his old friends at the university and met a nice girl. On weekends he worked for antiwar organizations.

One night Andrew was coming out of a campus movie theater with his girlfriend when he looked up the street toward his car and saw something that frightened him. "There were all kinds of people standing around my car," he said. "I immediately knew they were bad guys and had found my car. I asked my girlfriend to drive around all night. I left town the next day and drove to Detroit, where I had an aunt and uncle. They were not particularly friendly. He was a World War II veteran. It was the usual left-right generational thing."

In February 1970, Andrew drove across the border at Windsor, Ontario, and went to Toronto, where he landed a teaching position almost immediately. "I was helped immeasurably by sympathetic people in Canada," he says. "There was virtually no hostility whatsoever. I had heard I could expect a sympathetic reception, but I did not know a soul in the country. People took my resume and skipped the first couple of levels and I got a job right away. Canada was really booming then, and they had a very liberal government. I was a mainstream kind of guy [in Canada], but over there [in the United States] I was a radical, pinko dreg."

In fact, there was a large American population in Toronto by the time Andrew arrived. Many Americans, such as the Reverend Robert Gardner, had moved to Canada in order to help the war resisters. Gardner had been an Episcopal chaplain at Michigan State University for more than a decade when he wrote to the Anglican Church of Canada to volunteer his services to American war resisters and deserters. His offer was passed on to the World Council of Churches and the Canadian Council of Churches, which approved his relocation to Canada. Already in his late forties, Gardner packed up his family and moved to Toronto. "Some of these kids needed food and a bed to sleep in," he told newspaper reporters. "Some needed advice on how to become landed immigrants, while others required counseling during the lonely separation from their families."

Gardner's first task was to raise money to help feed and clothe the war resisters. He was able to raise a quarter of a million dollars from Canadian, American, and European churches, an amount he found "just about right" to set up aid centers across the country. One of the first things Gardner noticed were the differences in the backgrounds of the war resisters and the deserters. "The draft evaders tended to be educated, middle class and skilled. For Canada this is the reverse of the brain-drain that once went to the United States. Many of the deserters, on the other hand, were working class, less educated and skilled. Guys from Small Town U.S.A., who just ended up in military service and split for Canada impulsively. Naturally, they have had greater difficulty in adapting."

Not everyone fit either of Gardner's molds, however. Christopher Youngs had grown up in Watertown, Connecticut, where he attended Taft School, an Episcopalian prep school. While he was attending college, he received a notice from his draft board to report for his physical. Knowing that he would likely be drafted a short time afterward, he enlisted in the Marines. He was sent to Camp Pendleton, California, for his initial training.

The drill instructor stood on a platform with a loudspeaker and told him and the other recruits to imagine that an army of "slant-eyed gooks" were coming over the hill toward them. Then he told the recruits to thrust their bayonets into the air at the imaginary enemy and scream "Kill!" at the top of their voice. Christopher fought the imaginary enemy, as he was told, but when the time came for him to scream out the word "kill" he faked it.

After completing basic training, Christopher was transferred to Camp Lejeune, North Carolina. He knew his next stop would be Vietnam. By that time, he was convinced that the war was immoral and that it would be wrong for him to participate. He was also concerned about the quality of leadership he had witnessed in boot camp. He later told a newspaper reporter that the Marine officers he had encountered "were not the sort of people I would want to follow anywhere."

Christopher deserted. First he went to Long Island, Colorado, where he consulted with friends, then it was on to California, where he was welcomed by friends in San Francisco as a contemporary folk hero. He was not comfortable with that sort of adoration and, when told by friends that FBI agents had been making inquiries about him, he surrendered. He was transported back to Camp Lejeune, where he served thirty days in the brig.

Once he was released, he deserted again, only this time he fled to Canada, crossing the border at Buffalo, New York. Soon he met a Canadian girl named Molly. They fell in love and got married. While Molly taught school in a suburb of Toronto, he enrolled in the Ontario College of Education for day classes and went to night school at York University to complete work on a degree program in English literature.

Crossing the border at Buffalo was risky, but Christopher, like many other war resisters and deserters, did not have enough information to be concerned. In an incident that occurred in August 1969, two bus loads of Canadian teenagers and their chaperons were subjected to a nightmarish confrontation with American authorities. The incident was reported by the Canadian media but was ignored by American newspapers.

The students were on their way to the Woodstock Pop Festival when their buses were pulled over by U.S. customs officials and Buffalo police officers. The first bus was pulled around behind a building out of sight of the second bus. Authorities told the passengers on the second bus, which contained the chaperons, to close all the windows and doors and wait until they were called for. Police officers were posted outside the bus as guards.

As the chaperons waited on the second bus with nearly two dozen teens, the teens on the first bus were taken into the customs office and strip searched, a procedure that took three hours. One of the chaperons, Juanita Hunter, a forty-seven-year-old immigrant from Amsterdam, was concerned about her fifteen-year-old daughter but was told that the bus had been released.

When the Canadians on the second bus were led into the customs office, Mrs. Hunter was singled out by a female customs official. "You old hippie, get over here and strip," she said. Mrs. Hunter did as she was told—and it was a good thing she did, for, as she later learned, there was a police officer standing behind her with a nightstick. "The customs lady asked me, 'Have you got those sunglasses on to cover how you're doped up?'" Mrs. Hunter later told Canadian reporters. "I explained I had an eye infection and showed her how it swelled my face up. She didn't make me take my brassiere off, but I had to lower my panties."

The teenage girls were not so lucky. They were all forced to strip completely nude. One of the tour organizers, nineteen-year-old Ossie Parsons, said he counted eight Buffalo detectives and about twenty uniformed officers. Parsons knew a police officer when he saw one. He had worked for awhile as a civilian teletype operator for the Toronto police department. After they were searched, they were herded back to the buses.

Frank Grieco, another tour organizer, said he witnessed a confrontation between a twenty-one-year-old passenger and a customs officer. It began when the passenger leaned over and whispered something to the customs officer. The customs officer did not react, he said, but a narcotics officer did. "He grabbed [the passenger] by the neck and started to choke him," he said. "Four others started to beat him up." Several of the teens jumped off the bus to aid the passenger, but they, too, were beaten by police.

In the end, three American youths, whom tour organizers said were never passengers on the bus, were arrested and charged with narcotics violations, and the two busloads of Canadians were sent back to Canada. "The way we were shoved around, I thought I was back in the war again with the Nazis," said Mrs. Hunter. "But this was more scary—at least with the Nazis you expected it. I'll never cross that border again. I never want to see the United States again."

In July 1969, there was sort of a party atmosphere at Saigon's Tan Son Nhut airport as the United States took the first steps in withdrawing troops from Vietnam. The *Colonel Bogey March* blared across the tarmac and gaily dressed Vietnamese women paraded about with placards that read FAREWELL TO THE OLD RELIABLES. It was the nickname of the Ninth Infantry Division. Not one of the young girls present, most of whom were probably prostitutes, would have thought of that slogan on their own. Besides, the lettering was distinctly U.S. Army. Everything in Vietnam was orchestrated by public relations specialists, even humiliating departures.

With his sleeves rolled up above his elbows, General Creighton Abrams made a small speech, his voice gruff and commanding. Also, there was South Vietnamese President Thieu, who handed out plastic flowers and gifts wrapped in a floral paper that had a Christmas look to it. The men of the Third Battalion, 60th Infantry, were the first to go—all 814 of them— and they accepted the gifts with good grace, though not without considerable discomfort.

A month earlier, President Nixon had announced his intention to withdraw 25,000 troops from Vietnam after meeting with President Thieu at a naval officers' club on Midway Island. Most Americans believed Nixon when he said the troop withdrawal would be the first of many. Not many war resisters believed him nor did many news reporters. John Osborne, writing for the *New Republic*, voiced concern that the withdrawal was only a token gesture. He gave Nixon credit for breaking with the Vietnam policies embraced by presidents Kennedy and Johnson and for stating publicly that the United States no longer wished to support a non-Communist regime simply because it was non-Communist. But he was reluctant to put too much faith in Nixon and in his still-secret plan to end the war.

When Nixon returned from Midway, he told reporters that he and Thieu had "opened the door to peace," and he invited the leaders of North Vietnam to "walk with us through that door." Nixon was a consummate politician. He knew that was exactly the language the American public wanted to hear. It had a ring of fairness and conciliation to it. The Viet Cong and the North Vietnamese were not impressed.

The Paris peace talks were at a complete standstill. Besides, they knew what the American public did not know—namely, that Nixon had ordered bombing raids that extended into Cambodia. The operation was so secret that not even high-ranking Air Force generals were notified of the bombing raids. The operations were omitted from the daily battle reports that went to the military command center at the Pentagon and were known to only a handful of officials in the White House. Nixon trusted no one, not even the Pentagon—and the distrust was mutual.

The secret bombing in Cambodia would have been enough to stall any peace process, but that was only the tip of the iceberg as far as the North Vietnamese and the Viet Cong were concerned. It would take several more years for the American public to know what they knew, but slowly, by bits and pieces, the story was coming out.

In August 1969, *Esquire* published a story by Normand Poirier entitled "An American Atrocity" that provided Americans with their first glimpse of the reality of Vietnam. It told the story of a nighttime raid by U.S. Marines into a South Vietnamese hamlet. The soldiers were searching for Viet Cong and contraband. They raided nearly a dozen huts but found nothing incriminating. Each time they beat the men and women in the huts. The last hut they entered contained an eighteen-year-old mother, Bui Thi Huong; her three-year-old son, her twenty-year-old husband, a farmer who had a debilitating skin disease; her fifty-year-old mother-in-law; her twenty-nine-year-old sister-in-law; and her five-year-old niece.

When the American soldiers found no contraband, they focused their attention on the young mother and her husband. He was beaten by five soldiers, and she was held down and raped. "She had heard her husband's protests of innocence and his cries as he was beaten and the cries of the mother-in-law and sister-in-law and the wailing of the children," wrote Poirer. "When there were five men around her they forced open her legs and ripped her pajamas pants away and tore open the top of her pajamas. She felt rough hands on her breasts and strained to break free but the grips on her arms and legs were like steel clamps." All five men took turns raping her. Then, when the men were done and had washed their genitals with water from a canteen, she heard a burst of gunfire—and the wailing of her family, suddenly cut short. Then she felt a burning pain in her arm and breast and felt her body lifted up and spun around by the impact of the bullets.

Bui Thi Huong lived to tell her story to a Marine court martial panel. All five members of her family had been murdered—and she had been raped by five soldiers, shot, and left for dead—but the most severe sentences imposed on the soldiers by the judge advocate amounted to less than three years imprisonment, and even those sentences were later overturned on appeal. Such stories only inflamed the antiwar movement and made opponents of the war only more determined to bring it to an end. This was not the army that had fought so gallantly in World War II. It was not made up of soldiers who fought for truth and justice and freedom.

General Abrams announced that he was going to limit large-scale operations to about three battalion actions a day. His orders, he said, were to keep American casualties at a minimum and turn the war over to the South Vietnamese army. Abrams's reasons for doing so were not all based on directives from Washington. American soldiers were becoming increasingly difficult to control.

The story told by Bui Thi Huong was not an isolated event. Rapes, murders, and assaults were commonplace. Abrams shocked everyone at one point by arresting Colonel Robert Rheault, the former commander of the Special Forces (better known as the Green Berets) and seven of his men on suspicion of murder and conspiracy to commit murder in the death of a Vietnamese double agent. The Green Berets were under the authority of the army but actually worked for the CIA, according to an article by L. Fletcher Prouty in the *New Republic* (August 23, 1969). Abrams's action was as much directed at the CIA as it was the Green Berets.

Despite the announced intentions of President Nixon to reform the draft, students and antiwar protesters stepped up their activities, their passions inflamed by the atrocities that were being committed against Vietnamese women and children in the name of American patriotism. One hundred black students at Cornell University in Ithaca, New York, shocked authorities by staging a protest in which they appeared with shotguns, rifles and homemade spears.

On October 15, peace activists held a massive, daylong nationwide protest against the war called Moratorium Day. For the first time, the tide was turning in favor of the protesters. A Gallup poll reported that fifty-seven percent of those questioned supported a proposal by New York Senator Charles Goodell calling for the return of all American troops from Vietnam by the end of 1970.

Nixon tried to counter the moratorium by announcing the withdrawal of another 35,000 troops from Vietnam and the suspension of draft calls for November and December; but nothing Nixon did or said stemmed the growing protest against his war policy.

The Moratorium Day protest was the most massive demonstration in American history. The protesters held events in all fifty states. One hundred thousand demonstrators gathered at the Boston Commons, many with their hands raised in the peace sign. In New York City, crowds filled Wall Street. Police estimates placed the New York crowd at 250,000. In Lexington, Kentucky, nearly 3,000 people stood silently in front of the county courthouse.

In city after city, Americans stood shoulder to shoulder, often silently, sometimes taking turns reading the names of American servicemen killed in Vietnam. Before the moratorium began, Nixon had told reporters: "To allow government policy to be made in the streets would destroy the democratic process."

Feeling the pressure, Nixon told the directors of the Associated Press that he could say with confidence that "looking ahead just three years, the war will be over." But he seemed to miss the point: Most Americans did not want to wait three years for the war to be over, they wanted it to end immediately. Former United Nations Ambassador Arthur Goldberg called on the president to order a unilateral cease-fire. Even the Pentagon went on record with newspaper reporters to say that a unilateral cease-fire would create no great risk to American troops in the field.

Very few Americans, with the exception of hard-line right-wingers, voiced public support for Nixon's war policy. Most of the president's supporters were behind the scenes: They were defense contractors who had a financial interest in the continuation of the war; Southern Democrats who had constituents who had invested heavily in the armament industry; retired military officers who thought that the nation's honor was at stake; and a sizable population of ordinary Americans who believed with all their hearts that there would be something unpatriotic about bringing the war to an unilateral termination.

As the year drew to a close, news reporters became more aggressive in their coverage of the war. Instead of accepting the military's view without question—the policy of most news organizations for the past several years—reporters went out into the field to see for themselves. *Newsweek* reported that a Vietnamese farmer was killed by an American solider who was driving by the man's rice field. The playful soldier tried to shoot his hat off but missed and blew the innocent man's head completely off. The soldier received a five-year prison sentence. A brigade commander ran a contest to rack up his unit's 10,000th kill, with the prize being a week of luxury in the colonel's own quarters. Another officer bragged that he liked to shoot at Vietnamese civilians from his helicopter.

In December, reporters broke the story that something dreadful had happened in the village of Song My. Americans were horrified by accounts of what would later be named the My Lai Massacre, but it would be well into the new year before the public knew just how atrocious the crimes were. My Lai was a turning point in the war and in the peace movement's efforts to bring the conflict to an end.

In an article entitled "The Stupidity of Power," which was published in the December issue of Canadian news magazine *Saturday Night*, writer James Eayrs said it was difficult to tell which superpower had done more to "mess things up"—the Russians or the Americans. "By the end of 1969, their slate [Richard Nixon's and Henry Kissinger's], so far from being clean, was smeared by slime and blood," he wrote. "And now so are their hands." Eayrs pointed out that Kissinger had met at the White House with a delegation of college students and had pleaded for their patience in ending the war. "Come back here in a year," Kissinger said. "If nothing has happened, then I can't argue for patience." Wrote Eayrs, speaking for many war resisters, "His year is up. His game is up."

Andrew Collins adjusted quickly to his new life in Canada. After a couple of part-time teaching jobs in Toronto—he worked for the *Financial Post* for a short time and taught English to French-Canadians at the Toronto French School—he secured a full-time position teaching English at Algonquin College in Ottawa.

"It was a real fun period," he said. "The school was developing new curriculum, and my students were only three or four years younger than myself. I liked what I was doing, but I was grossly overpaid."

Andrew met a Canadian woman, Janice, shortly after he moved to Ottawa, and they started living together. They had a son, Oliver, who was born in 1972, and a daughter, Melissa, born in 1974. The following year, they were married and settled into a normal routine. Like most of the other war resisters, he did not actively seek out the company of other Americans, preferring to make a new life for himself among the people of his new country.

Andrew had been part of the biggest exodus of the war. The winter of 1969 and the spring of 1970 saw the largest group of war resisters to enter Canada. Toronto alone was receiving 350 to 400 people a month, according to *EXNET*, a weekly newsletter published by the Pan Canada Conference of Deserters and Resisters.

New patterns were beginning to develop. More exiles were heading toward the West coast into British Columbia than into the eastern provinces of Ontario and Quebec, and more deserters were heading north than ever before. A typical breakdown of new arrivals in Vancouver at that time, according to *EXNET*, could be found in one week's tally in July: Three Vietnam veterans; forty-two men classified 1-A; twenty-four deserters, nine with draft notices, fifteen nondraftable men; and seven women, four of whom arrived with war resisters.

There were several reasons why deserters were arriving in increased numbers. The draft was switched to a lottery system in late 1969, with officials at Selective Service headquarters holding the first draft lottery since World War II. They drew 336 birth dates from a mammoth glass bowl. Those men with high numbers could expect exemption; those with low numbers could expect draft notices within the year; and those with number 122 to 244 were left in limbo—maybe they would be called and maybe they would not be called. No one was happy with the lottery system, which was designed primarily to reduce the number of war resisters fleeing to Canada and to dampen campus protests. "Reforming the draft is like reforming slavery," said a college newspaper editor in Colorado. "It doesn't solve a great deal."

With opinion polls showing that most Americans wanted an immediate end to the war, Nixon announced his intention to end the war. Yet still the slaughter continued in Vietnam, on both sides. Not many soldiers wanted to be the last to kill a Vietnamese. Not many soldiers wanted to be the last killed for a lost cause.

Morale in Vietnam was at rock bottom. Officers were taking orders from their men. The result of all those factors was a record number of desertions, with Canada receiving an estimated 100 deserters a week. *Weekend* magazine sent reporters to visit antiwar groups in Toronto, Ottawa, and Montreal and estimated the number of deserters to be slightly higher, averaging about 500 a month in the later part of 1969.

In late 1969, U.S. Representative Edward Koch of New York went to Canada at the request of several constituents whose sons had fled to that country. Upon his arrival, he had lunch with several members of the Canadian Parliament, all of whom told him they were delighted to have the Americans. In Ottawa, he met with a group of war resisters. Later, he wrote, "My whole feeling about those with whom I spoke was that they nourished no hatred for their country. Neither were they cowards—indeed, some of them have fought in Vietnam."

Andrew's mother, Dixie, visited him several times in Ottawa. "Sometimes we went to Montreal just for fun," said Andrew. "One time she called Jimmy [Jesse Winchester] because his mother had said, 'Now you be sure and look up Jimmy if you are in Montreal.' " By 1970, Jesse had succeeded in performing with a number of successful groups such as The Band, and he had released his first album, *Jesse Winchester*. The album, which *Variety* called the best record of 1970, contained self-penned songs such as "Yankee Lady" and "Brand New Tennessee Waltz." *Rolling Stone* called Jesse the most promising new artist of the year.

Interviewed that year by Roger Neville Williams for his book *The New Exiles*, Jesse said he was having a hard time adjusting to his newfound celebrity status. "I just want to do some simple things, but sometimes being an entertainer kinda works a thing on your head, you just get so self-centered and eccentric," he said. "There've been pressures from people to go back so I could do my music trip in the States—a doctor wanted me to go back and have myself declared insane, but I told him I didn't want to do that. I want to remain true to my convictions about the draft."

Shortly before Christmas 1975, Andrew decided to fly from Ottawa to Florida to meet his mother for the holidays. There was still a warrant out for his arrest, but Andrew decided that the benefits of visiting his mother far outweighed the risks of being apprehended. He was so confident that he did not bother to use a fake ID. His flight took him from Ottawa to Baltimore, where he was required to go through customs and immigration.

To Andrew's surprise, authorities ran a computer check and discovered the outstanding warrant. He was arrested and taken to the Baltimore County jail. "I had a very good left-wing lawyer, and he got me out of the Baltimore County jail and arranged it so that he could keep me under house arrest at his home," said Andrew. "Then the next day, the prosecutor in Memphis asked for a change of venue because they wanted to try it in Memphis."

The U.S. magistrate in Baltimore agreed to a change of venue, but he also released Andrew on a $10,000 cash bond on the condition that he not leave the United States. Andrew continued on to Florida, where he met his mother, then after spending a few days there, they went to Memphis for a January 8 court date. At the hearing, Andrew's attorney, Phillip Kuhn, argued that Andrew had a wife and two children and a teaching job in Ottawa and should be allowed to return. U.S. District Judge Harry W. Wellford said he would not allow Andrew to leave Memphis to return to Canada unless he met certain strict conditions. The judge said that if Andrew wanted to leave Memphis he would have to post an additional $5,000 bond, which could come from his putting his home in Canada up as security, and he would have to sign a request that asked Canadian officials to extradite him if he did not show up for trial. Andrew took the stand and said that if he had wished to return to Canada under those conditions he could have done so while in custody of the attorney in Baltimore. "I could have gone back to Canada then if I had wanted to," he told the court. "There was nothing to stop me."

Assistant U.S. Attorney Hickman Ewing argued against allowing Andrew to return to Canada, saying "Canada nor any other country will extradite anyone on Selective Service charges." United States District Judge Harry Wellford agreed to allow Andrew to return to Canada on the conditions that he post an additional $5,000 bond and that he agree to report each month to immigration officials in New York state. Andrew protested the high bond, saying "I understand that people charged with murder and robbery have bonds one-fourth of what mine is."

Andrew returned to Canada, but crossed the border once a month to report to American immigration officials. "I had two trial dates set—and hitchhiked to Memphis twice—and in neither case did the trial occur," he said. Meanwhile, Bishop Dozier, an outspoken and early critic of the Vietnam War, offered public support to Andrew. He said he did not think the court had taken into consideration Andrew's conscientious objections to the war, and he expressed concern about a justice system that would deal more harshly with Andrew than with violent criminals. In an article for *Common Sense: The Catholic Weekly*, the bishop called upon churches to "pay more attention to our society's disregard for moral values and moral absolutes."

In the fall of 1976, Andrew finally got a court date that stuck. One of the reasons for the ever-changing court dates was that most of the federal judges knew Andrew's family. Judge Wellford recused himself from the case after it was pointed out by prosecutors that he lived only about 100 yards from Andrew's mother's house.

Finally getting the case was U.S. District Judge Robert M. McRae, who conducted a nonjury trial that lasted only one day. The judge said he found it a "very difficult case, made more difficult by the discussion going on now of candidates for president of the United States." The judge's comments were based on the statements made by presidential candidate Jimmy Carter, who had repeatedly said he would grant pardons to all Vietnam War draft resisters if he were elected.

Andrew viewed the trial as a waste of time, and he was not surprised when the judge found him guilty and gave him five years probation. "I was guilty as hell," he said. "The trial didn't last long. I wasn't allowed to say anything. It was very short—no jury, no nothing. My lawyer didn't care anything about me. I was not happy with his counsel. He [the judge] gave me the maximum, five years, but he said that since Jimmy Carter had announced that he would pardon people like me, it would be unfair for me to start my sentence pending an election in November that was two months away."

After the trial, Andrew returned to Canada and waited for the election returns to come in. President Gerald Ford already had declared an amnesty, but the two-year public service requirement did not appeal to Andrew, and he had rejected that offer. The ordeal in Memphis had been neither a victory nor a defeat—just more of the same harassment that seemed unending to him at the time. He never had to serve any time for his conviction, but he knew that was because President Jimmy Carter had promised to grant pardons.

Even so, for Andrew, the outcome of his trial was nothing to celebrate. He had paid a stiff price for his convictions. "I became divorced from my family," he said. "If you don't see people for months and years on end, you lose commonality. To this day, my brothers and I are strangers. My mother kind of held us together. I don't really feel I have any family left. I have my own family. But as far as being a child of a family, I lost that a long time ago."

Andrew retired from teaching at the age of thirty-five—"It's a demanding occupation"—and started buying real estate during the Canadian land boom. He quickly made money and was able to retire at a young age. In 1981, he received an offer from the Canadian government to go to Zimbabwe, South Africa, to revamp their English texts, most of which were academically tainted by years of institutional racism.

Eager for adventure, Andrew took his family to Africa. "I was teaching and consulting, and my son and I became interested in the landscape and the animals, so I gave up the teaching thing after a year and started taking tourists and corporate clients around South Africa. My son and I became guides."

One day Andrew and Oliver decided to try something that had never been done: They would attempt to drive from South Africa to England. The trip had been made from England to South Africa, but never in the opposite direction. They obtained corporate sponsorships for their trip—Dunlop Rubber (British) and Total Petroleum (French)—and set out in 1983 for England in a Toyota land cruiser. It was a successful trip.

When they returned five months later, they were heralded as the first Zimbabwean registered vehicle ever to make the trip. They made the newspapers and were celebrities of sorts. In 1989, Janice discovered she was pregnant, so they returned to Canada so that she could receive proper medical care. When the child was born, they named her Dixie after his grandmother and his mother, who subsequently died in November 1996.

Andrew and Janice were able to survive nearly two decades of exile, isolation, and African adventures but were ultimately not able to survive the *absence* of exile and isolation; they eventually filed for divorce. Today, Andrew has two grown children and one grandchild. He spends most of his time looking after his investments—and looking for new adventures. "I feel optimistic [about the future]," he said. "I take care of myself. . . . I have the resources to do whatever I want to do . . . you just move on."

3

1970
Charles Sudduth:
Saying "Hell, No" to the KKK

Charles Sudduth was standing at his bedroom window early one morning, having a cup of coffee, when he saw Johnny Pierce, the Mississippi highway patrol officer assigned to the area, approach his house in a patrol car, slow down, and point in his direction. Behind the patrol car was an unmarked car with two men in business suits. As the unmarked car pulled up opposite the house, it slowed down, then stopped. The men inside the car stared at the house a moment, then drove off. Charles did not like the way that looked.

After dressing—he wasn't used to wearing a coat and tie, but proper attire seemed appropriate for his mission—Charles drove around town until he found the unmarked car that had stopped in front of his house. It was parked outside Jones's Diner. Finding the car had not been difficult. He lived in a small Delta town of around 3,000 people.

You could count all the cafes and restaurants on one hand (and have fingers to spare). Half the population was African American, but there were no black-owned businesses on the white side of town. Segregation was still the rule, and the two races were separated by more than historical tradition. They were separated by a railroad track that drew a dividing line between the haves and the have-nots.

When Charles found the unmarked car, he went into the diner and sat down on a stool at the counter beside the two men in business suits. "What's up?" he said cheerfully.

The men did not answer.

Several times, Charles tried to start a conversation with the men. They only ignored him. Finally, he said, "Did you guys want to speak to me about something?"

The men stared straight ahead.

Charles went outside and wrote down the license number of their car. When he got home, he called the state Motor Vehicle Bureau in Jackson and told them someone had sideswiped his car. He gave them the license number of the car parked outside the diner. It was a lie, but he was being watched by men in suits, and this was no time to quibble over small details.

"I wouldn't worry about it," said the motor vehicles clerk, after she had looked up the ownership of the car. Her voice was reassuring. "I'm sure they will pay for any damages. The car belongs to the FBI."

Charles knew why the FBI was checking out his house. The previous year he had filed for conscientious-objector status with his local draft board. What he couldn't understand was why the FBI wouldn't talk to him about it. "Even though I went there and offered to talk to them about anything they wanted to talk about, they shut up," he says today. "That seems like dishonesty in the extreme."

The FBI was the least of Charles's problems.

The previous summer, while taking a break from his studies in philosophy at the University of Mississippi to work for the State Department of Vocational Rehabilitation, he was labeled a subversive by his employer, and his name was turned over to state officials, most likely the super-secret Mississippi State Sovereignty Commission. It was a summer job, the type created for students wanting to get experience in the field. Part of the department's mission was to provide medical services to poor people, many of whom were African Americans.

In the 1960s, to be labeled a "subversive" in Mississippi was to be identified as an advocate of civil rights, a "crime" of which Charles certainly was guilty. The Sovereignty Commission had been created in 1956 to combat racial integration, but, over the years, as the civil rights movement had merged with the antiwar movement, it began targeting political dissidents, often using illegal means to accomplish its goals.

Charles still has a good recollection of the incident.

"I recall we were at a meeting discussing individual cases," said Charles. "We talked about one woman who needed to go into the hospital. The doctor said to the director, 'You want me to fix her up, too?' "

"The director responded, 'Yeah, go ahead; she's got four children and she don't need no more.' "

"I realized they were sterilizing those people while they were under anesthesia without their permission. I went back to the office and asked our people if they were doing that, and they said they were. The next morning, the director called me into his office and asked me to sign a loyalty oath to the State of Mississippi. I told him I had no loyalty to any town, country, state, nation or organization whatsoever. My only loyalty was to humanity as a whole, without regard to race, sex, or nationality."

"I appreciate your response," said the director. "I am going to report you to the state as a subversive."

That was how many files were opened by the Sovereignty Commission: Mississippians reporting other Mississippians for being disloyal to the cause of racial separation. At the time, Charles did not know what it meant to be reported as a subversive, other than that it meant trouble. The year before, while a student at Delta State University at Cleveland, Mississippi, he made enemies by refusing to sign a petition in support of the Vietnam War.

"It made the students so hot because everyone signed it but me," he said. "They offered me fifty dollars to sign it, and I still wouldn't do it. I was almost lynched. Five students came after me with tire irons. I remember one guy in particular. I had thought he was a nice guy. He said he had flown bombers in Vietnam. He told me he knew what to do about me. He told me he was going to report me to the Sovereignty Commission."

Although the commission had been in operation for twelve years, few people understood the scope of its powers. In later years, evidence emerged from the commission's secret files that it was involved in an assortment of illegal activities and was, in fact, under the direction of former FBI agents.

Charles's most immediate problem was with the draft board. He knew many of the members by reputation, but one he knew personally. He was one of the wealthiest planters in the area. He was generally well thought of, but Charles knew another side of the man.

When he was eleven or twelve, a neighbor took him to the man's house for what he was told was a meeting of local Klan sympathizers. "The meeting was organized like a sermon in a church," Charles recently recalled. "[The board member] would stand at a podium and preach to his audience. I don't remember what he talked about, except I do remember him saying that Klansmen were justified to do anything to drive federal people out of the state. He said they were entitled to lie and cheat and steal and murder—anything to drive them out."

Charles attended three or four of those meetings, then stopped going. Several years later, he was called, along with all the other students, to the school auditorium to listen to a special presentation by the board member and his wife. The program, as he later learned, was sponsored by the Citizens Council, a nationwide organization that worked during the 1950s and 1960s to block racial integration.

The board member's wife was fond of speaking about the town's history to anyone who would listen. Her father was one of the area's earliest settlers. When Charles first saw the two on stage that day, he thought, "Oh, my good friends."

What transpired changed his mind.

"I remember that day I was wearing my favorite shirt," he said. "It was a Kingston Trio shirt. No one else had a shirt like it. When the curtains on the stage opened, there was [the board member's wife] in the center of the stage sitting on a stool. Standing behind her was [her husband]. She gave us a history [the area]. Then she started telling about the lynchings that occurred.... She told us how there was a store downtown next to the bank and that a black man went in the store and stole this necklace. They knew his wife was involved because she distracted them while he stole the necklace. She said they caught them and built a cage out of poles on the outskirts of town. She said they stripped them naked and took them into that cage and kept them there for three days. She said the people from town came there and tortured them with sticks.

"At the mention of each new atrocity, [the board member], who was behind her, puffed up and thrust his chest out and held his head higher. When the lecture was over, I ran out the front door of the school and tore my favorite shirt off and wadded it up and buried it in the ground. It seemed to me incredible that any person could inflict that kind of misery on another human being. At that instant, I felt [they] were my enemies from then on out. I just didn't realize how great an enemy they were."

That realization occurred when the board member summoned him to the draft board office to question him about his application for conscientious-objector (CO) status. "Looking back, I was extremely naive to file such a thing because that did little more than attract attention and make them more determined to grab [me] above all others," he recalls. "I always tried to say that I could make no universal condemnation of war, but I opposed the Vietnam War."

Charles tried to explain his beliefs to the board member.

"He was hard to talk to," said Charles, who, as a precocious youth, had immersed himself in the writings of Friedrich Nietzsche, Ralph Waldo Emerson, and Bertrand Russell. "There was hardly any intelligible conversation between us. They had a policy, in particular, of drafting people who were opposed to the war. Those who supported the war, they all got out [of the draft]."

In 1963, Charles's high school had a graduating class of twenty-three—thirteen men and ten women. Among the men, two or three had enlisted rather than be drafted. However, three had voiced opposition to the war in Vietnam, an unusual number of dissidents from a rural Mississippi farming town. Charles Sudduth was one of those three.

By 1968, the board member was reaching back into the class of '63 to select draftees for service in Vietnam. He looked at the list of thirteen draft-age men from the class of '63 and decided that the only three men in that class eligible for the draft were the three who had expressed opposition to the war in Vietnam. Concerned about his draft status, Charles wrote to a friend: "I'm still trying to get a deferment but things don't look too good. If a deferment comes through, then I will go to the University of Tennessee, where they have offered me a $1,800 yearly research assistantship. . . . When I took my draft physical in May, I refused to take the loyalty oath and refused to support the U.S. Constitution. . . . Most likely I'll wind up in Canada."

The draft board sent induction notices to the other two men in Charles's class. Both refused induction—one was already living in Canada and the other went to prison. The board member was not pleased that the only two men he had drafted from the class of '63 had turned down Uncle Sam's invitation to go into military service. That was why the FBI was shadowing Charles at his home. He didn't want this third target to slip away—at least, not to Canada.

For the time being, the board member was content to play cat and mouse with Charles. If he had known Charles was going to fight back, he might have made other choices. It was that lack of decisiveness that opened the door to the board member's past and lead the Justice Department into what must have been an uncomfortable silent partnership with him.

Charles gave up any hope of convincing the draft board to accept his application for CO status. He had pretty much made up his mind to move to Canada. He had been in contact with friends in Canada for almost a year, requesting information about immigration procedures. In May 1969, Sudduth said good-bye to his mother and father and drove to Ottawa. On June 1, he wrote a letter to the Selective Service System office in Watertown, New York. "I will not report for induction on June 2 as ordered," he said in the letter. He provided the board, as required under law, his new address in Canada, then he explained why he was not reporting for induction.

"I do not believe that my request [for conscientious-objector status] was given fair consideration because . . . the man who signed my induction papers is a member of the Ku Klux Klan in my home town," he continued in the letter. "Furthermore, he is not only a member of it, he is head of the Ku Klux Klan. . . . This man has known me for some years, and he knows that I was involved with black people in civil rights activities for the past four years."

Charles's letter was dutifully forwarded to the Mississippi draft board, which declined to alter his A-1 draft status. Their position was that board members, all of whom were appointed by the president, were entitled to belong to any organization they chose. It was their right as Americans. From the local board office, Charles's letter eventually made its way to the office of the U.S. attorney.

The letter created a dilemma for the federal prosecutor. Would he conduct an investigation into allegations of KKK involvement with the draft board, knowing that would probably lead him to the super-secret Mississippi State Sovereignty Commission and then possibly to the former FBI agents employed by the commission? Or would he forget he ever saw the letter and leave the man seated on the board?

Charles stayed in contact with his family by writing letters that reported on his whereabouts and activities. Like most war resisters, he wondered if authorities were intercepting his mail, but it was the sort of thing that was impossible to prove at the time. Not until 1976 did a Senate investigating committee uncover evidence that both the FBI and the CIA had illegally intercepted the mail of political dissidents.

The CIA conducted mail opening operations in four cities, said the Senate panel, in which it opened and photographed nearly a quarter of a million first-class letters. "The stated purpose of all of the mail opening programs was to obtain useful foreign intelligence and counterintelligence information," said the panel, but peace and civil rights activists were "specifically targeted," along with "journalists, authors, educators, and businessmen."

The FBI had a mail opening campaign similar to the one carried out by the CIA, but it went a step further with "black bag jobs" that allowed FBI agents to illegally enter private residences and businesses for the purposes of obtaining information and installing hidden microphones. "Like the CIA, the FBI did not secure the approval of any senior official outside its own organization prior to the implementation of its programs," said the Senate panel.

On January 4, 1970, an army radio announcer in Saigon was removed from duty after telling his listeners that he was "not free to tell the truth." When a reporter for the *New York Times* asked a reporter for the army-run *Stars and Stripes* about the incident, he was told that the army felt that telling the whole truth about the war would be "bad for morale."

In fact, the military had become a battleground between antiwar and prowar elements. That same month, the *New Republic* ran a story under the headline "The Man Who Beat the Army" that told the story of a young GI named Harris Tobias who successfully challenged the army's policy on granting conscientious-objector status to men already in uniform.

Tobias was a Specialist Four in the 203rd Transportation Company, a Long Island reserve unit that had been called up for active duty in May 1968. Antiwar sentiment among the entire company ran high, and as they sat about the base at Fort Eustic, Virginia, awaiting orders to go to Vietnam, many of the soldiers began petitioning their congressmen and the president, claiming that the call-up was illegal.

Tobias's opposition ran deeper. Before being called up, he had spent a year in the Peace Corps working in a village in Guatemala. The call-up of his reserve unit troubled him. He told friends he just did not have it in him to kill other people. He finally summoned the nerve to make a formal CO application, only to have it rejected.

Instead, the army ordered him to Vietnam. Tobias went AWOL, then hired a prominent New York attorney, who filed a lawsuit in federal court to block his transfer to Vietnam. Meanwhile, Tobias was placed in an army stockade and was found guilty by a court martial board. That conviction was overturned by a three-judge panel of the Fourth Circuit, which ordered the army to grant Tobias's application for CO status. In their ruling, the judges characterized the army's treatment of Tobias as "arbitrary and capricious." Tobias was granted a discharge from the army, but the conviction was left on his record.

For the first several months of 1970, the news media backed off on coverage of the war and President Nixon's efforts to end the fighting through his "Vietnamization" plan. News magazines stopped running Vietnam-themed covers, and where they had once placed coverage of the war at the front of the magazine in high-profile positions, they now pushed it back to the middle of the magazine and kept the stories brief and rosy. Not much had changed during Nixon's first year in office, but most newspaper and magazine editors seemed to have made editorial decisions to give the president space to bring the war to an honorable end as he had promised.

In its January 12 issue, *Newsweek* ran a feel-good piece headlined "The President: Happy New Year" that told readers everything they could want to know about Nixon's outings with Jimmy Stewart, Fred MacMurray, and Bob Hope. Even the liberal *New Republic* seemed weary. Its January 24 issue contained a feature on Nixon's first year by *New York Times* columnist Tom Wicker. "It can well be argued that the people have had quite enough of Roosevelt-Kennedy-Johnson style 'leadership' toward goals that were not commonly accepted or understood," wrote Wicker in a piece that seemed to be pleading for the public to give the president a break.

All that changed dramatically in May when Nixon invaded Cambodia. Instead of winding the war down, he was now expanding it. Instead of sending American men to die in one country, he was now sending them into two countries. Accompanying the invasion of Cambodia by thousands of American troops was a return to bombing in the north. The war was not cooling down, as everyone had been led to believe; it was heating up.

Many Americans felt an enormous sense of betrayal. The wave of protest began with the news media. *Newsweek* put Vietnam back on the cover with the headline "Now It's the Indochina War." Inside were photographs of dead soldiers, with their bodies bloated beyond recognition. Under the headline "Staying Alive Until 1973" [a reference to the next presidential election] the *New Republic* began its story on the cover with the words "Richard Nixon is going down in history, all right, but not soon enough. That he is no commanding genius was long suspected; but that he should come to believe in May 1970 that the United States can blast and bomb a military victory . . . all this came as a shock, even to the long-headed."

America was stunned. Only three weeks before the invasion, the Vietnam Moratorium Committee had shut down its central office in Washington, declaring that the era of mass protests was over. With news of the invasion and expanded bombing in the north, college campuses across the country erupted in protest. At the University of Maryland, more than 400 police officers descended upon the campus, beating sixty-three students and arresting twenty-five.

Just when police thought they had it under control, the protests began again. This time National Guardsmen were sent on campus, resulting in injuries to 75 students and 157 arrests. The same thing happened at the University of Ohio and the University of Wisconsin. Most college campuses experienced protests of one kind of another.

Among those was Kent State University. The day after Nixon announced the invasion of Cambodia, students held peaceful protest rallies across the campus. The college was located in the green hills of northeastern Ohio and did not have a reputation for radicalism. When the protests spilled over into the town of Kent that night, the twenty-man police force responded violently, and students retaliated by breaking store windows. Eventually, the protest made its way back to the campus, where the ROTC building was fire-bombed.

Ohio governor James Rhodes declared martial law in Kent and sent National Guardsmen from the 107th Armored Cavalry Regiment and the 145th Infantry Battalion to the campus. The soldiers were armed with .45-caliber automatics and automatic .30-06 rifles with bayonets affixed. The men were issued gas masks, which they donned when they confronted the unarmed students.

As the guardsmen charged the students, they fired canisters of tear gas; the students responded with stones and bottles and by tossing the canisters back at the soldiers. Without warning, the guardsmen opened fire, sending more than thirty-six shots into a crowd of students, all of whom were no more than seventy-five feet away from the soldiers.

When the shooting stopped, nine students were wounded and four lay dead, including Allison Krause, a nineteen-year-old student from Pittsburgh who was shot as she walked to class; Sandy Scheuer, a twenty-year-old student from Youngstown who was shot moments after she finished walking her dog; William Schroeder of Lorain, Ohio, a nineteen-year-old ROTC student and former high school basketball star who had paused to watch the protest; and Jeffrey Glenn Miller of Plainview, New York, a twenty-year-old student who had gone home during spring break to tell his parents that he would never go to Vietnam to kill.

Officials defended the actions of the soldiers, and no one was ever prosecuted for the killings. The attitude of the guardsmen was indicated by the unremorseful soldier who was interviewed by a reporter from *Newsweek:* "It's about time we showed the bastards who's in charge," he said.

Before the month was out, the Gallup Organization conducted a poll that found that fifty percent of Americans approved of Nixon's invasion of Cambodia, sixty-five percent were very satisfied or fairly satisfied with Nixon's job as president, and fifty-eight percent felt the students at Kent State were at fault for the killings.

The families of the students were besides themselves with grief. Bewildered and angry, the mother of Jeffrey Miller told *Life* magazine that she blamed the government for the killings, especially Richard Nixon, whom she said "acts as if the kids had it coming." Following burial of her daughter Allison, Doris Krause wrote to a war resister in Canada, saying "I do not recognize the world any longer; it has changed beyond all nightmares." Referring to the war resister, she wrote, "how sad to have to give up one's homeland because of such differences in belief."

Ten days later, students at Jackson State College, a predominately black institution located in Jackson, Mississippi, held rallies on the campus to protest the invasion of Cambodia and the escalating demands of the draft. Mississippi governor John Bell Williams called up the National Guard, but since they could not be assembled until the following day, he sent state highway patrol officers to the campus, where they were joined by city policemen.

Before marching on the campus, the officers gathered behind an armored vehicle sent to the scene by the Jackson mayor. Inside the tank, ten men were armed with Thompson submachine guns capable of firing 700 rounds per minute. The men behind the tank also carried shotguns. As the army approached the campus, it was greeted by shouts from dormitory windows.

"Pigs!" the students shouted. "White sons-of-bitches!"

The army and the tank pulled up outside one of the dormitories and stopped. One of the police officers addressed the students with a bullhorn. He was greeted with a bottle tossed from one of the windows. The bottle crashed harmlessly into the street, bursting in small pieces. The police responded by opening fire with their machine guns and shotguns. The gunfire fanned out across the campus, mowing down students caught in the open, tearing through the thinly constructed walls of the dormitories as if they were made of paper.

When the firing stopped, police discovered they had killed two students and wounded twelve others. Attorney General John Mitchell asked J. Edgar Hoover to send FBI agents to Jackson to investigate the incident. Later, Mitchell went to the campus to see for himself. No one was ever prosecuted for the shootings—both a county grand jury and a federal grand jury refused to indict the police officers—but the President's Commission on Campus Unrest subsequently found that the highway patrol and the police had used "unreasonable" force against the students. One of the commission members said Mississippi was a police state, "ruled by terror." Governor Williams dismissed the report as a "slanderous diatribe" against the state of Mississippi.

The commission's report on Kent State declared that the board's members were "impressed and moved" by the students' idealism and commitment to social causes, but it suggested they should be more respectful of their elders. The killings were viewed as the result of inadequate training for National Guardsmen. No punishment was suggested for the soldiers who gunned down the students. The remedy, said the report, was for the president to call together all the governors to discuss ways of upgrading the guard. "One Kent State," concluded the report, "is far too many."

In the minds of many, America had become a police state—and the commission's report only demonstrated the vastness of the no-man's-land that existed between those over thirty and those under thirty. Those over thirty said they were standing up for God and country. Those under thirty said they were fighting for their lives.

Charles Sudduth was working as a tree surgeon in Ottawa in November 1970 when he received a letter from the Mississippi draft board. "[We] received a letter from the U.S. attorney declining prosecution of you," said the letter. "In view of the above, it is important that you meet with the local board to discuss your classification."

Charles was stunned by the letter. Why would the United States attorney abruptly decide not to prosecute him?

Charles communicated with the draft board, but he did not cross the border and return to Mississippi as they requested. Instead, he corresponded with the Mississippi board for a while, finally establishing that it was willing to accept his application for conscientious-objector status.

Even then, Charles did not rush back to the States, not after what had happened at Jackson State and Kent State. After the killings had taken place, Charles stopped by to visit a friend in Brockville, Ontario. The killings were very much on Charles's mind. They had galvanized the antiwar movement, making everyone involved even more determined to prevail. Viewed from Canada, America had become a war zone, with students now public enemy number one.

In March, a delegation of Mennonite leaders went to Ottawa to meet with Prime Minister Trudeau to ask him to encourage American draft dodgers and deserters to come to Canada. The church leaders presented him with a brief on the subject and then left to await his reply. After reading the brief, Trudeau said it was the most "beautiful brief" he had ever read and had expressed views "close to my heart." Said Trudeau to the Mennonites: "Your motivation is like mine. It stems from a belief in a transcendent God. The young radicals are looking for the same thing too, whatever existentialist and nihilist elements there may be in their thinking." To the press, he said, "The government is welcoming U.S. draft dodgers and deserters to Canada." Then, referring to a Mennonite concern about the growing influence of the military, he said, "I, too, hope Canada will become a refuge from militarism." Most Canadians seemed to agree with Trudeau's position on war resisters, although there were pockets of resistance among some lower-level government officials.

Earlier in the year, two student radicals from Columbia University in New York had flown to Toronto to attend a conference on student revolt called The Year of the Barricade. When they arrived at the airport, the two students—Bob Bossin and Laura Jacknick—were taken by authorities into separate rooms for questioning. The ordeal lasted about an hour. They asked the two everything imaginable. Repeating the questions to a writer from *Maclean's* magazine, Bob said they asked him: "Do you believe the pen is mightier than the sword? Are you aware of an international conspiracy to overthrow the Canadian and American system?" Laura responded to her questioners by trying to convert them to feminism. Both said they felt flattered by all the attention.

Maclean's reported later in the year that contrary to Trudeau's instruction, the RCMP had established a six-man squad to work with the FBI in tracing deserters. The squad was instructed to report directly to an FBI liaison. The magazine also said the RCMP had taken an "unmistakably right-wing stance" and had "severely questioned" a thirteen-year-old Montreal girl whose mother helped a deserter.

That summer, retired Brigadier-General E. S. Light, archdeacon of Saskatchewan and general secretary of the Anglican Church of Canada, turned heads when he moved to Toronto to work with American war resisters. Before becoming a padre in the Canadian armed forces during World War II, he had earned his parachutist's wings and trained for a year as an air bomber in the Canadian Air Force. When he arrived in Toronto, he told shocked reporters that he had learned there were over 20,000 resisters in the city, and that he, and the church, felt they were in need of help.

"I'm convinced the majority are concerned and bewildered, especially the younger ones," he told the *Toronto Star*. "Their reasons for leaving their country are probably not well defined in their own minds. It may be that if I were one of them, I'd be in the same position. It may be that it's absolutely the only way to protest. I don't know."

Also coming to the war resister's aid was Canon Maurice Wilkinson, the associate secretary of the council of churches, who, like Light, was also an Anglican and a former combat officer during World War II with the Royal Canadian Army Service Corp. One of the young Americans who impressed Wilkinson was a deserter who had spent seven months in Vietnam. He was looking forward to going home at the end of his tour of duty, but then one day he came across a school filled with dead children. It was an experience that changed his life. The children had been napalmed by American pilots, and many of them were still at their desks. "He was sick to his stomach, [and] promptly signed on for another tour of duty, which meant an automatic thirty-day leave in the

United States," Wilkinson told Ron Lowman of the *Toronto Star*. But the re-enlistment was just a ploy. After the man arrived back in the United States for his leave, he crossed the border into Canada on the first day.

By 1970, Canadians began to question their government's indirect participation in the Vietnam war. Since 1950, Canada had sold $2.5 billion worth of war materials to the United States under terms of the Canada-U.S. Defense Production Sharing Agreement, which allowed Canadian firms to bid for military contracts issued by the American military. Included was everything from ammunition to complex electronic gear to clothing (the caps worn by the Green Berets were sewn in Toronto).

In March, *Maclean's* staff writer Walter Stewart wrote a tongue-in-check piece critical of that arrangement. He said he felt the "quiet thrill of pride" when he read about an American solider firing a clip of tracer bullets into a group of women and children. "An eyewitness account of bombs wrenching at rice paddies along the Ho Chi Minh Trail stirs me like the cry of bugles," he wrote. "After all, I tell myself, it's our war, too." He concluded with, "So, the next time you see a picture of a Vietnamese baby lying in a puddle of his own blood, don't let the Americans take all the glory. That blood is ours, too."

Back in the States, the same type of national introspection and analysis was beginning to take place in the American media. *Look* magazine, normally conservative and personality-oriented, published an issue that contained both a profile of Trudeau—it discussed his policy of allowing war resisters in the country and ran a photograph of the fifty-year-old prime minister turning cartwheels on the lawn of the official residence—and a diary of a draft resister who chose to live underground rather than go to Canada. The resister, Richard Gooding of Chicago, had worked as a newspaper reporter in Chicago and New York before receiving his induction notice. The article was titled "An Exile in My Own Country" and contained thoughts, written in an impressionistic literary style, of Gooding's internal odyssey into America's underground. Shortly after publication of the article, Gooding sought asylum in Montreal with his wife.

As the year ended, the Associated Press obtained Defense Department documents that outlined a secret military intelligence operation at a Texas Air Force base. The documents revealed that military intelligence officers were ordered to report on any personnel making sympathetic statements about antiwar demonstrators and expressing opposition to the war in Vietnam. North Carolina Senator Sam Ervin, a long supporter of privacy rights, received copies of the documents and protested to the Pentagon. He said he had evidence that military agents

also had been spying on United States senators and other elected officials.

   The wave of popularity garnered over the Cambodian invasion and
his handling of student dissidents—Gallup polling data gave President
Nixon a higher rating than Roosevelt received after the bombing of
Pearl Harbor—provided Nixon with a sense of invincibility. Buoyed by
the results of the new poll, Nixon scurried about Washington, dropping
in unexpectedly on organizations he thought might be sympathetic.
   Not impressed by the polling data were the tens of thousands of war
resisters in Canada—it seemed to confirm their worst suspicions that
their fellow Americans had gone over the edge—and a growing
number of congressmen. A bipartisan group of five senators, led by
South Dakota Democrat George McGovern, purchased a half-hour of
television time to discuss their amendment to end the war, which
would cut off funds for combat operations in Vietnam. A second
amendment sponsored by senators Frank Church of Idaho, a Democrat,
and John Sherman Cooper of Kentucky, a Republican, would prohibit
use of any appropriations to maintain U.S. troops in Cambodia after
June 30.
   Vice-President Spiro Agnew called McGovern's amendment "a blueprint for the first defeat in the history of the United States" and the administration sought to undermine the Church amendment by telling
congressman that it had been the president's plan all along to withdraw
the troops from Cambodia in July.
   Meanwhile, the war raged on. Initially, Nixon had sent 20,000 American troops into Cambodia, according to *Newsweek* (May 25, 1970). They
met stiff resistance, resulting in the deaths of 53 American soldiers.
Soon they were joined by additional troops, according to Professor Loren Baritz, bringing the American troop strength up to 32,000 and the
South Vietnamese troop strength up to 48,000.
   Within Vietnam, the war continued unabated, although with slightly
lower causalities that averaged about seventy-five dead and seven hundred wounded American soldiers a week. Nixon did pull American
troops back from Cambodia in July, but to his horror, antiwar sentiment
in the Senate continued to grow. He may have scored points with voters
with the Kent State and Jackson State killings—and with his intimations
that the war could be concluded with a victory—but he was rapidly losing ground in Congress. In September, his most vociferous critic, Senator George McGovern, set up a small office near the Capitol, a move
reporters interpreted as an indication he might run for president in
1972.

If Congress was gradually gravitating toward the side of the war resisters in its assessment of the war, the mood of the country as a whole was not. There was a spirit of meanness afoot, an understanding among state and local police officers that they had a free hand to deal with dissidents in any manner they chose.

Two incidents in Dallas, Texas, were indicative of that mood. Two men were jailed under a state law that made flag desecration a felony. Nineteen-year-old Gary Deeds was arrested after he burned an imitation flag (it was actually a piece of bunting) at a demonstration held to protest the war and the city's treatment of hippies. State prosecutors were successful in getting a felony conviction, but they were unable to get the twenty-five-year sentence they sought. Deeds was sentenced to *only* four years in the state penitentiary.

Another man, Robert Jones, was arrested after he went to the Dallas County District Attorney's office to complain about the police department's refusal to investigate a complaint he had made. The district attorney took one look at Jones, who was wearing bell-bottom trousers with flag material sewn into the cuffs, and had him arrested for flag desecration. He was placed in a section of the jail called "queen's walk," where homosexuals were customarily held.

When Deeds protested, he was told with a wink that he could not be transferred unless he attempted suicide. He did as they suggested, but it was a trick. As a result of the "suicide attempt," he was stripped naked and put in solitary confinement in a cell that had no bunk or running water. His toilet was a drainage hole in the corner. He was later freed on bond.

This type of hostility toward the youth of the country was even extended to the soldiers who served in Vietnam. The public did not like the soldiers any more than they liked the protesters. These feelings would escalate in the final years of the war, but as early as 1970, there were indications that returning veterans would be cut no slack, not even the dead ones.

In Florida, a twenty-year-old black soldier killed in Vietnam was denied burial in a cemetery at Fort Pierce. The grave had been donated to the soldier's family by an elderly white woman, but cemetery officials refused to honor the donation on the grounds that they were only allowed to bury white people. At the soldier's eulogy, a black student from Los Angeles described his friend as a "man without a country." So felt many Americans.

That fall, veteran *Newsweek* reporter Maynard Parker, who had served as the magazine's bureau chief in Saigon, wrote an article entitled "Vietnamization Is Not Peace," in which he said he was convinced that several thousand more Americans would die before the United States would be able to extricate itself from the war. The only solution he saw was for the United States to announce a deadline for the withdrawal of all troops, one that would shock the South Vietnamese leaders into the realization that America's commitment to their cause was indeed limited. Concluded Parker: "If the South Vietnamese, with a million-man army and with one of the world's largest air forces, cannot defend themselves within a year or two years' time, then there is very little reason to think they ever will be ready to stand alone."

As the year ended, President Nixon, his ego puffed up over his high ratings in the opinion polls, sent out signals that he was going to reverse course and resume massive bombings in the north. To reporters, Nixon seemed strangely belligerent. After weeks of hints and obscure threats from White House officials, Nixon finally said it outright: If the North Vietnamese "increase the level of fighting in South Vietnam, then I will order the bombing of military sites in North Vietnam."

Political commentators were baffled. If Nixon was serious, and did resume the bombing, the war would again escalate, and America would be subjected to a new round of demonstrations and civil unrest. If he was only bluffing in an effort to confuse the North Vietnamese and the Viet Cong, then he risked confusing the people of his own country to an even greater degree.

On an October trip to the Mediterranean designed to flex U.S. military muscle overseas, particularly in the Middle East, Nixon stopped off in Rome for a visit. While there, he asked for an audience with Pope Paul at the Vatican. Photographs taken of the two men together show Nixon looking unusually stern and tense. At one point during their visit, Nixon leaned over to the Pontiff and said: "Tonight, after I leave the Vatican, I will be flying to sea and there I shall see the mightiest military force which exists in the world in any ocean." Pope Paul ignored his strange comment and did not respond.

Nixon's critics had always disliked Nixon because of his politics. Now there was a growing suspicion among their ranks that there was something really out of kilter with the man. They could not quite put their finger on it, but they had the uneasy feeling that the president might not have a firm grasp on reality—and that was frightening indeed.

Canadians were not immune to the insanity of 1970. Militant members of the Quebec separatist movement kidnapped two government officials and plunged Canada into a major political crisis. The separatists said that if their demands were not met, the two officials—British trade commissioner James Cross and Quebec Labor Minister Pierre La-porte—would be killed.

Prime Minister Trudeau shocked the entire country, especially the American war resisters who had come to think of him as a friend, by re-acting with strong force against the separatists. He invoked Canada's War Measures Act, which allowed him to suspend constitutional limi-tations on search and seizure, and called his critics "weak-kneed, bleeding-heart liberals" who were afraid to take a strong stand.

Convoys of steel-helmeted troops were sent into Quebec to raid separatists headquarters and more than 300 individuals were arrested at gunpoint. Later, newspaper reporters were told by the separatists where they could find the body of one of the men. They had promised to kill their hostage if Trudeau did not meet their political demands—and they did. Trudeau eventually succeeded in restoring order in Quebec, but Canadians were divided over whether he had overreacted, and in the end, he admitted he might have walked into a "trap."

In December 1971, Charles Sudduth loaded up his MG roadster and headed back to Mississippi, crossing the Canadian-U.S. border at Wa-tertown, New York. When he arrived in Jackson, he stopped by the American Friends Service Committee, which was counseling war re-sisters on their options with the draft. There he met Rick Abraham, a na-tive Mississippian who had just returned to Mississippi from California to work for the antiwar movement. Abraham let Sudduth stay with him until he could find a place of his own. He also got him a job at the same tree service where he was employed.

"My information was that draft boards in Mississippi were all white and racist and targeted people who were involved in civil rights work or antiwar work or any other unpopular activities," said Abraham. "Charles Sudduth was one of those. . . . I never understood why the U.S. attorney declined to prosecute Charles. Obviously they didn't want to prosecute because they were afraid to." It would take time for him to understand why.

Meanwhile, Abraham put together a citizens' advisory committee to offer suggestions to the state Selective Service organization and worked as director of the Mississippi Draft Information Service. "One of the is-sues I raised was participation of the KKK on the draft boards," said Abraham. "I remember raising the issue of [the board member from Charles's district]. I was told by Davis [James Davis was state director of the Selective Service System] that was not a problem. He said a Jew could get fair treatment from a Catholic and . . . a KKK member could be just as fair with a black as a Jew was with a Catholic. He saw [the KKK] as an innocent organizational affiliation. I was astonished."

In 1970, there were no blacks on any of the state's eighty-two local draft boards, but by 1972, the figures had changed somewhat, nudged along by complaints from activists such as Abraham. As of May 1972, the figures supplied to Abraham by the state headquarters indicated that of 400 board members, 326 were white, 67 were black, 4 were Oriental, and 3 were Indian. The ten-member appeals board was composed of nine whites and one black.

When Abraham discovered that the state Selective Service board employed no blacks on its staff—in a state in which forty-two percent of the population was classified as nonwhite—he protested, and they agreed to hire blacks, although they were assigned to menial jobs that Abraham said made them little more than "paper shufflers."

Abraham never found evidence of a direct link between Selective Service and the Mississippi State Sovereignty Commission, but he knew it was there. "We didn't know who was in the Sovereignty Commission [thus making it difficult to connect them to the draft boards], but there was no question in my mind that Selective Service was used as a tool to undermine the civil rights and antiwar movement. It was used to keep people in line."

An example of how that worked, he said, can be seen in the political candidacy of Benny Thompson. When Thompson, an African American, announced his candidacy for alderman in the town of Bolton, Mississippi, in 1970, he was ordered to report for induction. Thompson challenged the induction order in court and won. He later was elected mayor of Bolton.

While Abraham was involved in the antiwar and civil rights movements, he was contacted by the FBI and asked to become an informant. "They wanted to know about people organizing poor blacks," he said. "I think they assumed I might be receptive [to them] because I was from Mississippi. Anyway, I declined. I said I didn't see anything wrong with what they [civil rights activists] were doing. . . . They were aggravated at my response."

One day the FBI stopped by Abraham's house, which he was still sharing with Sudduth, and spoke to their landlord. "They told him that Charles was a member of the SDS [Students for Democratic Society], was known to carry explosives and was a questionable dangerous character," said Abraham. "The purpose of the visit was to get Charles and probably me, too, thrown out on the street."

When they did not succeed in getting them evicted, the FBI approached the tree service where both Abraham and Charles were employed. By then Abraham had figured out that both he and Charles had become targets of Cointelpro. "The whole thing [Cointelpro] was designed to disrupt the lives of people like Charles and myself," he said. "This time they told our employer that there had been a bank robbery in town and Charles was a suspect."

The FBI agents asked where Sudduth was working and then left to find him. At the time, he was working in the front yard of a house in a residential neighborhood. Just before the agents arrived, Charles noticed that the homeowner pulled down all the window shades. He recalls thinking how strange that was; that it gave him such an eerie feeling that something bad was going to happen.

Two men got out of a car and identified themselves as FBI agents. "I believe one of them was named Joe Jackson," said Charles. "They asked me to sit down and talk to them. I said, 'If you don't want to talk about the draft or the war, I'll answer any questions you have.' " The agents told him there had been a bank robbery that morning. "Did you do it?" they asked. Taken aback, Sudduth said, "No, of course I haven't robbed any banks."

Years later, Charles read a newspaper interview with FBI agent Joe Jackson. In the interview, Jackson admitted that he had once arrested a man for robbing a bank because he was on the FBI agitators list. He said the man was innocent. "He said they got their orders out of Washington to keep an eye on these people, so I would assume it was all inspired by the Sovereignty Commission," said Sudduth. "It would give your name to Washington, and they would send it back to their agents."

In the spring of 1971, Abraham's Mississippi Draft Information Service received a call for help from Charles Jenkins, a black man who was being prosecuted by U.S. attorneys for draft evasion. Jenkins had refused to serve on the grounds that he was being drafted illegally, and the chairman of the draft board was the head of the KKK.

By then, Abraham knew all about draft board activities in the Delta. Sudduth had shown him his correspondence with the draft board and he was well versed on its ties to the KKK. Charges of KKK affiliation were not the only complaints. One mother described how a board member had once told her he could do something about her son's draft status if she went out on a date with him. She turned down his offer, and her son was drafted.

Before he went to the Delta, Abraham received a tip that a Leland policeman had informaiton about the KKK. Since Leland was about ten miles from Greenville, the county seat, he made an appointment with Leland Police Chief William Burnley. "I had heard that Chief Burnley was not sympathetic to the Klan—he had a reputation as a Klan buster," said Abraham. "I thought he might have knowledge of [the board member]. I also knew that the [police officer] was on his force there in

Leland." Burnley had once served as the police chief of Greenville and he did, in fact, have a reputation for being tough on the Klan.

Abraham went to Leland and met with Burnley at the police station at nine o'clock one night. The chief said he did not have any information on the board member. Then Abraham told him about his tip, about the police officer on his force who had knowledge of Klan activities. After listening to his evidence, Burnley summoned the police officer in question to his office. "The chief didn't want the embarrassment of it coming out publicly he had a member of the Klan on his force, so he agreed to call him in," said Abraham. "The chief told him to tell me what he knew about [the board member]."

The police officer told Abraham that the board member was not just a member of the Klan; he was the head of the Klan. He had seen him wearing robes and a hood at meetings on Lake Washington, a rural area in the southern part of the county. "I asked if he would sign an affidavit and he said he didn't want to do that," said Abraham. "He said he was an undercover agent and didn't have to sign anything."

At Jenkins's trial, the police officer was called to the stand by defense attorneys. Abraham was there in the courtroom when the police officer testified. "He was asked about [the board member] and basically he said the same thing he told me," said Abraham. "The prosecution objected, saying it was not relevant, and the judge upheld the objection." The police officer was dismissed from the witness stand and no legal action was ever taken against the board member by the Justice Department. KKK infiltration of the draft board was allowed to continue unchallenged.

4

1971

Richard Deaton: Making Protest a Family Affair

At the end of the summer of 1967, Richard Deaton and his entire family—his stepfather, his mother, and his three younger brothers—loaded up their car and left their Staten Island, New York, home to find a new life in Canada. Together they headed for the nearest border crossing into Quebec. After passing through U.S. Customs, where they were questioned by immigration officials, Richard's stepfather, Robert, spun about in the car and expressed his outrage by giving the customs officials the finger.

Richard was not the only member of his family who felt strongly about the Vietnam War. The family exodus to Canada had begun the previous year with a quiet conversation on the front stoop of their home in Staten Island. Richard was in his junior year at the University of Wisconsin. A pre-law student, he had come home for the two-week Easter holiday to pick up applications to enroll in the New York University School of Law. As they sat out on the stoop, watching the day recede into dusk, his stepfather asked the big question: "What are you going to do about Vietnam?" Richard thought about it for a moment, then matter of factly said, "Oh, I don't know—probably go to Canada."

His stepfather told him that was probably a good idea. "We had a long discussion about it," said Richard. "My father's feeling was that I had two younger brothers and if it wasn't Vietnam, it would be South Africa or Central America, and he had no intentions of having his sons fight colonial wars." Suddenly, the law school applications were no longer important.

Richard returned to the University of Wisconsin, and while he was gone, his family decided to emigrate to Canada en masse. Richard came back home that summer and rode with them across the border and on to Montreal, where the family settled. Then he went back to the University of Wisconsin to complete his senior year. He was active in the antiwar demonstrations that took place on the campus, but he was never involved with the counterculture that revolved around drugs and rock music.

Richard took a more intellectual approach to his radicalism, a natural by-product of his early university-based upbringing. His natural father was a prominent university professor who came home one day to be told by his wife (Richard's mother) that she had fallen in love with one of his students. They divorced when Richard was nine and his mother married the student, a younger man named Robert Deaton. They moved to New York City, where Robert, who had been trained as a criminologist, became a stockbroker and moved his new family into a home in Manhattan. Richard and a younger brother were subsequently adopted by their stepfather (the reason he refers to him as "father") and later they were joined by twin brothers born to their mother and stepfather.

Richard describes his background as "solid middle class." His Jewish parents were committed progressives and active in the union movement in the 1940s and 1950s. According to Richard, their experience living through the McCarthy Red-baiting period influenced their thinking and made them highly political. "My mother was a self-styled literati, a fan of the *New Yorker*, and I grew up with politics. Some people would probably refer to me as a red-diaper baby." After living in Manhattan for three years, they moved to a house on Staten Island, where they lived until they emigrated to Canada.

Richard finished out his final academic year at the University of Wisconsin as his stepfather found work as a stockbroker in Montreal, and his younger brothers were accepted as students at McGill University. Before joining his family in Montreal, Richard went to the Canadian consulate in Chicago to apply for landed immigrant status. It was not the recommended way to go, since consulate officials have a greater opportunity to reject applicants before they enter the country than they do after they arrive, but it seemed the most sensible thing to do under the circumstances.

"I played the charade of why I was going to Canada—to join my family—and it was quite clear, based on what they showed me, that they had seen my FBI file." That did not surprise Richard. "I was never confronted by the FBI, never hassled, but I assumed there were times when my phone was tapped. I assumed that because of my civil rights and antiwar activities at the University of Wisconsin. I knew I was being photographed."

Despite his stern, humorless demeanor—and his access to Richard's confidential FBI file—the senior officer at the Canadian consulate in Chicago was not the ogre that he appeared to be. He had, in fact, already admitted numerous draft-age Americans into Canada. Richard was no exception. Based on the point system then in use, he easily qualified for landed immigrant status.

Richard crossed the Canadian border on June 10, 1968. Shortly before he left, Robert Kennedy was assassinated. "At that stage, my reaction was, 'What else is new?' I never believed it was a sole gunman. I'm not a conspiracy freak. I just find it odd that it is always a lone gunman." Before that it had been the Kent State massacre. And before that, the assassination of Martin Luther King, an event that affected him profoundly.

"I remember his death very vividly," he said. "I had gone home to my apartment. I lived across the street from the Wisconsin football stadium. I heard it on the radio and then went down to a diner on the street and watched the riots. Given the times, I understood the rage. It was obvious to me. Maybe it is generational folklore, but I think John F. Kennedy's assassination and King's and Bobby's and Malcom X's really marked the end of American innocence."

Two days before he left the University of Wisconsin campus, he attended a Joan Baez concert at Agricultural Hall. At the beginning of the concert, she said men opposed to the war should go to jail and not Canada. Recalled Richard: "Eight thousand people booed her."

When he arrived in Montreal, he enrolled at McGill University to do graduate work in economics. He was not there long when a family friend sent his parents a brief article that appeared in the *Staten Island Advance*. The article reported that Richard had refused to report for military duty. Soon a woman he had dated at the University of Wisconsin joined him in Montreal, and they were married. "We found integration [into Canada] very easy. But it was a very tumultuous period, personally as well as politically. Soon after we got married we realized that the marriage was a failure and would be a short-term one."

Not long after the Deaton family relocated in Montreal, they learned Canada had social and political problems of its own, particularly with the Quebec separatist movement, which wanted to see the province sever its relationship with the national government and the English-speaking provinces. Elements of the separatist movement were quite radical and loose talk of armed revolution was not uncommon on the streets of Montreal in the late 1960s.

"I had a lot of mixed feelings in some ways," said Richard. "I watched the Democratic convention in 1968 on television and then shortly after that watched the riots in Montreal. That situation was quite volatile. Still, there was a feeling that Canada was more progressive, more civilized. Canadian streets were relatively safe."

As tensions in Quebec were mounting in 1970, Richard completed his studies at McGill University and moved to Ottawa, where he was offered a job as the assistant director of research at the Canadian Union of Public Employees. Shortly after he left, the country was thrown into turmoil when separatists kidnapped two Canadian officials. Prime Minister Trudeau's invocation of the War Measures Act created a crisis of a different sort as it played into the hands of his political enemies and caused his supporters to feel palatably uneasy.

In particular, the crisis sent a tremor through the large population of American war resisters, who began to wonder about their own status in Canada. In January 1971, the *New Republic* published an article by American war resister Roger Neville Williams entitled "Strong-Arm Rule in Canada." Williams, who lived in Montreal, wrote about seeing soldiers with submachine guns patrolling the alley behind his apartment. Under the provision of the War Powers Act, they had the power to stop and search anyone they chose. Williams's concerns were amplified when he saw soldiers take a young man out of his house in handcuffs. Behind him marched soldiers carrying boxloads of books.

The American exile group with which Williams had been associated had openly supported the Quebec independence movement. When he saw members of that movement being arrested, he wondered if American war resisters would be next. He was especially concerned about what he interpreted as self-censorship by Canada's liberal media. The War Measures Act contained a censorship provision, but Trudeau had not applied it when he invoked martial law.

Nonetheless, Williams pointed out, "there had been control, and it came from two sources: frightened editors, and the police." In Williams's eyes, it was a dangerous precedent. "One wonders what will happen to freedom in Canada should the people one day elect a prime minister from the right who (ironically) has no record as a civil libertarian."

As it turned out, Williams was wrong about the media. From early 1971, newspapers and magazines and television commentators, none of whom felt any philosophical kinship to the Quebec separatists, called Trudeau to task for invoking martial law. The *Ottawa Journal* protested what it considered the "un-British" actions of the government, saying "this Chicago-like flaunting of firearms, is a scene that smacks more of fascism than of Canadian constitutional authority."

Writing in *Saturday Night* magazine, James Eayrs blamed the government for the subsequent death of one of the hostages. "It lay within the power of the government of Canada to save the life of Pierre Laporte," he wrote. "It chose instead to gamble with his life . . . the government of Canada bears inescapably a measure of responsibility for his death." Eayrs's article was entitled "Dilettante in Power: The First Three Years of P. E. Trudeau" and was among the first to question Trudeau's suitability as prime minister.

Maclean's magazine published an excerpt of an upcoming book, *Rumors of War* by Ron Haggart and Aubrey Golden, that provided a moment-by-moment look at what happened to four Quebeckers during the crisis. One of them, Pauline Julien, was a prominent Canadian and her story of being awakened at five in the morning by soldiers who appeared in her bedroom without knocking was particularly effective in destroying the credibility of Trudeau's decision to react so harshly during the crisis.

Trudeau seemed stunned by the criticism. It never occurred to him that Canadians would fault him for using right-wing tactics against an enemy everyone agreed was vicious and a threat to society. He thought his credentials as a liberal would protect him from such criticism. Physically, he looked different after the crisis. His playful arrogance transformed into stern standoffishness. In the midst of the public criticism of his leadership, he left Ottawa on the morning of March 4, 1971, after telling his cabinet that he was going skiing, and he flew to Vancouver, where he met and married twenty-two-year-old Margaret Sinclair.

Two months later, the two boarded a Canadian Armed Forces Boeing 707 bound for Moscow. Trudeau would become the first sitting prime minister to pay a state visit to the Soviet Union—and with him was his stunning new bride. For twelve days, the couple toured the Soviet Union, bedazzling the diplomatic and press corps and startling the wives of Soviet officials, who, as the press gleefully pointed out, seemed twice as big as the prime minister's rock 'n' roll bride and nearly three times as old.

The marriage caught the country completely off guard. There had been no inkling that the prime minister was even considering marriage. No one had ever heard of Margaret Sinclair, much less considered her a potential mate for the prime minister. Now, suddenly, literally overnight, she had become the "First Lady" of Canada. Margaret was young and beautiful, and the country was so enamored by her striking presence that the media put Trudeau's misstep in Quebec on the back burner and proceeded at full speed with the instant deification of Margaret Trudeau.

American war resisters were left speechless as well. The Prime Minister's wife was *their* age. Hell, she was one of *them!*

When American troops pulled out of Cambodia in the summer of 1970, President Nixon said that all future activity in that country would be limited: "We will conduct air interdiction missions against the enemy's efforts to move supplies and personnel, but there will be no U.S. air or logistics support."

By the beginning of 1971, he had changed his mind—again. The year began with swarms of American helicopters crossing the border into Cambodia to provide direct air support for a joint South Vietnamese-Cambodian ground operation. Accompanying the air patrols into Cambodia was an escalation of the ground war in South Vietnam. Most Americans were shocked. They expected an end to the Vietnam War, not a new one in Cambodia.

The lead story in a February issue of *Newsweek* was on Vietnam and attempted to answer the question posed in the headline: "The Last Big Push—Or a Wider War?" The magazine noted that many Americans were perplexed by a policy that suggested that the best way to withdraw troops from Vietnam was to send more into combat. Nixon had promised to have all American troops out of Vietnam by 1972. "But however confusing the public might find the proposition, [the operation] was based on the assumption that the way to conduct a strategic retreat is to attack," concluded the magazine.

Hans Morgenthau wrote an article for the *New Republic* in which he said he saw only three options open to the United States: the use of tactical nuclear weapons; provoke China into entering the war as a means of garnering public support; or an unconditional disengagement. The respected University of Chicago professor noted that as vice-president in 1954 Nixon had advocated the use of nuclear weapons in Vietnam. He wondered if the signs were not there that he was again considering that option, only this time as president. The provocation of China seemed unlikely, he said, because of the disintegration of the American armed forces as an effective fighting force. That left only options one and three. "If military doubts and fears should crystallize into outright opposition to the war, such opposition might well turn into the decisive argument in favor either of the nuclear 'final solution' . . . or unqualified disengagement," he said.

Clearly, Morgenthau was uneasy about the way the war was supposedly winding down. Many Americans felt the same way, as evidenced by continued resistance to the draft. Newly released figures for the pre-vious year revealed that Selective Service was drafting nearly twice as many men as it needed to meet its quotas because so many men were failing the physicals or simply not showing up for induction. In April, for example, the Department of Defense had requested 19,000 men. In order to get that many men, Selective Service had to send out 36,500 in-duction notices.

Many men were obtaining medical deferments because their per-sonal physicians were writing them letters claiming ailments that would qualify them for exemptions. A favorite ailment was manic de-pression. It was the type of diagnosis that was almost impossible to dis-prove. The *New York Times* reported that one New York psychiatrist was writing about seventy-five such letters a week for a fee of $200 each, all to be paid "cash in advance." With the help of physicians, whether for financial gain or opposition to the war, the failure rate for Vietnam War-era inductees was triple what it had been during World War II.

In April 1971, public perception of the Vietnam War took a new turn with the court martial conviction of Lieutenant William Calley for his role in the My Lai massacre. There had been media coverage of the mas-sacre since 1969, but not until Calley's murder conviction did the brutal-ity of it really seem to hit home. He was sentenced to life imprisonment, but President Nixon ordered him released until he had exhausted his appeals.

To assess public response to his conviction, *Newsweek* commissioned a poll by the Gallup Organization. When the pollsters asked if people approved or disapproved of the verdict, seventy-nine percent of the Americans polled said they disapproved. Asked if they thought Calley was a scapegoat for the actions of others, sixty-nine percent answered yes. It was one of those odd moments in American history in which the nation's manifest destiny seemed lacking in any semblance of moral re-straints.

The massacre had occurred on March 16, 1968, when three platoons of Charlie Company entered My Lai, a small hamlet in South Vietnam. One of the platoons was under the command of Lieutenant Calley. When the soldiers entered the village, many of the families were gath-ered in front of their homes cooking rice over open fires. With no sign of Viet Cong soldiers, the Americans started gathering up the villagers for questioning. The killings began suddenly, without warning.

One of Calley's men dragged a civilian over to where the other sol-diers were standing and, without saying a word, stabbed him in the back with his bayonet. The man fell to the ground gasping for breath, and the GI stabbed him again. The same soldier then threw a middle-aged man into a well and tossed a M26 grenade down after him.

Then other soldiers pushed the women and children together and began firing their automatic weapons into the group. The women screamed, "No VC! No VC!" But no one listened—or seemed to care. When the shooting stopped, fifteen to twenty villagers, mostly women and children, lay dead. Hearing the gunfire, Captain Ernest Medina, the officer in charge of Charlie Company, rushed into the village. According to the testimony of one of the soldiers who testified at Calley's trial, Medina shot a woman with his M16 rifle, then ordered his men to "kill everyone—leave no one standing." With that, a machine gunner fired into the villagers without warning, mowing them down. By the time the slaughter was over, 102 innocent civilians had been gunned down in cold blood.

The massacre did not come to light until 1969 when an investigative reporter named Seymour Hersh uncovered the crimes and wrote a series of newspaper articles that were published in November 1969. That same month a second reporter, Joe Eszterhas, later to find fame as a Hollywood screenwriter, received a phone call from an old schoolmate, an ex-GI who told him he had photographs of the massacre.

After publication of the stories, the army sent a general to the village to determine if the incident had occurred and to find out if there had been a cover-up by American commanders. The South Vietnamese Senate passed a resolution that proclaimed that My Lai was not a massacre, but rather a "regrettable incident."

As the army investigation continued, American public reaction seemed to support the massacre. American Legion members in Columbus, Georgia, placed large newspaper advertisement in the local newspaper proclaiming support for Calley and Captain Medina, noted Hersh in his book *My Lai 4: A Report on the Massacre and Its Aftermath.* "The advertisement accused newspapers and television of trying to 'tear down America and its armed forces.' A week later a group of former servicemen in Atlanta, Georgia, began a petition movement to get the Army to drop its charges against Calley."

Not everyone defended the massacre. The *Philadelphia Inquirer* equated it with "the worst days of Hitler and Stalin." The *Washington Star* said the thought of American soldiers gunning down helpless women and children was "simply appalling." For American war resisters in Canada—and those who were still taking to the streets in the States—the massacre was confirmation of everything they had been saying all along.

For *Newsweek*, Calley's conviction was a crystal clear message that Nixon should give a definite date for the termination of the Vietnam War. "Who else is guilty?" asked the magazine. "For reasons that seemed to spring from the natural human tendency to translate moral dilemmas into personal terms, the Calley case was turned overnight into a symbol of the entire American tragedy in Vietnam."

In the wake of the Calley verdict, antiwar demonstrators planned a massive rally in Washington, D.C. It had been a year since the last gathering, and the My Lai massacre was an ugly reminder of the fact that human beings, women and children, were still being killed in Vietnam, despite President Nixon's pledge to end the war. As antiwar demonstrators converged on the capital, Nixon met with his advisors to devise a plan to deal with them. The meeting lasted an hour and a half. Should they order the demonstrators arrested? Or should they simply ignore them?

Secret tapes of the meeting, not released until 1997, reveal that Nixon and his advisors were anxious about the demonstration. Sometimes their conversations, reflecting their paranoia, descended into the absurd. "If . . . they come in and start breaking up the mimeograph machines, then that's a problem," said Nixon. "Then they should be arrested—no ifs, ands, buts or maybes."

"The press is going to be looking for some sort of angle to play, that the government is all upset, it's wringing its hands, it's putting mattresses in its halls, letting people sleep in, and this kind of thing," said domestic policy advisor John Ehrlichman, directing the conversation away from office equipment. "I think that a calm, deliberate sort of steady course is obviously the one to pursue."

"I know they want to be arrested but, Mr. President, I don't think that's any reason for not arresting them," said Attorney General John Mitchell, taking a harder line.

As Nixon and his advisors continued their discussion, more than 200,000 antiwar demonstrations filled the capital. An equal number took to the streets in San Francisco. Especially visible were 1,200 veterans from Vietnam Veterans Against the War. Some wore Purple Hearts. Some were amputees. All were fighting mad. The demonstration was originally scheduled for one day, but many antiwar demonstrators stayed all week, particularly the Vietnam vets.

At the end of the week, they gathered on the other side of a temporary fence that had been erected at the Capitol, and with some vets cursing bitterly, they flung hundreds of medals onto the steps. The vets had been prohibited from occupying the Mall, but they did it anyway. Initially, the White House pushed to have them evicted, but the police made it clear they did not have the stomach for that. "We are not going in there at one in the morning and pick up some wounded veteran and throw him in the street," one police officer told reporters. Fortunately, the White House backed down and rescinded the order.

A month later, the Vietnam Veterans Against the War gathered in Concord, Massachusetts, for a march into Lexington. Their plans called for them to camp on the Lexington Green. Told that would be against the law, one veteran said, "The only place I ever slept illegally was Vietnam."

When they arrived, they found that sympathetic townspeople had already gathered at the green and had arranged for a spaghetti dinner for the vets. The police arrested the vets, as promised, but many townspeople also demanded that they, too, be arrested, and more than 500 demonstrators were loaded into vans and trucks and carted off to jail. One of the demonstrators, a disabled vet on crutches, pleaded with police to take him, too, and they did, though reluctantly.

Observed the *New Republic* of the demonstration: "To governments that base their power on any silent majority, the Vietnam veterans are like a sore spot on a dog that he can neither scratch nor lick."

"It was a decidedly political and ideological decision," said Richard Deaton of his decision not to serve in the armed forces. "I look at the documentaries, and they say it was a bad war without saying why it was a bad war. I didn't do it as a statement of conscience. I did it as an explicit ideological act. I am not a pacifist. I never have been and probably never will be. I did it as a political statement. To differentiate from the good German syndrome, someone had to articulate that there was resistance to the war in Vietnam, what it represented in context of the cold war period. It wasn't just a matter of being a bad war."

Richard adapted readily to his new life in Ottawa and to his job with the Canadian Union of Public Employees, an employer he would have for over twenty years. In this environment, he met the woman who would become his soulmate. Her name was Marie-Claire Pommez. She had emigrated to Canada in 1962 from France to work as a progressive trade union organizer.

They were very different people—he was Jewish, she was Catholic; she was an anarchist, he had a more structured view of society; he was American, she was French—but it was their common interests that drew them together and, perhaps, their mutual link to Vietnam. They were married and eventually had twin daughters, Emmauelle and Shoshanah.

For those who revel in the ironic twists and turns of fate that life sometimes bestows on the unsuspecting, the romantic saga of Richard and Marie-Claire is almost without parallel. After meeting Marie-Claire and falling in love with her, Richard was astonished to discover that she had grown up in a village sixty miles north of Saigon. Her father was a Frenchman who had served in the Pacific with the French army during World War II. He was captured by the Japanese and sent to a prison camp. At the end of the war, he went to work for the French government and was sent to Vietnam, where he worked with the French administration that withdrew after the Geneva agreements in 1954. It was during that time that he met Marie-Claire's mother, who was born in Vietnam.

When Richard spoke of his opposition to the war in Vietnam, when he agonized over the battlefield atrocities taking place, he had a sympathetic listener in Marie-Claire, for she had learned that the village in which she had spent her childhood had been bombed by the Americans and, in fact, no longer existed.

A second great irony emerged in Richard's life, but it came much later. For the moment, simply getting on with his life was his greatest priority. Typically, American war resisters in Canada forged new relationships and established careers as new Canadians, not as Americans. Most did not seek out other Americans and only encountered them occasionally in a professional or social context. The most frequent contact with other Americans occurred in the media, for by the early 1970s, Canada's newspapers and magazines were profiling new families of war resisters on a regular basis, though after 1970 most of the focus was on deserters.

In 1971, the *Toronto Star* ran a question-and-answer feature on its editorial pages of an American couple, Sid and Faithe Johnson, who had fled to Toronto in 1970 after Sid had refused a direct order to board a plane for Vietnam. He had applied for conscientious-objector status, but his application had been rejected by the draft board in his hometown of Raleigh, North Carolina. After he was drafted and assigned to the army, he reapplied for a military exemption as a conscientious objector. The army spent three months trying to talk him out of it, then one day ordered him to report in uniform to a Seattle airport.

When he arrived, he was told to board a Flying Tiger troop transport that was bound for Vietnam. He refused to board the plane. The other soldiers screamed insults at him as he stood there on the tarmac, and a major gave him a direct order. Again, he refused. The plane left without him. For legal reasons, the army went through the same procedure with a second plane. When he refused the second time, he was placed in confinement to await court martial. One day in the post exchange, he told his escort that he hoped he did not have to fight him, but he had every intention of leaving the base. The escort was sympathetic and ordered a sergeant to give him a lift off the base.

Shortly after arriving in Canada with his wife, Faithe, he found work as the assistant manager of a hobbies and crafts store in Toronto. Faithe was a strikingly beautiful woman and easily found work as a fashion model. "The U.S. prides itself as a free country, but that's an illusion," Sid said in the interview, which the newspaper ran in a regular column entitled "As Immigrants See Us." "I learned in the army what freedom of choice an American can expect. It may sound melodramatic, but as an ex-American resident this quality of freedom found in Canada is what I enjoy most. Canadians are encouraged to live and react according to their personal beliefs."

Weekend Magazine, a supplement carried by newspapers across Canada, ran a sympathetic cover story on deserters entitled "There are thousands of deserters from the U.S. Armed Forces in Canada. Here are a few of their stories." Among those interviewed were Dr. Donald Bourke, a twenty-nine-year-old physician who deserted after his reserve unit was called to active duty. He went to Quebec, where he was given a position in a large hospital in Montreal. In his spare time, he worked for the American Deserters Committee. "They shouldn't be able to keep us out of our own country," he said. "They're denying us our basic rights."

Another deserter interviewed by the news magazine was Missouri native Jim Shearer, who had deserted after serving with the First Cavalry in the Mekong Delta. He had enlisted in the army after dropping out of high school in the eleventh grade. By the time he was assigned to Vietnam, he had made sergeant. It was while he was on missions with his men in the Mekong Delta that he decided to desert. His men were out of control and no longer satisfied with simply killing the enemy.

"In the field, they'd cut off a Viet Cong's ears, or penis and put it in his mouth," he said. "Sometimes they'd tear off their First Cavalry shoulder patches and stab it in his head with a bayonet."

After a year of that, he extended his tour so that he could get out of the army five months earlier than usual. He was reassigned to a helicopter unit as a door gunner, flying support for the infantry. When prisoners were taken by the infantry units, they were handed over to the helicopter crews for "questioning." "They'd go down and get these 'gooks' and tie a gunnysack and rope around them, and if they wouldn't talk they'd dangle them through the trees. If they still wouldn't talk, it would go on until they were dead."

Deserters were not the only Americans moving to Canada. In May 1971, *Newsweek* did a feature entitled "Canada's Other U.S. Emigrants." The story, which was written by James C. Jones, the magazine's Detroit bureau chief, focused on the thousands of Americans who were going north to escape the violence and political uncertainty taking place in America. Jones made a two-week swing through Canada to locate that country's newest group of expatriates.

One of those interviewed by Jones, Sidney Leinwant, left Brooklyn for Manitoba with his wife and two children because he felt overwhelmed by the crime taking place in American cities. The forty-five-year-old former World War II medic said he had seen enough blood during the war to last him a lifetime. Seattle native Judy Churchill told Jones she left the United States to take a job with Western Airlines in Calgary because she felt Canada had more of what she was seeking, namely a sense of "openness."

American expatriates were not the only headline fodder in 1971, of course. By midyear, the crisis in Quebec had cooled to a simmer, and most of the country's attention was still on Prime Minister Trudeau and his new bride. He was a brilliant man, a true intellectual, and an adroit political leader, but it was not those qualities that captured everyone's imagination. It was his ability to transform a drab political office into something totally unfamiliar.

With a beautiful woman on his arm who was thirty years younger than himself, the dapper prime minister "went Hollywood," mesmerizing his countrymen with his sense of style. The only equivalent in America would have been if Cary Grant or Gregory Peck had suddenly been elected president. Canadians were fascinated, if not always pleased, and pretty much told their prime minister, with a mischievous wink, to go for it, man.

In July 1971, the Viet Cong and the North Vietnamese offered the American delegation in Paris a plan that would allow the United States to withdraw its troops and account for American war prisoners. Said Le Duc Tho, a spokesman for the Hanoi delegation: "Our resistance war against the French lasted nearly nine years. But after the settlement of the war and the restoration of peace, there was no obstacle to the building of friendly relations between the Vietnamese people and the French people. I believe it's the same way with the American people."

The proposal was turned down. A White House spokesman said there were elements of the proposal that were attractive—especially the opportunity to retreat with honor and the repatriation of prisoners of war—but no peace plan could be agreed to that did not address the political future of the officials in South Vietnam. Many Americans were every bit as baffled by the White House's response as were the Viet Cong and North Vietnamese. Wasn't the point to get out—and as quickly as possible?

America had lost the war, but Nixon wanted to pretend that was not the case. Each day that he spent attempting to devise a sleight-of-hand maneuver to disguise the reality of the situation, more American soldiers died. The editors of the *New Republic* were blunt. "How did the government of the United States come to accept as fact, this fiction that America has the power (and the right) to deliver Vietnam into the hands of some Vietnamese and deny it to others?" said the magazine. "Even assuming, and it is a very large assumption, our manifest destiny to save the Vietnamese from themselves . . . what fine and sure calculation convinced successive presidents that the Vietnamese would be happier, freer, friendlier, richer if they were governed by Thieu and Ky rather than their adversaries?"

In London that summer, more than 200 off-duty American servicemen marched from Hyde Park to the American Embassy to present petitions to end the fighting in Vietnam. Later in the day, one of the marchers, Air Force Captain Thomas Culver, a thirty-two-year-old Vietnam veteran, was arrested when he returned to Lakenheath Air Force base and charged with violating a regulation that prohibited servicemen from participating in demonstrations in foreign countries. At his trial, Culver wore a silver ring that bore the peace symbol. His attorney challenged the prosecutors' assertion that Culver had participated in a demonstration.

What happened in front of the embassy, said the attorney, was nothing more than an expression of his constitutional right to petition for redress of grievances. The attorney concluded his argument before the eight-man military panel with a quote from Richard Nixon: "I believe that every man in uniform is a citizen first and a serviceman second, and that we must resist any attempt to isolate or separate the defenders from the defended." The panel deliberated for just four hours before convicting Culver, but they sentenced him to a reprimand and a $1,000 fine, the lightest penalty they could impose.

Courageous officers such as Culver became the focus of the antiwar movement in the final two years of the war and made supporters of the war decidedly uncomfortable. Another officer who created a stir in 1971 was Colonel David Hackworth, a five-year combat veteran of Vietnam and the most decorated soldier of the Indochinese war. Hackworth stunned his superiors by submitting his resignation from the army at a time when he was in line for promotion to general. Hackworth told reporters that he was disillusioned. Only by getting out of Vietnam, he said, could the army restore some of its pride.

"I was an extreme hawk—a real superaggressive, airborne-all-the-way, let's go-get-the-dirty-Communists type," he told *Newsweek*. "But later, after seeing the enemy and watching [South Vietnamese troops] perform, I concluded: no, we shouldn't have gotten in. It was just an absolute waste."

Increasingly, people working in government and in the military began to speak out against the war. One of the mightiest blows to the war effort came from a research associate at the Massachusetts Institute of Technology, Daniel Ellsberg, who leaked Pentagon documents to the news media that proved that government officials had lied to the public about the war.

Later dubbed the "Pentagon Papers," the documents showed that President Johnson had planned all the war's escalations months in advance and had lied to Congress about them. They also showed that the Kennedy administration had acquiesced in the coup in which South Vietnam President Diem was murdered.

When summaries of the documents were published by the *New York Times* and the *Washington Post*, the Nixon administration went to court to block publication of additional documents. At issue was the White House's attempt to impose prior restraint on the newspapers. The case went to the Supreme Court and was ultimately resolved in the newspapers' favor by a six-to-three vote.

One result of the ruling was that the Pentagon installed security officers on the roof with long-lens cameras and sent other officers prowling throughout the building in search of untended documents. Staffers were told to tilt the Venetian blinds in their offices and turn their papers upside down whenever they left their desks. Another result was that Nixon became obsessed with Ellsberg, ordering his staff to "get him" at all costs.

The Pentagon and the White House both felt under siege from the American public. Years later, it was revealed that this was the time period during which the president began to come emotionally unraveled under the pressures of the office.

The Ellsberg incident infuriated Nixon. He told aides he wanted Ellsberg destroyed. "We are going to use any means necessary," he said, pounding on his desk. He also blamed the Brookings Institution, a liberal think-tank that often issued position papers critical of his policies. "I want a break-in," Nixon told his aides. "I want the Brookings' safe cleaned out. And have it cleaned out in a way that makes somebody else look bad."

The more he thought about it, the more convinced he became that the National Archives had documents that would incriminate President John F. Kennedy in the Cuban missile crisis of 1962. He ordered his aides to arrange for a break-in into the National Archives to get the goods on Kennedy. The aide told him he could send the director out of town and send people in while he was gone. That sounded good to Nixon and he wondered aloud if it might not be a good idea to have a man in the White House who could carry out his orders.

"I need a man, a commander, an officer in charge here in the White House that I can call when I wake up, as I did last night, at two in the morning, and I can say, 'Now look here, I want to do this, this, this and this. Get going' See my point?" Nixon asked. One of his aides said he knew just the man, a retired CIA agent named Howard Hunt.

That news delighted Nixon, but he cautioned his aides that he would still be the boss. "I'll direct it myself," he said. "I know how to play this game. And we're going to start playing it."

At another meeting, he instructed his aides to have the IRS go after prominent Democratic campaign donors. "Please get me the names of the Jews," he said. "You know, the big Jewish contributors."

Politically, the news centered on the 1972 presidential campaign. George McGovern, the first announced candidate for the Democratic nomination, was largely ignored by the news media and the pollsters. Getting the most attention were Maine senator Edmund Muskie and former vice-president Hubert Humphrey. Although he had not declared himself a candidate, Massachusetts senator Edward Kennedy was often included in the opinion polls and mentioned as a possible candidate.

One poll taken in October showed that if the election were held then Nixon would handily defeat Kennedy, Humphrey, and Muskie. McGovern was not included, said the pollsters, because of his low name recognition. When pollsters focused on new voters—those eighteen to twenty-three who would be voting for the first time in a presidential primary—they came up with different numbers. Kennedy, Humphrey, and Muskie defeated Nixon among that group of voters. By the end of 1971, it became clear to Nixon campaign strategists that young voters—and there were twenty-five million of them—could be pivotal in the general election.

The draft was still very much an issue in 1971, as Congress engaged in a ferocious debate over whether to extend the draft another two years. The more dovish Senate voted to extend the draft, but attached a rider to the bill that required President Nixon to pull out of Vietnam within nine months, provided Hanoi agreed to release all prisoners of war. The more hawkish House of Representatives voted to extend the draft, without the withdrawal provision.

As the senators and House members met in conference to iron out their differences, the existing draft law expired. For the first time in twenty years, the United States was without a draft. Selective Service headquarters sent out telegrams to the local boards, ordering a halt to the call-ups, but that would only be temporary, since the congressmen eventually reached an agreement. The uncertainty made the White House noticeably nervous, not just because its only option was to use the president's emergency powers to call up men with deferments, but because it would give Nixon a high-profile on a sensitive issue at a time when his campaign advisors were warning him of the volatility of the youth vote.

The draft legislation that passed did not contain a withdrawal date, but it did contain provisions that made it more difficult for unscrupulous draft boards to deny due process to draftees. For example, the new law required the boards to meet in quorum to hear the appeal of any registrant who wanted to make a personal appearance, and it required them to allow the registrant to bring witnesses to speak on his behalf. Even though Nixon's strategy of "Vietnamization" was supposed to be progressing at full speed as 1971 drew to a close, the Pentagon was still sending about 4,300 fresh troops a month to Vietnam.

Richard Deaton became a Canadian citizen shortly after the five-year waiting period expired, and although one of his uncles—an assistant attorney general in New York State—has urged him to reapply for dual citizenship, he has not done so. His wife, Marie-Claire, holds dual Canadian-French citizenship, but he is content—for the moment at least—to be a citizen of only one country. One reason why he has not applied for dual citizenship may be because he has only visited the United States four times since leaving the country, and those visits were to see an elderly uncle. He just does not have much desire to return. Another reason may be because there was an active warrant out against him for ten years.

Once, when the warrant was still active, he had occasion to visit Acapulco, Mexico. At the airport, Mexican authorities told him that American agents were looking for him, and they advised him that he would be safe in the international lounge. It is understandable that incidents such as that—and the fact that American authorities seemed more interested in pursuing political dissidents than organized crime chieftains— would influence his feelings toward his homeland.

"Actually, I have no reason to [return]," he says today. "All my family in the States are dead. The family I have is here in Canada. Thomas Wolfe is right—you can't go home again. After living in Canada for so many years, I realized I would never fit in there again, even if I wanted to. I wouldn't fit in either culturally or politically. I've seen too much of the world to believe that American consumerism and ethnocentrism has much to offer the world in terms of solving its problems. My roots are all now here in Canada. My family—mother, brothers, wife, children, and friends—are all here in Canada. Life is comfortable—I've had a fairly good run."

By 1971, the United States had become a significant issue in Canada as government officials, the news media, and private citizens agonized over the degree to which American business interests had infiltrated the economy. In December 1971, using statistics gathered by the government in 1968, *Maclean's* magazine took a hard look at American influence in Canada. The soul-searching had begun with the realization that Canadian businesses had contributed to the Vietnam War effort by manufacturing items purchased by the American military. A closer look at the economy suggested to many that Canadian independence was under attack.

The good news for Canadians in 1971, concluded the magazine, was that they owned seventy-one percent of the investment companies, eight-one percent of the public utilities, and sixty-nine percent of the retail trade in their own country. The bad news was that foreigners, mostly Americans, owned ninety-nine percent of the booming petroleum industry. While nonresident corporations made up only three percent of the companies, in terms of numbers, they owned twenty-seven percent of the assets and made forty-one percent of the profits.

For Canadians, those were scary numbers. "We own industries such as those in the financial sector, those protected by law; they have a strong and growing grip on everything else," said the magazine, which also noted that the country's universities were "being taken over by foreign-born teachers."

Ironically, that same issue of *Maclean's* contained an opinion piece from a *New York Times* assistant editor that made the case that presidential candidate Edmund Muskie would be the best choice for Canada. The editor had two reasons for that suggestion: First, since Muskie was from Maine, which was reasonably close to Canada, it could be assumed he had a better understanding of things Canadian; second, he favored the expansion of overland Canadian oil imports to the United States.

Earlier in the year, a Vancouver newspaper, sporting a headline that read "IF CANADA VOTES, NIXON DID IT," suggested that Nixon's economic foreign policy policies were creating so much concern in Canada that it made a Canadian election inevitable. At issue was the Vietnam War, which after so many years, was seriously eroding confidence in American political leadership, and the fact that although Canada was the United States's biggest trading partner—ahead of both Japan and Europe—American economic policies seemed to take Canada for granted. The result was a growing distaste among Canadians for everything American.

These Canadian sentiments did not surprise *Newsweek* writer William Bundy, who went to British Columbia to talk to people about the growing rift between the two countries. The tendency of Americans to take Canada for granted, he concluded, was almost certain to create pockets of anti-American feeling.

Maclean's approach to what was clearly a problem was typical for the times. On one hand, Canada genuinely welcomed American immigration; on the other hand, it feared American influence on things cultural and endeavored to preserve its identity. Canada eagerly sought American investment, but it devoted countless hours to devise ways of preventing those investors from assuming too much control in any one sphere of the economy. The result was a perpetual love-hate relationship that continues to this day.

In 1994, Richard Deaton became curious enough about his old classmates from Curtis High School on Staten Island to compile a sociogram on them. At first, he had a difficult time locating them. Then, using a Staten Island telephone directory, he was able to locate one former classmate. That contact led to another and eventually he was able to track down a dozen classmates.

"Of the twelve people I located, I was the only male who was drafted," he said. "All the others bought certificates from shrinks. One was turned down for the draft because he had allergies. Another was legitimately considered unstable. All of the people, except two, had gone through divorces. Two or three had become disabled in terms of occupational ability. But none of them were drafted or served in Vietnam." The lesson he learned from the sciogram was that if he had been more conniving, he could have found a legitimate way to escape the draft.

In most instances, according to Richard, the war resisters who went to Canada improved the quality of their lives by doing so. "They ended up being big fish in a small pond," he said. "I would hypothesize that their career ability was better in Canada. For example, one-third of the faculty at the University of Ottawa law school has American degrees.

My children have a high school English teacher whose husband, it turns out, is a lawyer in Ottawa. Once the children were asked to write an essay, and they wrote about me coming to Canada. My daughters got excellent grades, but the teacher said she didn't want to compromise me by naming me [to the other students]."

Like many war resisters, Richard resents being lumped into a category that draws its definition from a set of perceptions that are defined by the group as a whole. Most war resisters were staunchly antigroup. Very few ever defined themselves in terms of their actions as war resisters. It was their opinions that were important—and those opinions existed apart from what amounted to a political act. "It would be an analytical mistake to treat that generation as a homogeneous group," Richard said. "I had nothing to do with the counterculture."

After serving as the assistant director of research at Canadian Union of Public Employees (CUPE) for more than twenty years, Richard resigned in the early 1990s, first to work for the government's income security program, then to teach at Carlton University in Ottawa. During that time, he published numerous academic articles and books and took on a variety of work assignments.

"When I left the union movement, it was on very bitter terms. I had a chance to re-evaluate what I wanted to do with the rest of my life. I had always wanted to go into law. The work that I had handled for CUPE involved a lot of litigation, and it made the transition easy. Americans, more so than Canadians, view law as a catalyst for change. For example, when I was at the University of Wisconsin, there was a generation of radical lawyers. The idea of . . . radical lawyers is laughable today, especially here in Canada where they never had a strong civil libertarian tradition."

In 1995, Richard took a position that offered him the second great irony of his life. He was hired as an associate professor at the Royal Military College in Kingston, Ontario. "One of the courses I taught was in military ethics—it was the twentieth century's ultimate oxymoron. I had three lectures to prepare. One was on My Lai. I remember the agony that I went through in preparing those lectures. I did it a month in advance and I remembered the day I came to Canada. There was a part of me that was hermetically sealed and would never be opened again—not until I had to prepare those lectures on My Lai. I knew I would be emotionally vulnerable teaching that course. I knew I had to be quite controlled. The whole point was to watch a documentary on My Lai and to raise the ethical issues involved. It was interesting to watch the cadets. Both the men and the women broke down and cried."

The experience made Richard intensely introspective, sending him to corners of his emotional self he had not visited in years. The fact that his own experiences overlapped with those of Marie-Claire and included a shared perspective of the atrocities of My Lai gave him a rush of complicated feelings that surfaced without warning and pulled him back for a reexamination of not just his own life but that of his entire generation. "Look, I was right [about the war]. I could have said that [in the class]. That gave me no satisfaction. But it was a reality check to see how other people reacted."

Perhaps only in Canada would a government hire an American war resister to teach a course in military ethics to young army cadets. It makes a certain amount of sense, but it is the type of logic that would be impossible in the United States, where political considerations intrude more into military decision making than does logic. It is one of the great strengths of Canada that it can—and often does—make sense at the drop of a hat, and usually without apology.

In 1997, Richard made a decision that in some ways took him back to the point where he had begun his life's journey. He enrolled in law school. Whether the experience of teaching military ethics at a military college had anything to do with it, he is not certain. He was ready for a change, a new challenge, and he went for it.

5

1972

Jim Thomas: "I Didn't Want to Kill Other People"

Jim Thomas grew up in the city of Chicago, where his father was the general manager of a metal products company and his mother was a homemaker. He had a younger brother and an older sister. He underwent what he calls an "entrenched middle-class upbringing." It was the kind of family that was celebrated on a daily basis on television with the likes of *Leave It to Beaver* or the *Donna Reed Show*. The only thing that set his life apart from others in middle America was that he lived in Chicago, a city with a long history of political bossism and gangsterism.

Jim learned about politics at an early age. "I grew up in Chicago and you can't be not aware of politics," he said. "Chicago has politics unlike any other place. There was politics at the grassroots level . . . petty corruption." Hearing himself say that, Jim laughed. "Well, in the Democratic Party it was more than petty corruption." His mother was a Republican and his father was a liberal Democrat. "We always had great discussions around the dinner table at night."

Vietnam first intruded on his consciousness in 1964 when Congress passed the Gulf of Tonkin resolution. He decided then that he was against the war and told his family so. After graduating from high school he received a draft deferment to attend college. The first few years he attended several different schools.

At one school, he decided to give the military a try by enrolling in Air Force ROTC. The classes gave him visions of soaring through the sky at the throttle of a powerful jet. Maybe a career as a jet pilot would not be all that bad. It did not take long for him to realize that soaring through the air and dropping bombs on civilians were conflicting visions, so when he transferred to Roosevelt University in Chicago, he put aside his association with the ROTC.

Jim was not a Quaker, but in the mid-to-late 1960s he got involved with them and attended their meetings. Although he was not overly political, he participated in demonstrations and silent vigils during that time. His favorite targets were the FBI and CIA recruiters who came to the campus. "I had a view that the best thing you could do to slow the FBI and the CIA down was to take up their time, so I went to interviews for the FBI and the CIA on campus. I wasn't interested [in working for them]. I just wanted to take up their time."

The war was a personal issue for Jim, so the politics of the hawks and the doves did not play a major role in his day-to-day activities. His opposition to the war came from the heart. "I didn't want to kill other people," he said. "It's wrong. I can't find a circumstance that makes it right."

In 1967, Jim married his girlfriend, Mary, who said she would stick with him no matter what. All along, Jim had talked to Mary and his family about his options after graduation. He made it clear he would not go to Vietnam. "I wasn't going—and I wasn't going to prison," he said.

The following year, Jim was still attending Roosevelt University when Martin Luther King was assassinated. There was a memorial service for him that day on the campus. "I was very impressed with Dr. King," he said. "I remember when he came to Chicago. It was still a segregated city. One of the activities he undertook was to integrate the segregated housing markets in the neighborhoods where I lived. I thought that was a great thing. I can still remember the chills going up and down my back when I heard his voice. I think his assassination was a turning point in history."

Two months later, Jim was further traumatized by the murder of Robert Kennedy. Although he was not a Kennedy supporter—most antiwar activists at that time felt Kennedy entered the presidential race to ride on the coattails of Eugene McCarthy—he mourned the loss of Kennedy and feared it was a sign of even worse things to come. That spring he graduated from Roosevelt University and was accepted into the graduate program at the University of Illinois, where he intended to pursue a master's degree in labor relations. His draft board granted him a deferment to continue his education.

To earn money for the fall term, he worked that summer as a roofer. Chicago was preparing for the Democratic Party convention and the rhetoric from Mayor Richard Daley and the leaders of the antiwar movement was as hot as the sun on the rooftops on which he worked. "I remember I had never seen so many helicopters, and they all had big, pointy things sticking out [machine guns], and there were Jeeps with machine guns mounted on them, and I thought, 'Geez, this is strange.' "

Jim did not go downtown to participate in the demonstrations, but he received first-hand reports on them from friends who had gone into the National Guard to dodge the draft. "It was a police riot, but there were two sides to it," he said. "There was a lot of taunting going on, but at the end of the day people like Eugene McCarthy had a right to speak and to be denied that opportunity was a terrible thing. I never had a great deal of respect for the Chicago police. They had a thing called the Red Squad, and they used to do surveillance of various organizations. They called our university the Little Red Schoolhouse."

Jim was finishing up work on his master's degree in 1970 and giving consideration to pursuing a doctorate when the draft switched over to a lottery system. When the lottery numbers were drawn, Jim found himself near the top of the list with a low number. That did not leave him many options. He wrote to the Toronto Anti-Draft Programme to get information about emigrating to Canada. He also applied for a draft-deferred job at Wisconsin Electric. He was hired to work in the labor relations division, but two days before he was scheduled to begin work, he received his draft notice. By then, Mary was five months pregnant with their first child, Kathleen.

Jim went to the University of Illinois and checked out four books on Canada. Actually, the library had only four books on Canada. He located a map so that he could find Toronto. He had no idea where it was and started his search in the Yukon. When he found Toronto, he was pleasantly surprised. "It's near Buffalo, for heaven's sake," he said.

Once they knew where it was, Jim and Mary loaded up their car and drove straight to Toronto, crossing the border at Windsor. No one in their families was surprised. They had been talking about it for a couple of years. Once he arrived in Toronto, he wrote his draft board a letter, declining their generous invitation to include him in the war effort. "The FBI called my family and got a hold of my dad, " he said. "The FBI chap wanted to know where I was living. My dad said, 'Well, you've asked me some questions. Can I ask you some questions?' "

"I don't know if I will answer them," answered the FBI agent.

"So, what do you earn?" Jim's dad asked.

"That's personal," said the FBI agent.

"Well, so is my son's address."

When Jim and Mary pulled up in front of the office of the Toronto Anti-Draft Programme on Yonge Street, they were not sure at first if they should go inside. "I can remember being apprehensive about it, that it might be some kind of front for the FBI," he said. "But I went in anyway. They said, 'Here are the rules on how to immigrate.' "

The Toronto Anti-Draft Programme was the largest of several organizations in Canada that assisted war resisters in obtaining landed immigrant status, jobs, and housing. They worked with a network of 2,000 draft counselors in the United States and volunteers across Canada. In Toronto alone, they had 200 Canadian families who provided food and housing to the exiles, lawyers who gave legal advice, and physicians who offered medical care.

Jim and Mary read over the information given to them, then took the counselor's advice and drove back to the immigration office in Windsor to apply for landed immigrant status. "They granted us landed immigrant status on the spot," said Jim. "I think it was because Mary was pregnant."

Almost immediately, Jim found a part-time job as a clerk in a Toronto factory, then found a full-time job in the economic research division of the Canadian Ministry of Labor. "Toronto was great," he said. "No one ever said anything unpleasant." When they first arrived, the country was undergoing the trauma of the Quebec kidnappings and the imposition of the War Measures Act. They saw occasional troops on the streets, and it gave them pause. "I commuted by train," Jim said. "I remember sitting on the train and really thinking about what it meant to have a Bill of Rights."

If the presence of troops on the streets made Jim and Mary wonder if they had traded one nightmare for another, those thoughts quickly disappeared that spring with news of the killings at Kent State. Jim saw the killings as a natural outcome of the government's policy toward war resisters. It was open season on anyone opposed to the war. For years, it had been acceptable to club them and beat them senseless. Now it was acceptable to shoot them down in cold blood.

Jim was not interested in shooting anyone—not the Vietnamese; not the American government; not his friends hiding out in the National Guard. He just wanted to be able to live his life in a manner that was compatible with his own moral beliefs. America would not allow him to do that. Canada would.

The Kent State killings sent a new wave of Americans into Canada, not all of whom were eligible for the draft. When Jeff and Lynne Sallot moved to Canada in 1971, Jeff had a high lottery number, which meant he was unlikely to be drafted. Both were students at Kent State when the killings took place.

"The killings were bad enough, but it was the aftermath that did us in: The 'they shoulda' shot more o'youse' reactions," wrote Lynne in a column for the *Toronto Star.* They stayed at Kent State for another year so that Lynne could finish work on her degree, then with their young son they moved to Canada, where Jeff found work as a staff writer at the *Star.* "We left to come to a freedom we couldn't find in the States—a freedom from fear," she wrote. "Living in the United States, paying Uncle Sam's taxes was in a way condoning what the country was doing—a tax too high for us to pay."

Senator J. William Fulbright of Arkansas was one of the earliest and most disarmingly eloquent critics of the Vietnam War. The fact that he represented a state known for its arch-conservatism—one that had V.F.W. and American Legion posts in every city, town, and hamlet—surprised almost everyone, except, of course, the people of Arkansas, for despite its rural, hillbilly image, that state had long been a sanctuary for rugged individualism.

Growing up in that environment, and in the shadow of Fulbright's inspiring leadership and stubborn liberalism, was Hot Springs native Bill Clinton. When Clinton left Arkansas to attend Georgetown University, he did not leave the sphere of the senator's influence. He found work in Fulbright's Washington office. Clinton was an outspoken opponent of the war and when he went to England to attend Oxford University as a Rhodes scholar, those feelings seemed to intensify. To study abroad, he obtained a student deferment from his local draft board (a rarity at that time; it was not especially difficult to obtain a deferment for undergraduate studies, but draft boards across the country were stingy with deferments for those who wanted to study abroad or enroll in graduate school); later he received a high number in the draft lottery that enabled him to return to the States with little risk of being inducted.

Upon his return, he enrolled in the Yale University law school, where he met his future wife, Hillary Rodham. In 1970, he was a coordinator in Joe Duffy's antiwar Senate campaign in Connecticut. Then in the spring of 1972, he and Hillary both got involved in presidential politics by going to Texas to work in Senator George McGovern's antiwar campaign. At that point in the campaign, no one gave McGovern much of a chance. Senator Edmund Muskie was considered the front-runner, with Hubert Humphery a close second.

McGovern held solid credentials as a liberal, but the fire of his campaign lay in his opposition to the war. In early 1972, historian Arthur Schlesinger published an article in the *New Republic* entitled "The Case for George McGovern." Schlesinger said he had nothing against Muskie and could live with his nomination, but he said he felt McGovern had leadership qualities—namely, a predisposition to telling the truth—that made him more deserving of the nomination.

When McGovern lost in Texas, he pushed on despite the ridicule of the news media that seemed to view him as somewhat of an ineffectual outsider to the political process. McGovern's fortunes changed literally overnight when Muskie broke down in tears in New Hampshire outside the *Manchester Union Leader*'s office while taking exception to something published by the newspaper.

By May, the news media was all abuzz about the "new" Democratic race between McGovern and Humphrey. Soon, first-place victories by McGovern in Wisconsin and Massachusetts had him going into the July convention as the distinct front-runner. Throughout the campaign, the Vietnam War continued unabated.

By early 1972, President Nixon had established a withdrawal plan for American troops, with approximately 22,000 soldiers a month being pulled out and assigned duty elsewhere. Nixon announced in January that he intended to bring American troop strength down to 69,000 by the first of May. All three major Democratic candidates criticized Nixon for the way he was conducting the withdrawals. Said Humphrey: "It is taking Mr. Nixon longer to withdraw our troops than it took us to defeat Hitler. Had I been elected, we would now be out of that war."

In April, Nixon met with a group of Republican senators in the Cabinet Room to discuss his war policy. Tennessee Senator Howard Baker made an impassioned plea to the president to end the war. He said he was more concerned about the future of America than he was with victory or defeat in the Vietnam War.

"Our posture vis-à-vis Berlin, China, Japan . . . is worth a hell of a lot more to me than the question of how long or how short that we stay in Vietnam," Baker said. "I've never said that before to a living soul, but I felt obliged to say it to you now." Also in the room were senators Bob Dole, Barry Goldwater, and John Tower, all of whom stayed out of the conversation. After Baker made his plea, Nixon told him he agreed with his political assessment and was aware of the problem.

In May, Nixon was jolted by news that the North Vietnamese and Viet Cong had captured Quang Tri, making it the first provincial capital to fall since the United States entered the war. As enemy troops headed toward the ancient imperial capital of Hue, Nixon was told there was a possibility the entire country could fall. The South Vietnamese army, the backbone of Nixon's "Vietnamization" plan, was having little success stopping the advancing armies. Said Nixon: "If the United States leaves Vietnam and allows a Communist take-over, the office of the president of the United States will lose respect and I am not going to let that happen."

Nixon dispatched Henry Kissinger to Moscow to discuss details of an upcoming summit with the Soviets and to seek help in getting the Paris peace talks back on track. Kissinger returned with word that the talks would resume, then discovered that would not be the case. The White House issued statements saying the president was not surprised by the battlefield victories in Vietnam and was confident the South Vietnamese government would stand firm. Privately, the president considered options to escalate the American military commitment to South Vietnam.

By the end of May, Nixon had decided to retaliate by planting mines in North Vietnam harbors and by ordering the resumption of heavy bombing strikes. American military officials claimed that the U.S. planes had destroyed a key bridge on a major North Vietnamese rail route. The North Vietnamese claimed that the planes were targeting dikes on the Red River, causing heavy civilian casualties. More American planes were shot down, adding to the number of prisoners of war held in the north.

All of a sudden, the Vietnam War was back in the headlines. Did the new military operations ordered by the president mean America was slipping even deeper into the morass? To address the uncertainty, President Nixon asked for time from the television networks to address the nation.

In his speech, Nixon all but admitted that his Vietnamization policy had failed. "The risk that a Communist government may be imposed on the seventeen million people of South Vietnam has increased," he said, adding that he feared the South Vietnamese would face "a long night of terror" unless the United States succeeded in stopping the advance of the North Vietnamese and Viet Cong. Then, in statements directed as much to the North Vietnamese as the American public, he said the United States would end all "acts of force" in Indochina once Hanoi released all Americans prisoners of war and allowed an internationally supervised cease-fire to be established. Once that happened, he said, he would agree to withdraw all American troops within four months.

There was no immediate response from the Viet Cong or North Vietnamese.

By that point, most Americans, realizing that victory was out of the question, had stopped discussing the war, except in terms of what would happen once it ended. The most hotly debated issue was how to deal with the thousands of war resisters who had fled to Canada and Sweden. Unlike President Nixon, who said he would never grant an amnesty to those who opposed the war, George McGovern said early on that would be one of his first acts as president.

In January, *Newsweek* ran a cover story on the subject of amnesty in which it released results of a Gallup poll that showed that seventy-one percent of those questioned favored amnesty of some kind. Only seven percent of those favored amnesty without qualification, while sixty-three percent favored it only with a service requirement (one percent were unsure about whether there should be a requirement). "It is not a declared war and the boys are not traitors," said one of the respondents Another said, "If the war were just I would feel different. In this war, think people should decide for themselves."

Despite the rather large pro-amnesty results of the poll, individual Americans opposed to amnesty made their feelings known. At a campaign stop in Columbus, Ohio, McGovern was confronted by a thirty-year-old Vietnam war veteran who demanded to know why he wanted amnesty for "traitors." McGovern told him he was not for traitors but was for justice for those who opposed the war. With that, the man thrust his arm out at McGovern and pointed at a bracelet on his wrist that contained a man's name. According to Nicholas C. Chriss of the *Los Angeles Times*, the man angrily said, "This man right here is a prisoner of war," to which McGovern responded, "That's right. And Nixon's keeping him in jail by keeping this war going. He's been there since 1967 . . . what's Nixon done to get him out?"

Syndicated columnist Art Buchwald took a different approach. He wrote a column in which he created a conversation between himself and an "acquaintance by marriage" named Cedric Farfinkle. Not surprisingly, Farfinkle was against amnesty, Buchwald turned the conversation around by saying that he thought the "warmongers" should be given amnesty out of simple Christian charity. Buchwald was exerting the muscle of his well-toned wit, but for the war resisters, it was no joke. In their minds, it was the people who conducted the war who should have been the subject of debate over amnesty, not the people who opposed it.

In January, Charles Porter, a former Oregon congressman who had opposed the war from the beginning, formed an organization named Amnesty Now to work for support of general amnesty. He said he felt a responsibility to war resisters because of his public opposition to the war. "Myself and other liberals like me unwittingly forced a cruel dilemma [on] these young men," he told a reporter for the *New York Times*. "We opposed the war and generated resistance. Idealistic young men caught in the middle of that debate had to make a decision and some of them chose not to become involved in what has been considered an illegal and immoral war."

By that time, amnesty bills sponsored by Representative Edward Koch of New York and Senator Robert Taft, Jr., of Ohio had already been introduced in Congress. Writing in the February issue of the *New Republic*, James Reston, Jr., advocated unconditional amnesty. "The national guilt is total in Vietnam, and if this country wishes to balance that record with positive acts, it must wipe the slate clean," he wrote.

As debate continued, President Nixon began to backpedal from his earlier position. In an interview with CBS news correspondent Dan Rather, Nixon said: "We always, under our system, provide amnesty. . . . I for one would be very liberal with regard to amnesty, but not while there are Americans in Vietnam fighting to serve their country . . . and not while [prisoners of war] are held by the enemy. After that, we would consider it."

By 1972, Jim Thomas's American lawyer had filed a show-cause order with the federal court in the Illinois district in which he had been indicted for not reporting for induction, and the federal prosecutor had dropped charges against him, surprising everyone involved. Jim was free to live in any country he chose, including the United States. He chose to remain in Canada.

"When I left I was under the impression I would never see my parents again or my wife's parents," he said. "The court action meant I could travel anywhere I wanted to. Prior to that, it had been a real problem as far as my career was concerned."

Jim worked for a large Canadian company that had 4,500 employees in offices across Canada and in the United States. Jim and Mary lived in Toronto for a while, then they were transferred to Berry, Ontario, then back to Toronto. For a time they lived in Calgary, where there was a large population of Texas oilmen who had gone north to work for short stints in the oil fields. "You had to be a little more cautious in what you said around the Texas oil people, but, having said that, the company I worked for had holdings in the United States and I used to travel there all the time.

"I usually tell people I came [to Canada] because I turned down a job with the United States Army," Jim said. "You don't go to an army base and tell people that, but I was never not prepared to tell people why I was in Canada. I always wanted to talk about it. We had raging debates at university for so long it was not a fair battle for someone who did not have the background. I was always happy to talk about it."

By the time the *Newsweek* cover story on amnesty was published, Jim already had his freedom. "I thought the whole business of amnesty made sense, but I thought it should be unconditional," he said. One of his new friends in Canada was a man who had fled to the United States from Cuba when Fidel Castro came into power. He went to university in the United States, and when he graduated, he went to work for Head Start, teaching in the ghettos. Then he was drafted and sent off to boot camp. After he completed the training, he decided he had been pulled into exactly what he had wanted to get away from when he left Cuba. So he deserted and went to Canada.

When Jim heard talk of amnesty, he thought of his friend—and of the thousands of other exiles who had not been lucky enough to have their charges dropped. They needed help, too.

The Canadian news media, particularly the newspapers, devoted considerable time and space to the amnesty issue. The *Toronto Star* devoted several three-quarter-page features to the subject. One story, written by staff writer Margaret Daly, bore the headline "War Resisters: 'We Still Don't Want to Go Back.' " One of the men she interviewed was Peter Pacini, a minister's son from Cleveland, Ohio, who had chosen exile in Canada over service in the military. At the time he was interviewed, he was a partner in a successful radio production business in Toronto. Daly asked him what he thought of President Nixon's "peace" efforts. "Promoting these leaders who prolonged this thing for so long as men of peace now . . . makes me want to puke," said Pacini, who was only eighteen when he went to Canada. "The war itself is something I must admit I try to avoid thinking about. I was always against it—we had a French-Canadian teacher in high school who spoke against it long before it was at all acceptable to do so, and also, I'm a minister's son and brought up to think for myself about right and wrong."

In another issue of the *Star,* staff writer Trent Frayne interviewed a war resister who said he would not return to the United States if an amnesty were granted, and a war resister who said he would return to work for social change. Dan Zimmerman, a twenty-three-year-old New Yorker, said he was in no hurry to return. "If I can be useful in Canada, I'd like to stay . . . there's potential here I can't see in the States," he said.

Dick Burroughs, a twenty-five-year-old Texas resister who said he would return, felt encouraged by changing views in the States about the war and social issues in general. He admitted he was probably in the minority. "Anybody is crazy who thinks this country is full of Americans who've been standing at the border staring across with tears in their eyes," he said. "Guys that anxious to get back have long since gone." The only thing he did not like about Canada was the way in which government leaders allowed Americans to influence the Canadian economy. Said Burroughs: "America takes, you know, and gives very little back."

The Recorder and Times, a conservative daily in the small city of Brockville, Ontario, ran a lead editorial about amnesty that pointed out most of the debate on the subject was occurring in the United States. "Very little is coming from the exiles themselves," noted the newspaper (which had allowed a local war resister to write editorials on other subjects for its pages). "Perhaps in time the war resisters will lose some of their bitterness toward their former country. And perhaps, through the help of [books on the subject] . . . Americans can come to understand what motivated them. But first, both sides have to stop the deprecatory name-calling, the simplistic generalizations—and the hate."

Taking a different approach was the weekend newspaper supplement *Parade* magazine, which was distributed in newspapers on both sides of the border. In the spring of 1972, its editors sent writer Martin B. Margulies to Toronto to meet with exiles. Margulies's story, published in the April issue, pointed out that many of the war resisters from states with liberal prosecutors eager to close cases against draft evaders were already free to return to the States whenever they wished.

One of the resisters interviewed by Margulies had left Arkansas after his draft board rejected his CO application without a written explanation. Subsequently, the courts declared inductions under those conditions invalid. By the time the Arkansan learned he was no longer a wanted man, he had made a new life in Canada as a well-paid computer programmer analyst.

Some war resisters did return to the States in 1972 when they learned charges against them were no longer pending. After receiving a degree from Amherst College, Harry Pincus had gone to England in the mid-1960s to earn a master's in social work at the London School of Economics. He was working as a psychiatric social worker when he was drafted. He refused to return to report for induction and helped organize the first American anti-Vietnam War group in England. He was an active member of the GI "underground railway" in England and once achieved a degree of notoriety by slipping past Secret Service agents to present President Nixon with a petition during a state visit to England.

In 1970, Pincus learned charges against him had been dropped, and he returned to New York City to work with drug addicts and political resisters. In 1972, after learning that a close friend—and fellow war resister—had committed suicide, Pincus, who once was described by a friend as someone who was "on the side of the angels," grew despondent and took his own life.

From early to late 1972, Canada was still recovering from the prime minister's invocation of the War Measures Act to combat terrorists in Quebec. Canadians do not like their political leaders to make sudden moves of any kind. Trudeau's actions had made many Canadians uneasy, particularly the liberals who had put him into power. Trudeau's subsequent marriage to Margaret softened his image with voters, and the birth of their first child, Justin Pierre, earned him bushels of fuzzy feelings from the public and a raucous desk-pounding in the House of Commons, to which he replied: "This is one area where I am certainly very happy to receive advice from the opposition parties."

But, baby or not, Trudeaumania had lost its edge. Commenting on Trudeau's apparent fall from grace, reporter John Gray wrote a piece in *Maclean's* that asked the question, "Has the Prime Minister Changed Or Have We?" Gray was not certain what had changed, only that *something* had changed. He wondered if the shift was coming from Trudeau's own supporters. Concluded Gray: "In fairness, he might ask whether the change in public opinion is not just a caprice on the part of the smirking, smug and arrogant Toronto intellectual establishment which tried so hard to make of him a national hero in 1968."

Several months later, Walter Gordon wrote an article for *Maclean's* entitled "Last Chance for Canada," in which he concluded that "a choice between Trudeau and our country's survival is no choice at all." Gordon expressed fears that the spring of 1972 would someday be recognized as the "beginning of the end for Canada."

In the beginning, Pierre Trudeau had been a hero among American war resisters. He stood up for them when no one else would. As a result, the exile community embraced his leadership almost without question. Trudeau lost much of that support when he imposed the War Measures Act, for it demonstrated to the war resisters the truly fragile nature of their hold on freedom. Ironically, it nudged them into new roles as defenders of the traditional Canadian way of life.

In the summer of 1972, as the presidential campaign was heating up—and the Democrats and Republicans had yet to nominate their respective candidates—five men wearing surgical gloves and carrying walkie-talkies picked the lock of the basement entrance of the Watergate office complex in Washington, D.C., and proceeded to the office of the Democratic National Committee. The men jimmied the lock of the office and proceeded to rifle the files. Some files they stuffed into boxes; others they dumped onto the floor. Unfortunately, for the five men, their entrance was detected by an alert night watchman who promptly called the police.

Within minutes, three cops from the D.C. plainclothes squad burst in on the men and arrested them. "Don't shoot—you've got us," pleaded one of the burglars. When the men were booked, it was discovered that four of them had previously worked as operatives for the Central Intelligence Agency and the fourth, James McCord, was currently employed both as the security coordinator for President Nixon's re-election campaign and the Republican National Committee.

The Washington political and media establishment were stunned. Never before in American history had a national political party used illegal and totalitarian methods to spy on an opposition party. The break-in was identical in technique to those used by the FBI and the CIA to spy on antiwar dissidents, although at the time of the Watergate break-in, neither Congress nor the American public was aware of the illegal activities being conducted by the FBI and the CIA.

When confronted with the facts of the break-in, the White House denied any knowledge of the crime. Former Attorney General John Mitchell, who had resigned to head the Committee for the Re-Election of the President, told reporters there was no place in the electoral process for that type of activity. The Justice Department announced that the FBI had entered the case, and the public was assured by the White House that, whatever had happened, neither the president nor the Republican Party was involved.

With a big win in the New York primary in June, George McGovern was confident of victory the following month when he went to the Democratic convention in Miami Beach. He did not have enough delegate votes for a first-ballot victory, but he had enough to hold out for a win, especially if he was able to keep his coalition of young people and blacks and women together. When the McGovern supporters arrived at the convention, many of the old-timers complained to the candidate that his youthful followers were too arrogant and were making the party veterans uncomfortable.

Even defeated primary opponent Edmund Muskie went on record warning McGovern to keep his people under control. No one seemed to want to consider that what they saw as arrogance was nothing more than the exuberance of the disaffected, those who had been kept out of the system coming to believe, wrongly as it turned out, that the system really worked and they could make a difference with hard work and dedication and faith in the inherent goodness of the American people.

Life magazine sent Norman Mailer to the convention. For the novelist, it was sort of a Democracy on Parade street festival that left him both hopeful and depressed at the same instant. With apologies to Charles Dickens, he called it the best and worst of conventions. He looked for

the Big Picture but saw only small details and seemed genuinely dis-
tressed that the greatest "peoples' victory" in American history—it was
the first time that ordinary people, grass-roots activists, chose a candidate, leaving the party men in the lurch—did not take place under more
gentile circumstances that would allow for, at the very least, a meta-
phorical parting of the heavens.

Even so, Mailer concluded that the convention, "no matter how tedi-
ous, boring, protean, and near to formless, came out a rare and blithe
watershed in the civil affairs of men." No one was really sure what to expect. The *New Republic* ran an article by Alexander Bickel with the headline "Will the Democrats Survive Miami?"

McGovern's victory gave hope to an entire generation of Americans
who had come of age knowing nothing of the political process except its
deceits and dishonors. It also gave hope to Richard Nixon and his cadre
of campaign advisors who all along had picked McGovern as the
Democrat who would be the easiest to defeat. McGovern was *too good* to
be president. The Nixon people had only to examine their own lives to
see that the White House was no place for a man of decency and honor.
At some point, they even convinced themselves that McGovern would
make a terrible president because he was too moral to make the dirty
decisions that they felt all presidents had to make on a daily basis.

The following month, the Republican convention, also held in Miami
Beach, stood in mind-numbing contrast to the Democratic gathering.
America's youth were at that convention, just as they had been at the
Democratic convention, but they were there not to anoint a hopeful
leader but to scold a president who had promised them four years earlier that he would end the war and who had lied to them without remorse.

There were riots at the Republican convention, particularly at Fla-
mingo Park, where opponents of Nixon's war policy gathered to engage in guerrilla theater and political education. *Newsweek* ran
photographs of police officers beating the dissidents with clubs and
chasing them through the streets. There were photographs of police officers using their clubs like scissors to choke the protesters and lift them
by their necks.

One photograph showed a young women with her jeans pulled
down past the top of her panties, exposing her to the crowd of onlook-
ers, her hands handcuffed behind her back; her mouth was agape in agony, her eyes closed to the abuse of the male police officers. Her face was
the image of an entire generation of Americans for whom honor and
truth and justice were but abstract concepts enjoyed by previous generations.

Amid a cascade of red, white, and blue balloons, Richard Nixon accepted his party's nomination for president. In his speech, Nixon invoked the memory of past Democratic presidents—Franklin Roosevelt, Harry Truman, John Kennedy, and Lyndon Johnson—and there were those present who thought that maybe Nixon really wanted to be the Democratic candidate. To those Americans who felt they had been driven from the Democratic Party by extremists such as George McGovern, Nixon invited them into the Republican fold to enjoy "the great principles we Americans believe in together."

Early in the campaign, McGovern suffered a setback when it was disclosed that his running mate, Senator Thomas Eagleton of Missouri, had once undergone electro-shock treatments. At that time, there was a perception among most Americans that there was a big red button in the White House that, when pushed, would launch the nation's nuclear missile arsenal. Did they really want a man a heartbeat away from that office who had been subjected to electro-shock treatments?

Some of McGovern's advisors told him he should dump Eagleton and find a new running mate. Others advised him to keep Eagleton, for fear of appearing wishy-washy and disloyal to his supporters. McGovern anguished over the dilemma and decided to replace Eagleton with former Kennedy advisor Sargent Shriver.

For a time, it appeared McGovern might actually win the election. He visited Lyndon Johnson at his Texas ranch and was photographed with the former president. He mended fences with Mayor Richard Daley of Chicago, or at least presented the appearance of doing so. The Vietnam War was still raging. Nixon had had four years to end it and had not done so. Watergate was a tantalizing fester that summer but had the appearance of developing into a major scandal as the campaign progressed into the fall.

The Paris peace talks resumed in July, amid the pageantry of the conventions, and as if to underscore the fact that the war was still very much a reality, the northernmost province of South Vietnam, Quang Tri, fell to the Viet Cong and North Vietnamese. The only thing that had been agreed to at the peace talks was the shape of the table. As the public talks proceeded in Paris, Henry Kissinger met secretly with the North Vietnamese. Soon it became apparent that the only purpose of the public talks was to announce any progress made in the secret talks.

As a political issue, Vietnam simply would not go away. For weeks, news leaks out of Saigon hinted that peace was at hand. *Newsweek* ran a story that asked the question, "A Cease-Fire by Election Day?" Cynics suggested that Nixon might just end the war to spite McGovern. In mid-October, North Vietnamese Premier Pham Van Dong invited

Newsweek senior editor Arnaud de Borchgrave to Hanoi for an exclusive interview, at which time he said all American prisoners of war would be released as soon as an agreement was reached. Dong said he foresaw a three-stage settlement: a cease-fire, followed by a total American withdrawal; direct negotiations between Saigon loyalists and Communist leaders; and national elections to determine the composition of a new South Vietnamese legislature.

In the four months leading up to the election, more details surfaced about the Watergate break-in. It was learned that the team of men who had broken into Democrat headquarters had direct ties to the White House. As early as 1971, intelligence teams were being organized in the basement of the White House. *Newsweek* reported that Republicans had as many as twenty-five secret agents on its payroll. Investigators found that in addition to breaking and entering to steal documents and plant eavesdropping devices, the secret agents forged letters, disrupted Democratic campaign schedules, and investigated the private lives of Democratic campaign workers.

The week before the election, Henry Kissinger called a press conference at which he announced that "peace was at hand." The terms of the peace agreement he outlined were pretty much identical to the terms advanced by Dong to *Newsweek*. Kissinger was optimistic, but he was careful to say that there was still a lot of work to be done. Hanoi, on the other hand, was ready to sign on the dotted line. Nguyen Thanh Le, Hanoi's spokesman at the Paris peace talks, told reporters, "Peace is at the end of a pen. All that remains is for the United States to grasp that pen."

On election day, American voters were convinced that peace was at hand. Watergate was still a little confusing to them. Many considered it some sort of high school prank that the Republicans had played on the Democrats. McGovern did not stand a chance. Voters gave Nixon the biggest landslide victory in history. McGovern said he had done everything he could. "I've thought if I lost, it wouldn't be me that was really hurt, but others in the country," he told one of his aides.

Later generations found Nixon's victory puzzling. Wasn't McGovern clearly the better candidate? The fact that he lost was less a reflection on him as a candidate or as a man than it was a mirror image of a segment of the public that felt that if McGovern was right and the Vietnam War was immoral and a travesty of justice, then the 50,000 Americans who died there would have died in vain and they—the voters—would be to blame; no one in 1972 wanted to shoulder that responsibility.

Nixon was given four more years, prompting the *New Republic* to observe that "something very strange is happening in American politics." The November election faded into Thanksgiving and then Christmas.

By the end of the year, American troops were still in Vietnam and it was clear that Watergate was not going away.

"Something quite fundamental is beginning to happen in America," wrote deserter Jack Colhoun for the September 1972 issue of *Amex-Canada*, the magazine published by American exiles in Toronto. "There are definite rumblings of change." Colhoun was referring to the amnesty debate, which by that time had spilled over onto the front pages of most American newspapers. He was concerned because military deserters were not being included in the debate.

Since deserters, as a rule, were from families of a lower socioeconomic class, he felt they were being ignored for reasons of racial and class distinction. Said Colhoun: "Other than a class difference, there are no differences between one who resisted the war before induction and one who resisted it after induction."

Colhoun had reason for concern. The *Newsweek* poll conducted by Gallup did not include questions about deserters, although it did ask if amnesty should also be granted to First Lieutenant William Calley for atrocities committed against women and children in Vietnam. To the disgust of many, only twenty-four percent of those polled were opposed to amnesty for Calley. That question, more so than those about amnesty for draft evaders, was indicative of public opinion about deserters—and that made Colhoun and most war resisters uncomfortable. For many war resisters, Calley was the epitome of everything that had gone wrong with America. To be equated with him, if only in an opinion poll, was a moral affront of the highest order.

In that same issue of *Amex-Canada* was a letter to the editor from a Navy deserter, who identified himself only as "John." He said he had turned himself in to authorities in San Diego and had been released after ten days in the brig, while the Navy decided what to do with him. The big news in San Diego, he said, was the damage done to the USS *Ranger*, an aircraft carrier bound for Vietnam, when someone—presumably an antiwar sailor—tossed a ten-inch bolt into the gears, causing $250,000 worth of damage. Wrote John: "The brass is really shitting because the Navy is coming apart right in front of them."

Canada was also undergoing fundamental change in 1972. Prime Minister Pierre Trudeau's return to power was dependent on his Liberal Party maintaining a majority of seats in Parliament. When the votes were counted after the October 30 election, no party emerged with a clear majority. The Liberal Party was given a one-seat lead over the Conservative Party, with the New Democratic Party (NDP) holding the balance of power.

Trudeau was stunned, for he had expected to win by a comfortable margin. His only options were to resign—and allow Parliament to broker a deal for a new prime minister, most likely Conservative leader Bob Stanfield—or govern as the leader of a minority party by appealing to the NDP for support (help from the Conservatives was out of the question). He chose the latter, a decision that left him both bloodied and bowed.

The election provided an interesting lesson in Canadian politics. Pierre Trudeau was still prime minister, but Canadian voters, feeling that perhaps he was becoming a bit too arrogant in his use of power—the implementation of the War Measures Act, for example—made certain that the only way he could govern would be through a working consensus with those of opposing viewpoints. For Trudeau, it was a most humbling experience. When a reporter from *Time* asked him if he thought his arrogance might have been a factor in the election, Trudeau replied, "I certainly have many sins, but I usually confess them to my priest, not to the press."

By 1972, most of the war resisters in Canada had been there for several years and had forged new lives that seemed to have little to do with the amnesty debate. David Keller is a good example. When he arrived in Canada in 1970 in a 1951 Dodge panel truck, he stopped off in Toronto on his way to the Queen Charlotte Islands, where he and his wife meant to settle, and he never left. With $300 in his pocket, he found a partner who would help him to start up a T-shirt business. Two years later, when *Globe and Mail* reporter Martin O'Malley caught up with "Crazy David"—he had asked his clients to call him that as a marketing ploy—his factory was turning out nearly 10,000 T-shirts a day.

"Obviously, Mr. Keller is doing well in the T-shirt business," wrote O'Malley. "He is doing so well that he says he would like to retire in about two years, at which time he expects to be able to live off the interest of the $200,000 or $300,000 he hopes to have in the bank." Crazy David said he learned the value of promotion in the early days while driving around to shopping centers and race tracks to hawk his merchandise from the back of his truck. "I've always believed that for every dollar you spend on advertising you get ten dollars back in business," he said, adding that his next big project would be the formation of the Crazy David T-Shirt Band. He planned to sink $100,000 into that project.

Another draft resister, Allen Morgan, published a book in 1972 about his experiences. *Dropping Out in 3/4 Time* was published by a New York company and was yet another sign that the issue of draft resistance was gaining mainstream acceptance south of the border. Morgan's book was heavy on fantasy and whimsical musings—and light on substance—but it did offer a glimpse into the apolitical brain of at least one Canadian exile and received good reviews in both Canada and the United States.

After spending six years in Calgary, where he and his wife Mary had a second daughter, Caroline, Jim Thomas, returned with his family to Ontario and settled in London, a city of nearly 400,000 located halfway between Toronto and Detroit. Jim formed his own management consultant firm and started dabbling in politics. "Not in a big way," he said. "I support the people I like. I've helped run campaigns for friends. I've never run for office myself. I'm not into abuse that much. Frankly, it doesn't make any sense. Just look at the abuse someone takes in order to be a politician. I have friends who are provincial officeholders." Jim describes himself as a "Red Tory," someone who is "fiscally conservative but willing to say that we should be willing to take care of each other."

From the late 1970s to the time of this printing, Jim as worked as a negotiator for companies that have unions and as a "head hunter," for businesses looking for big-ticket personnel such as operations managers and company presidents. Never once has he considered moving back to the United States, except in one "fleeting incident" when he was angry at the National Democratic Party and thought about it for twenty minutes.

"But, no, I don't want to move back," he said. "I'm here because I want to be here. I should have come sooner. Canada is the best kept secret in the world. My family is in Montana now and there are some reactionary elements there. When I go there, I get, you know, 'This is the best country in the world.' I say, 'Do you really want to talk about that because I don't buy it.' I'm not at all unhappy here. I could leave anytime I wanted to, but I don't want to. When I look at my friends that I am still in contact with [in the United States], they have to plan their travels to take into account the undercurrent of violence [in America]."

Jim and Mary have been married for over thirty years. The interesting thing about them as a couple is the level of devotion they have maintained for each other over the years, despite a fundamental difference of opinion—in the beginning, at least—about Jim's decision to go to Canada.

"Mary never understood my decision not to serve," he said. "She says she would have served. She came with me, but I'm not sure she was happy about it." He paused and laughed, realizing that he has underplayed her feelings. "I *know* she wasn't happy," he said, correcting himself. "It wasn't the best day of my life. No one was talking to me. My wife was unhappy. My mother wasn't talking to me. My dad was supportive but did not understand. He said I should go and shoot over peoples' heads. But I knew that if someone was shooting at me and my friends, I would get angry.

"I get asked, 'Would you do it again?' "

"Yes, but it has to be the right issue. I wouldn't do it over whether my taxes are too high. When someone says you should go out and shoot other people, even if the reason makes sense, that's wrong. It's not exclusive to the United States. Look at what happened in Bosnia. I find it incredibly frustrating not to be able to do anything about what is happening there. . . . Look at the scholarship that surrounded the studies of Vietnam. The government lied and lied and lied. In Canada, there was an attempt by the government to cover up abuses in Somalia. You have to be ever vigilant.

"My kids get bored with this issue sometimes. It's not relevant to them, and I can understand that."

James Dickerson. Photo courtesy of James Dickerson. Used with permission.

Highway 137 from Ontario across the St. Lawrence River into New York; the sign seems to offer unsolicited advice of a political nature about how new arrivals are expected to behave in the United States. Photo courtesy of James Dickerson. Used with permission.

Diane Francis. Photo courtesy of Diane Francis. Used with permission.

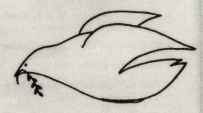

Antiwar booklet distributed during October 15 "Vietnam Moratorium." Used with permission.

A demonstrator's eye view of National Guard troops called out in the wake of the Martin Luther King assassination in Memphis. Photo courtesy of Mississippi Valley Collection. Used with permission.

National Guard soldier detains protestors during rioting in the aftermath of the Martin Luther King assassination. Photo courtesy of Mississippi Valley Collection. Used with permission.

Richard Deaton's family. From left, Emmauelle, Marie-Claire, Richard, and Shoshanah. Photo courtesy of Richard Deaton. Used with permission

Patrick Grady's family. Back row: Patrick and Jean Grady. Front row: Mark, Meghan, Jean's mother Ruth, and Heather. Photo courtesy of Patrick Grady. Used with permission.

This photo of Jean and Patrick Grady was taken on August 18, 1968—the day before they went to Canada. Photo courtesy of Patrick Grady. Used with permission.

Richard Deaton in 1970. Photo courtesy of Richard Deaton. Used with permission.

Michael Wolfson at Cambridge University in 1973. Photo courtesy of Michael Wolfson. Used with permission.

Within hours of taking office, President Jimmy Carter declared a pardon for Vietnam War–era draft resisters. Used with permission.

L-R, Richard Deaton, Patrick Grady and Michael Wolfson. Photo by James Dickerson. Used with permission.

Michael Wolfson with his wife, Eleanor, and two of their four children, Andrea, left, and Lynne, right. Photo by James Dickerson. Used with permission.

6

1973

Michael Wolfson: "I Felt the War Was Politically Wrong"

When he was sixteen, Michael Wolfson liked to hang out at the University of Buffalo to attend concerts by avant garde artists and poets. Often he was accompanied by his parents, who were fans of new and experimental music. On one visit to the campus—Michael thinks it was probably in 1963—he attended a "Teach-in" about the Vietnam War at which a professor first read a *Time* story about two South Vietnamese fighter pilots who had defected to the Viet Cong and tried to bomb South Vietnamese President Diem's palace.

The story made much of the president's claim that he had retreated to the basement of the palace with a photograph of Abraham Lincoln. The professor then read the same story as it was written by a reporter for a Toronto newspaper. The two stories were markedly different, and President Diem did not come across in the Toronto newspaper's version as being quite so enamored of American history.

"He made the point that the American media were manipulating the news about what was happening there—glorifying the American side of the story beyond matter-of-fact reporting," said Michael. "That was when I first began wondering whether American policy was right."

By Michael's reckoning, he had become radicalized by the tenth grade, though he is not entirely sure how it happened. His parents were progressive, mainstream Democrats who belonged to a reformed Jewish congregation. His father was an engineer; his mother had a bachelor's degree but never worked outside the home, except for a short time during World War II. Michael attended the temple with his parents and his younger brother and sister until he was barmitzvahed, then he stopped going when the rabbi could not answer his questions about the Kabballah or Bertrand Russell's atheism.

In 1964, while in tenth grade, he went to Sycacuse, New York, on the tenth anniversary of the Supreme Court's ruling against segregation in public schools, to participate in a civil rights protest. It was his first public demonstration, but he had friends who had gone South the summer before to work in voter registration drives, and they had kept him informed of their activities. It was a time of great expectations and a time of great violence, for it was in 1964 that three civil rights workers in Mississippi were murdered and buried in an earthen dam.

In Syracuse, he started thinking seriously about Vietnam and what he would do if he were drafted. "[In Syracuse], there was a literature table and pamphlets by the American Friends Service Committee about conscientious-objector status and that was the first time I started thinking about what I would do about the draft," he said. "When I was seventeen, I decided I would apply to be a conscientious objector when the time came."

The high school he attended in Amherst, a suburb of Buffalo, had a good reputation, but he was a precocious student and felt held back. After placing well in the Westinghouse National Science Talent Search, he was invited to apply to Cargnegie Institute of Technology (now Carneigie Mellon University). He studied grade twelve English in summer school so he could graduate from high school, and left in fall 1965 to study physics at Carnegie Tech, a co-educational school in Pittsburgh, Pennsylvania.

When he turned eighteen and registered for the draft, he discovered that applying for CO status was not a simple matter. The draft board did not care what he thought about the morality of killing. The CO exemption was based on religious grounds. "I tried to express it as a moral opposition and got in a philosophical tangle because to be classified as CO I had to have a religious opposition," he said. "I felt the [war] was politically wrong, an expression of American imperialism, and the violence was morally wrong, abhorrent and unnecessary."

When the draft board turned down his CO application, Michael accepted a student deferment. At least, with a student deferent, he would not be subjected to a grilling by FBI agents, who sometimes called on CO applicants, not so much to question them about their religious convictions as to intimidate them into withdrawing their application. Life as a student was more tolerable.

In spring 1966, Michael heard from a friend who had enrolled at the Berkeley campus of the University of California. She told him Berkeley was the place to be. Michael applied to the University of California and was accepted as a second-year transfer student. One problem was getting there. He asked around and found a professor who needed someone to drive his car to California. It was a rear-engine Corvair, a compact car that later was taken off the market because of claims that its design made it a death trap.

Michael made it safely across country in the Corvair and found Berkeley to be as advertised by his friend. In the middle of the fall term, the Navy set up a recruiting table in the student union. "A number of students, myself included, decided that was not an appropriate thing for the university to allow them to do," said Michael. "We called a general strike."

Those were heady times in Berkeley. For the first time in American history—maybe in the entire history of the world—a thriving youth culture emerged that literally made up the rules as it went along. Drugs, sex, rock 'n' roll: Everything and anything was available on an experimental basis. The youth movement had its own language, its own dress code, and its own media. New counterculture newspapers such as the *Berkeley Barb*, which focused on politics and gay rights, and *Rolling Stone*, which focused on music and grass-roots politics, hit the streets and spread the gospel for the under-thirty generation.

Even mainstream publications jumped on the bandwagon, churning out an endless string of features on the youth movement. *Newsweek*, *Time*, *Life*, and *Look* devoted space to what was happening on the streets, particularly in Berkeley. In January 1968, *Look* devoted an entire issue to the subject. With Beatle John Lennon on the cover, the magazine offered a series of articles and images by photographer Irving Penn that introduced middle-class readers to what was probably their first glimpse of the Hell's Angels, assorted hippies, and earth mothers in magnificent street plumage.

Penn arranged a group photograph of two of the bay area's favorite rock bands—the Grateful Dead and Big Brother and the Holding Company (with a baby-faced Janis Joplin). "Everybody has the ability to affect everything around them" said one unnamed member of the Grateful Dead. "Once we recognize this, that we can be a force on the planet, then we all may become more responsible. We'll realize that Western civilization has to have a spiritual reawakening." An unnamed member of Big Brother and the Holding Company told Penn that life was for the living and that if he had to go to Vietnam to die he would feel he was being "burned" by life.

It was not long before the excitement of what was happening in the streets of Berkeley Haight-Ashbury overwhelmed Michael's formal studies. He withdrew from school and found a job in a bookstore. Later he found a better job as a computer programmer in Lawrence Radiation Lab, working for a physicist.

"I had learned you could appeal your CO status," he said. "I knew I couldn't win, but as an act of civil disobedience—and as a way of clogging up the bureaucracy in Washington—I wrote back a letter saying I appealed. Every time the paperwork turned another notch, I wrote another letter of appeal, still hoping against hope that it would finally be accepted."

Meanwhile, he looked for more serious work. One of the places he interviewed was at Rocket Dyne Corporation in Los Angeles (related to the Jet Propulsion Lab). "They flew me down for an interview and gave me a test. I think it was an IQ test. They told me it looked like they had all kinds of interesting work for me and would be in touch."

"Two weeks later, I received a curt letter saying, 'We don't have an opening for someone of your qualifications.' My guess is they did a security check and at that point I was 2-F on my way to being 1-A, but what right did they have to go into my records? That certainly colored my thinking. I felt that my future was shot for a wide range of interesting jobs."

Michael's appeals to his draft board continued for two years. "At one point I was advised that I had to appear at the Oakland induction center for a physical. I went and said I wouldn't fight, and never got the physical. I just left." During the appeal process, Michael's relatives, landlords, and employers were all interviewed by the FBI. "Part of the process of appealing CO status is that you have the pleasure of being investigated by the FBI," he said. "The FBI was kind enough to send me a summary of the report."

In March 1968, he went home to Buffalo for his last appeal. After a week of contemplation, writing, and rewriting, he sent the letter to Selective Services headquarters in Washington. On the flight back, he stopped off in Chicago to change planes and picked up a newspaper. "The headline was something to the effect that Mayor Daley was that summer going to allow police to shoot [demonstrators] if there was trouble at the convention. It was the culmination. It just capped everything off."

Back home in Buffalo, he told his parents he had decided to go to Canada. "They didn't give me any hassle at all," he recalled. His parents drove him to Toronto to talk to antidraft counselors about how to emigrate to Canada, then they returned to Buffalo and he made plans to leave the country.

In April, the nation was rocked by Martin Luther King's assassination. King had written an article for *Look* magazine that was published the week after his death. In it, he said whites were welcome to join in the upcoming spring protests, and he warned that if the protests failed to bring about change, "holocaust" could follow.

The problems of African Americans were many, he said, but they were overshadowed by the Vietnam War. Wrote King: "We'll focus on the domestic problems, but it's inevitable that we've got to bring out the question of the tragic mix-up in priorities. We are spending all of this money for death and destruction and not nearly enough money for life and constructive development."

In Michael's eyes, the country was literally falling apart. King was dead, and the cities were burning. Soldiers were roaming the streets with bayonets and automatic rifles. Tanks and armored vehicles were taking up positions on the street corners of every major city in America. Demonstrators were being beaten senseless by club-wielding policemen. That May, Michael said good-bye to his parents and drove to Toronto with no hope—or desire—of ever returning to the United States.

The year 1973 began with the heaviest bombing campaign in history. On the orders of President Richard Nixon, more than 120 B-52s and smaller attack aircraft pounded the North Vietnamese cities of Hanoi and Haiphong, with each B-52 dropping over thirty tons of bombs. It was the first time the big bombers had ever flown over Hanoi. But it was not the first time that civilians had been bombed. One of the first casualties in Hanoi was a one-thousand-bed hospital.

During the first six days of the attack, a dozen B-52s were downed by North Vietnamese missiles, resulting in the capture of fifty-five American airmen. When that information reached the American public, embarrassed Air Force officials announced they could no longer provide figures on downed planes "for security reasons." Not shy about giving that information directly to the American public were the North Vietnamese, who arranged press conferences and trotted out the captured airmen for all to see. Attending one of the press conferences was folk singer Joan Baez, who serenaded the pilots with a rousing rendition of "The Night They Drove Old Dixie Down."

Most Americans were stunned by the escalation in the war. Just before election day, they had been told by President Nixon that "peace was at hand." *Newsweek* spoke for many Americans when it published a story on the bombing campaign with a headline that asked "What Went Wrong?"

As the bombing continued on a daily basis, the world reacted with outrage. The Canadian House of Commons unanimously passed a resolution deploring the raids. The Australian Parliament lodged a protest and maritime workers announced a boycott on American shipping. In Great Britain, Labor Party leader Roy Jenkins—who was ordinarily extremely pro-American—called the bombing "one of the most cold-blooded acts in recent history."

The international community was not alone in its expression of moral outrage. The antiwar movement had spread to Congress, with lawmakers considering legislation to cut off funds for military operations in Vietnam. Senate majority leader Mike Mansfield said the time had come for Congress "to bring about complete disinvolvement" in the war. Republican Senator Norris Cotton of New Hampshire said he had never seen Congress begin a new session "in such an ugly mood."

At issue now was America's image of itself. In North Vietnam, American pilots were bombing hospitals and civilians, and in the South, horror stories about atrocities toward women and children had only escalated with the revelations of My Lai. That was not the image of America that had been created by Hollywood.

Feeling the heat, President Nixon sent Henry Kissinger back to Paris for another try at the peace talks. Inaugural Day was approaching, and Nixon did not want to be sworn in for a second term without a peace agreement in hand. A week later, Kissinger returned to Washington and told Nixon that he thought peace was within reach. Nixon dispatched Kissinger back to Paris to wrap up the deal.

To Nixon's disappointment, Kissinger was unable to come through before the inaugural. In his speech, Nixon ignored any mention of Vietnam, though he did make several double-speak references to America's need to re-establish its traditional values. It was the beginning of a level of double-speak about the Vietnam War that would continue to the present day, whereby those opposed to the war—and those in favor of it—discussed it using identical words with opposite meanings.

On January 23, 1973—three days after Inauguration Day—President Nixon's familiar image flickered on television for one last address on the Paris peace talks. "Good evening," said Nixon. "I have asked for this radio and television time tonight for the purpose of announcing that we today have concluded an agreement to end the war and bring peace with honor in Vietnam and Southeast Asia." Unable to witness that "peace with honor" was Lyndon Johnson, who died of a heart attack a few days before the agreement was signed.

Just like that, the war was over on basically the same terms offered by the Viet Cong and the North Vietnamese all along. Under the agreement, the bombing would be stopped and the last remaining 24,000 American troops in Vietnam would be pulled out, a cease-fire would be implemented, the 600 American prisoners of war held in Hanoi would be released, and free elections would be allowed to take place in South Vietnam. To obtain that agreement, which amounted to basically the same terms agreed to in 1954 and a stinging defeat for the American military, more than 46,000 American soldiers were sent home in body bags, with another 300,000 wounded and maimed—all at a cost of $146 billion to American taxpayers.

As the nation prepared to receive the prisoners of war—the Pentagon named it "Operation Homecoming"—the wives, parents, and children of the captured soldiers were briefed by the military on how to act. Foremost, warned the military, do not ask, "Well, how was it?" The families were advised to go slowly and not expect too much. "Such questions as 'Should mother come and live with us?' or 'Should we send Johnny to such and such a school?' are just overwhelmingly complex for him," briefing officers told the families. "He's still living in the most important world he's ever known. That's his prison world, and it's going to take him a bit to come out of it."

As the prisoners of war were coming home, the issue of amnesty for war resisters arose anew, with *Newsweek* columnist Shana Alexander acknowledging that although it "may have taken as much or more courage to resist this war on moral grounds as it did to fight in it," consideration should be given to the feelings of those "who sacrificed all their freedom and even their very lives" for the war effort. That kind of logic may have appeared reasonable to Americans who had a middle-of-the-road opinion on the war, but to war resisters—those who cared one way or the other about amnesty—it was an admission that the real "lessons" of the war had yet to be learned.

The actual end of the war was anticlimactic. On March 29, 1973, the last 2,500 American combat soldiers in Vietnam boarded planes at Tan Son Nhut airport in Saigon. There to see them off was a small crowd of Vietnamese civilians and Ambassador Ellsworth Bunker, who also was departing. Addressing the small gathering, General Frederick Weyand, the last U.S. commander to serve in Vietnam, said simply, "Our mission has been accomplished."

Not paying much attention to the ceremony or the speech were the soldiers, who at that point were passing around bottles of champagne and grinning ear to ear. Hours later, President Nixon went on television to report the event to the American people. "For the first time in twelve years, no American military forces are in Vietnam," he said. "All of our American POW's are on their way home. . . . We have prevented the imposition of a Communist government by force on South Vietnam."

If President Nixon thought there would be parades in *his* honor to celebrate his role in the peace agreement, he was mistaken, for accompanying the de-escalation of the war was an escalation of his troubles related to the Watergate break-in. Three weeks after his announcement about the end of the war, the Senate voted to launch its own investigation into the espionage that took place during the presidential campaign. Nixon continued to deny any knowledge of the Watergate break-in and of any other illegal spying that took place during the campaign. Few Americans felt great affection for Nixon, the politician, but most refused to believe that the president was a crook or would lie to them.

On March 17, 1973, just a little over a week before the last troops left Vietnam, Nixon met with one of his top aides, John Dean, in the Oval Office to discuss the break-in of Daniel Ellsberg's psychiatrist's office. They discussed Congress's request for CIA files on the subject. Dean told Nixon the secret operation took place under John Ehrlichman's watch, but he wasn't sure he even knew about it.

"I've never asked him if he knew," said Dean. "I didn't want to know."

"I can't see that getting into, into this hearing," said Nixon.

"Well look. No. Here's the way it can come up." said Dean. "In the CIA's files which they—which the Committee is asking for—the material they turned over to the Department of Justice—there are all the materials relating to [Howard] Hunt. In there are these pictures which the CIA developed and they've got Gordon Liddy standing proud as punch outside this doctor's office with his name on it. And this material, it's not going to take very long for an investigator to go back and say, well, why would this—somebody be at the doctor's office and they'd find out that there was a break-in at the doctor's office and then you'd find Liddy on the staff and then you'd start working it back."

"It's irrelevant," said Nixon.

But Nixon was wrong. It was relevant, and by the end of April, his administration had been shaken to its foundation. *Newsweek* ran a story under the headline "Watergate: The Dam Bursts," in which Watergate was called "the most damaging scandal to befall the Presidency since the Teapot Dome." At a press conference, Nixon conceded that there was a possibility of indictments at the top level of his administration. The only reason Nixon faced up to the issue, reported *Newsweek*, was the release of a confidential report that stated that his deputy campaign manager, Jeb Stuart Magraduer, had told federal prosecutors that John Dean and campaign chairman John Mitchell had approved the Watergate bugging in advance and were aware of efforts to pay off the operatives after their arrest.

Inevitably, the Watergate case spilled over into the Daniel Ellsberg case, with the presiding judge ordering the case dismissed because of misconduct by the Nixon administration. By that time, the CIA had publicly admitted that it had provided assistance to the burglars, and the FBI had admitted that it had installed wiretaps on Ellsberg's telephone long before the Pentagon papers were ever published.

By summer, Nixon had issued a four-thousand-word white paper on Watergate in which he admitted that his men had attempted a cover-up of the scandal and that he might—inadvertently, of course—have set it in motion. The language of the white paper—and Nixon's confession—amounted to a plea for mercy from the American people. Asked by a reporter if Nixon planned to resign, press secretary Ron Ziegler scoffed at the suggestion: "The President of the United States has a lot to do and a lot to accomplish in his second term and he fully intends to do just that."

Among Nixon's "confessions" in his white paper was an admission that his men had designed a super-secret police operation that was unprecedented in American history. Under the plan, the FBI, CIA, and intelligence units of the armed forces would be allowed to engage in bugging, burglary, and even blackmail in an effort to destroy the lives of antiwar activists, foreign students, and federal employees and office holders considered disloyal to the administration's war policy. Nixon assured reporters that the plan was never put into operation, but few, if any, antiwar activists or war exiles in Canada believed a word he said. To them, Nixon was a liar and a disgrace to the country.

"Welcome to Toronto, and please forgive Torontonians' jubilant amazement about our metamorphosis," read the introduction to the 1968 Toronto edition of *Mapdigest*, a booklet provided to visitors by the city's convention and tourist bureau. "You see we've suddenly become truly cosmopolitan after years of a rather drab existence. In fact we used derisively to be called 'Toronto the Good' ... but we've changed our face and outlook now ... and it's all yours, too, our most welcome visitors."

That warm welcome was extended to Michael Wolfson—and tens of thousands of other American war resisters—with the same energetic hospitality offered to other new arrivals in the city. The contrast between the two cultures was staggering. Toronto had a hippie district called Yorkville that was similar to what war resisters had left behind in Berkeley and San Francisco, but with a major difference: Toronto proudly advertised its hippie district in its tourism brochures, although it did refer to it, tongue in cheek, as a "questionable tourist asset." Most revealing of all, the city paid tribute to the "influx of New Canadians."

"I felt like a huge load had been lifted off my shoulders," said Michael about crossing the border into Canada. "I went to the Toronto Anti-Draft Programme, and they offered me advice on how to fill out the form to get enough points [for landed immigrant status]. The critical thing was to have a job offer, and they had a number of volunteers who were helping place draft dodgers. In my case, since I had computer programming experience, they put me in touch with a professor at the University of Toronto. I went and had an interview with him and—lucky for me—he said, 'Why don't you be my research assistant.' So I got a job working for him the same month I arrived."

Michael found a place to live near the university and a little later looked into the requirements for entering the university as a student. He made an appointment with the head of the math department, who gave him an armful of materials to study over the summer. At the end of the summer, the professor said he would test Michael on the materials and, if he passed, he would enroll him that fall as a second-year student. The Ontario education system is different from its counterpart in the United States in that it has a grade thirteen that must be completed before admission to college. University of Toronto officials wanted to treat Michael's first year of college in the United States as equivalent to grade thirteen in Ontario.

Within weeks after Michael's arrival, Robert Kennedy was shot to death in Los Angeles. It was big news on Canadian television and in the newspapers. In the eyes of many Canadians, American politics had become an extension of the gunfight at the OK Corral. First, there had been Martin Luther King, followed by Robert Kennedy; then, at the end of the summer, the Democratic convention in Chicago.

America seemed to be falling apart, right before their eyes. In contrast, life in Toronto was unbelievably sweet. It was, in many ways, what America was like in the old days of Jimmy Stewart and Gary Cooper movies. Canada was what America used to be—or at least what it *thought* it used to be. It was a good place to live and raise a family.

The University of Toronto is located on the western perimeter of Queens Park and the Ontario Parliament Buildings. In the summer, the park is lush and green and usually filled with students and office workers from nearby buildings, all lounging lazily about on the grass. In the 1960s and 1970s, the students wore jeans, and the office workers wore mini skirts and well-tailored suits.

Just east of the university is Yonge Street, the city's main north-south artery. Many of the city's office buildings and hotels are located on the

street, but during the 1960s and 1970s, there was a four-block district between Queen and Gerrard streets—Torontonians called it the "strip"—
that was as outrageously flamboyant and decadent as anything offered on
New York's Times Square. There were six topless bars, four adult book-
stores, a lounge where secretaries moonlighted during their lunch hours as
nude, body paint-by-number models, assorted triple-bill movie theaters,
and a nightclub, Le Coq D'Or, that was famous for the black soul bands it
imported from Mississippi and Alabama.

Once, while researching a feature on the strip joints, a Toronto newspaper reporter came across a stripper at a club named Starvin' Marvin's who
said she was the girlfriend of an American draft dodger. The woman, who
danced under the name Rita del Rio, would not allow the reporter to photograph her. Since most draft dodgers and their wives and girlfriends
were generally not shy about having their pictures taken, it seems likely
that Rita del Rio, who said she was from the Midwest, was probably one of
the handful of female deserters who sought asylum in Canada.

Just walking the street was usually entertaining, for interspersed
among men in business suits, members of the provincial Parliament,
leggy fashion models, and wide-eyed American war resisters were
clusters of street people, roaming bands of Hare Krishnas in flowing, orange robes, and a middle-aged amputee and veteran of the Canadian
army who constantly prowled the street in search of men to punch in the
groin with his fist. The man's legs had been cut off at the knees, and as
he thundered along the sidewalk, his leather knee-pads thumping omi-
nously against the pavement, men with briefcases ran for their lives. It
said something about the Canadian temperament that the amputee's
actions were usually ignored by nearby police officers and tolerated by
his victims, who seemed to relish the challenge.

Michael passed the math professor's test at the end of the summer
and enrolled at the university as a student. By then, his draft board in
Buffalo had sent him an induction notice. He ignored it and was indicted by a New York grand jury. One day he received a telephone call
from the RCMP. "They said they would like to talk to me," he said. "We
set a time for a meeting and I made sure I had a friend with me, and, of
course, the man I spoke to brought a buddy with him."

Michael was not sure what to expect. He had a friend who worked at
the University of Toronto library, which was located across the street
from the International Students Union. His friend told him that the
RCMP had taken a room facing the student union and was filming everyone going in and out of the building. "They were tracking people,"
said Michael. "At the time, no one, certainly not my parents, believed
that the CIA and the FBI were operating against people such as myself."

Understandably, Michael was suspicious of the RCMP's interest in him. After a perfunctory greeting, the two Mounties asked him if he intended to stay in Canada.

"Why?" asked Michael.

"The FBI asked us to find out," said one of the Mounties.

"I have no intention of going back," Michael answered.

The Mounties left, and he never heard from them again. Michael thrived in Canada and excelled at the University of Toronto, graduating in 1971 with an honours bachelor's degree in computer science, math, and economics. By that time, he had found a job working for an economics professor at the university. The professor became Michael's mentor, and when Michael told him he wanted to apply for admission to England's Cambridge University to continue his studies, the professor wrote him a letter of recommendation.

By the time Michael left for England in 1971—despite being an indicted felon in the United States, the American consulate in Ottawa provided him with a passport—he had been subjected to a constant stream of nightmarish news from across the border. Following on the heels of the King and Kennedy assassinations were the police riot at the Democratic convention in Chicago and the My Lai massacre, then the killings at Kent State and Jackson State.

The Kent State killings had a major impact on Michael. "It was the epitome of how far the situation had deteriorated, the fact that they were now using lethal force," he said. The difference between the King and Kennedy murders and the violence at Kent State and at the Democratic convention was the difference between individual acts of violence, and a much more troubling pattern of state violence against its citizens, he reasoned, giving a greater "political" significance to the events at Kent State and Chicago. "It seemed a clear indication that the United States was falling apart," he said. "I thought, if this is what I am leaving—good riddance."

In 1971, Michael left for England to work on a Ph.D. in economics at Cambridge University. He did not have a scholarship or a grant, but he had saved enough money working for the professor to pay his way for the first two years at the university. It did not bother him—or the university—that he was an indicted felon back in the United States. In those days, anyone worth a damn was under indictment for opposing the war in Vietnam. If anything, it was a badge of honor.

The fact that American combat troops had pulled out of Vietnam did not mean that the Indochina war had ended. F-4 Phantom jets based in Thailand continued to make bombing runs into Cambodia throughout the spring and summer. Not until late August did the order go out to terminate the air raids.

President Nixon ended the fighting only after Congress ordered a halt in the bombing. Angrily, he accused Congress of "abandoning a friend." In a statement released the day after the bombing halt, he said: "This Congressional act undermines the prospects of world peace by raising doubts in the minds of both friends and adversaries concerning the resolve and capacity of the United States to stand by international agreements when they are violated by other parties."

Noting that American planes had dropped three times more bombs in Indochina than they had dropped during all of World War II, *Newsweek* compiled a tally of the costs of the air war: 4,240 American airmen killed; 4,866 helicopters lost; 3,706 planes lost; over 7 million tons of bombs dropped—a total cost of 16 billion dollars to the American taxpayer.

Meanwhile, the fighting continued in Vietnam. One provision of the peace accord reached in Paris called for the creation of a national reconciliation council to pave the way for elections. Without the support of the U.S. military, South Vietnamese president Thieu was in no hurry to engage in a popularity contest with the Viet Cong. By late 1973, the elections still had not occurred. As a result, more than 50,000 Vietnamese died in battle during the first nine months of the "cease-fire." Soon it became obvious that there would be no cease-fire anytime soon and that both sides were stalling to improve their respective battlefield positions.

When news reporters contacted the Pentagon for information on the situation in Vietnam, they were told by military officials that Vietnam was no longer its public-relations problem. Inquiring reporters were referred to the State Department for answers to their questions.

Dodging questions from a federal judge in Baltimore was former Vice-President Spiro Agnew, who had been accused of selling favors for pay-offs. Trembling, according to the reporters who were present, he stood before the judge like any other street felon and pleaded no contest to one count of tax evasion. It was part of a plea-bargain deal. In exchange for not contesting the charge of tax evasion, he would not be prosecuted on charges of betraying his country by taking kickbacks from back-room powerbrokers. It was the same sort of corruption that had fed the Vietnam War machine, only on a smaller scale.

For five years, Agnew had led the Nixon administration's charge against antiwar demonstrators, opponents of the draft, intellectuals, and others opposed to administration policies. He became the first vice-president in history to leave office a convicted criminal. His sentence—three years probation and a $10,000 fine—was viewed by most observers as a supreme act of charity. Of course, not everyone considered him worthy of charity. U.S. Attorney James Thompson of Chicago, a Republican who had been brought into the case at the request of officials in Washington, offered what was perhaps the best take on Agnew's departure: "He was simply a crook. The country is well rid of him."

Fighting off allegations that everyone associated with his administration was a crook of one kind or another, President Nixon sought to head off another confrontation with Congress by selecting one of its own members to replace Agnew. His choice was House Minority Leader Gerald Ford, a career congressman who had never shown any aspirations for higher office.

As expected, Ford's appointment as vice-president was handily approved by the Senate. There were fears among some that Nixon and Ford had a secret understanding that in the event Nixon was removed from office, and Ford ascended to the presidency, Nixon would receive a full pardon from Ford for any crimes committed against the country; but both sides vigorously denied that any such under-the-table understanding existed, and critics adopted a wait-and-see attitude.

By summer, the Watergate scandal had become so pervasive that newspapers were devoting full pages to it, and magazines were offering entire sections. Watergate had become the Super Bowl of crimes committed against the American people. It was no longer simply about break-ins and petty pay-offs; it was about a conspiracy at the highest level to take over the country. Testifying before Congress, John Dean told of secret files labeled "Opponents List" and "Political Enemies Project" that contained the names of individuals targeted by the government for harassment, income-tax audits, and wiretaps.

Among those on the lists were heart transplant pioneer Dr. Michael DeBakey, comedian Bill Cosby, New York Jet quarterback Joe Namath, and an assortment of editors and reporters, including several at the *Washington Post* and the *New York Times*. Nixon even had his own brother, Donald, put on the list for Secret Service wiretaps. When the names of those on the lists were released, most told reporters they considered it a badge of honor. Actor Paul Newman, sounding as if he were receiving an Academy Award, thanked all those in the White House "for making this award possible."

In contrast, President Nixon was not reacting with good humor; he was beginning to feel the heat of the congressional investigation. In September he held a press conference—his first in over five months—at which he defended his administration and counterattacked his opponents. He came across reasonably well before the cameras, but when the press conference ended, and he was caught by the cameras shoving his press secretary, he looked desperate and needy—and, perhaps worst of all, unstable. Was Nixon having an emotional breakdown? It was the question on everyone's mind.

About three weeks after the press conference, a federal grand jury handed down indictments against two former White House aides— Howard Hunt and G. Gordon Liddy—and the five men arrested at gunpoint at the Democratic national headquarters. The speculation had ended: Watergate—and its many associations—was now a federal case.

In the weeks that followed, Nixon fired Watergate special prosecutor Archibald Cox, the man who had sought the indictments, prompting the resignation of Attorney General Elliot Richardson. "It Looks Very Grim," said a *Newsweek* headline. Above the headline was a photograph of a man in prison stripes and a Nixon mask holding up a sign that read "Honk for Impeachment."

Indeed, for the first time, there was talk of impeachment in the halls of Congress. It seemed an unthinkable remedy, but with each new revelation of wrongdoing, the alternatives fell away in fast order. Everyone wondered if Nixon could survive. Nixon offered an answer to reporters, though it was wrapped in false bravado: "The tougher it gets, the cooler I get. I have what it takes."

Nixon hit the road to make his case directly to the American public. At a convention of the National Association of Realtors, he walked out on stage before a gigantic American flag decorated with electric lights. He told the cheering crowd that he fully intended to do the job he had been elected to do. The realtors rose to their feet, cheering and shouting their approval. Then he went to Orlando, Florida, to address an Associated Press Managing Editors' convention. His message to that gathering of 400 cynical journalists was simple and to the point: "I am not a crook."

In the minds of most Americans, it was a case of too little, too late. Even Barry Goldwater, the dean of the Republican Party, had misgivings about Nixon. In an interview with the *Christian Science Monitor*, he said, "I hate to think of the adage 'Would you buy a used car from Dick Nixon?' But that's what people are asking around the country."

A few days before Christmas, Nixon invited several people to the White House to have dinner with him and his family. Among those attending were Goldwater and Nixon political advisor Bryce Harlow. Throughout dinner, Nixon talked about his problems, most of which he blamed on power-hungry Democrats and the media, who he said were working together to destroy him. According to authors Bob Woodward and Carl Bernstein, Goldwater phoned Harlow the next day to talk to him about the dinner.

"Is the President off his rocker?" Goldwater asked.

"No," answered Harlow. "He was drunk."

"The President was drinking more than usual and phoning [Chief of Staff Alexander] Haig, and others late in the night," wrote Woodward and Bernstein in *The Final Days*. "The President was overexcited, filled with anxieties, carrying on. Nixon's inability to handle more than one drink was well known to his intimates. During campaigns he had wisely chosen not to touch alcohol. But now, on too many afternoons, he started sipping in his office."

By the time Michael Wolfson returned to Canada in 1973, after two years at Cambridge, he found that the political and social landscape had been altered almost beyond recognition. The last of the American troops were being pulled out of Vietnam, President Nixon was under siege for crimes related to Watergate, and there was a growing movement to grant amnesty to war resisters.

Upon his return, Michael got a part-time job at Statistics Canada and used the rest of his time to work on his Ph.D. dissertation. At Statistics Canada, his work centered on the measurement of income inequality and the sources of inequality in the distribution of wealth. Although his political views at that time were considered radical in the United States, that was not the case in Canada, where he was viewed as a mainline player concerned about the welfare of his fellow countrymen.

Once the last of the troops were pulled out of Vietnam in March, the news media on both sides of the border descended on the amnesty issue. Opinions among the war resisters varied, sometimes swinging to polar extremes. A Toronto deserter, David Lewis, wrote a letter to the *Toronto Star* in which he said he was offended by all the talk about amnesty (actually deserters were not being included in much of the debate). "Anybody who came here not thinking it would be a permanent move should not have come here," he wrote. "These are the people that are, in most cases, contributing absolutely nothing to Canada."

Lewis said he thought antidraft publications such as *Amex-Canada* served a purpose during the war, but he thought they were no longer relevant. "Canada was an alternative to every person of draft age in America at the time. Some of us chose it. Most of us, I'm sure, are better for having made that choice. I personally think that all the time, energy, and money being invested in amnesty promotion would be better spent on the Committee for an Independent Canada—or something similar."

Accompanying Lewis's letter was a large, four-column photograph, an indication of the importance the newspaper put on the topic.

Responding to Lewis's letter was war resister Alex Scala, also of Toronto. Scala said he had no intention of becoming a Canadian citizen and—in the unlikely event amnesty was offered—would be on the next plane to New York. "No one [in Canada] has taken exception to my answer or suggested that I'm somehow morally obligated to become a Canadian," he wrote. "Lewis, however, gives me the impression that if it were up to him he'd have me deported. His letter supports the truism that nothing surpasses the bigotry and righteous self-congratulation of the convert." The photograph accompanying Scala's letter was only three columns wide.

Lewis's letter did raise an interesting question about *Amex-Canada*, whose masthead declared it was "published by Americans exiled in Canada." It was a well-organized, professionally run magazine that usually ran about forty pages per issue. In 1973, the author of this book was curious enough about the publication to write a letter inquiring about its mission and its focus on political issues. Editor Dee Charles Knight responded by letter: "We have never been able to support the magazine on the following of people here [in Canada], and have had to have it supplemented by political support from the U.S.," an explanation for why political and social questions "held the ascendancy."

It probably does not matter from what source *Amex-Canada* received the bulk of its support—it was, after all, a quality publication that provided an articulate voice to many new Canadians—but if war resisters themselves had realized the basis of the magazine's financial support at the time, the publication probably would have been encouraged to shut down.

When President Nixon backed away from the position he took on amnesty during the campaign and said draft evaders and deserters would have to "pay the price for deserting their country," *Time* magazine sent its correspondents to Montreal, Toronto, and Vancouver to find out what the war exiles were thinking. Ed Starkins, who worked at a Vancouver medical clinic, said he would never go back, except to visit family and friends: "The problem is not just the Vietnam War. It is the whole social structure that's screwed up."

Dr. Donald Burke, a pathologist at the Jewish General Hospital in Montreal, said he would only agree to return to the United States when "there is a general recognition that the war was an immoral and illegal exercise." When reporters asked Nixon to comment on statements from war resisters about not wanting to return to the United States, he said,

"If they don't want to return, they are certainly welcome to stay in any country that welcomes them."

There were instances of some war resisters returning to the United States in 1973, long before the amnesty issue was resolved. Thomas Lee York had left Little Rock, Arkansas, in 1962 to relocate in Canada, a year or two before most Americans had an awareness of Vietnam. His reasons for going to Canada were mostly of a spiritual nature. While a student at Little Rock High School, he had been one of twelve semifinalists in a nationwide Voice of Democracy contest. He also worked as a copy boy at the *Arkansas Gazette* and won a Reserve Officer Training Corps scholarship to Tulane University. He was well on his way to a military career as a right-wing zealot, when he took a detour to Duke University and ended up in a doctoral program that left him confused about his political and his spiritual life.

One day, he and his wife, Lynn, packed their bags and moved to Ottawa. He had been to Canada once on a canoeing trip and thought it would be the ideal place to find himself. "I am a nature mystic, and if one is to find God anywhere he has the best chance in the bush," he told a reporter for the *Toronto Star*. "One is undistracted there—you can reach a consensus of mind."

Not impressed with York's search for God was the Little Rock draft board, which sent him an induction notice in 1964, the year of the Gulf of Tonkin resolution. By that time, York was a minister of the United Church of Canada. The induction notice never reached him, and he did not know it had been sent until 1968, when warrants were issued for his arrest.

In 1972, York led a government-funded expedition through the Arctic in search of musk-ox wool; it was a research project designed to determine the feasibility of collecting wool in the wild as a commercial venture for the Eskimos. If his initial move to Canada had been for the purpose of finding himself, then it was the expedition to the Arctic that made him realize he wanted to return to Little Rock to set the record straight.

The following year, he crossed the border with his wife and family and drove to Little Rock, where he turned himself in to authorities. He stood trial and was convicted of failing to notify his draft board of a change of address. He was sentenced to three years in a federal penitentiary and released on bond while his lawyers filed an appeal. He went to New Orleans to await his fate. It was there that Martin O'Malley, a reporter for the Toronto *Globe and Mail* caught up with him.

In a story that the Canadian newspaper ran on a full page, York said he intended to return to Canada when his ordeal was over. "I don't want to go to jail," he said. "But if I have to go to jail, I . . . won't feel bitter and resentful and say I'm innocent. I'm not innocent. I may be innocent of what I'm going to jail for but as a person I'm not innocent. That's real self-delusion, to consider oneself innocent."

Such stories were in the newspapers on a daily basis when Michael Wolfson re-established himself in Canada in 1973. But war resisters were not the only Canadians in the spotlight. Prime Minister Trudeau was still holding onto power, to the bafflement of the Conservative Party members, who seemed to feel they had been deprived of their place in the sun by the New Democrats, who continued to provide Trudeau with the parliamentary majority he needed.

Trudeau tried his best to stay out of trouble that year and succeeded beyond anyone's expectations. For an intellectual, he could be astonishingly realistic when pressed by necessity. In May, *Time* ran a story that focused on "The Remaking of Pierre Trudeau." It noted that he was working to "shed the image of short-tempered arrogance that cost him so heavily" in the last campaign. To the leader of the Conservative Party, *Maclean's* had this advice: "Please grit your teeth, Mr. Stanfield."

Aside from the war resisters, the only person who could garner full-page spreads in the newspapers that year was Margaret Trudeau. In June, she sat out on the steps of her Harrington Lake home and poured her heart out to *Toronto Star* writer Dan Turner. Unlike the war resisters, who often received full-page spreads for their stories, Margaret received two full-pages, accompanied by five full-color photographs of herself and baby Justin. Canadians had never seen anything quite like it. Never before had a prime minister's wife been photographed barefoot in rolled-up jeans.

"I sort of feel right now that we are in some kind of vacuum—Pierre and I—in a very lovely bubble, except for his job," she said. "But I envy my friends who are still very much involved in making their lives happen the way they want them to. The so-called glamorous trappings of this life don't fit in with my values, so they are not to be what I want."

Margaret was not alone. It was a year of soul-searching for all Canadians. The economy needed major adjustments, and the influence of the sleeping giant to the south remained an issue with Canadian nationalists. Then there was Quebec, where the separatist movement was as strong as ever. When Margaret said being the wife of the prime minister did not fit in with her values, it was a feeling many Canadians felt about their own lives, though they were not entirely sure why.

Like many other resisters, Michael Wolfson was not interested in the prospect of receiving an amnesty, but when two friends—one in the States and the other in Canada—phoned him out of the blue to suggest that he look into his draft status, he checked with the Toronto Anti-Draft Programme to see what all the fuss was about. They suggested he check with the U.S. attorney's office to see if his case was still active. He did.

"I said, 'Can you tell me what my draft status is?' "

" 'Oh, yeah,' they said. 'We found a procedural error and all the charges have been dropped.' "

Michael asked them to put that in writing, and they did. "My hypothesis is they observed that I had no intention of coming back . . . and I think they were tired of the paperwork."

Michael has found life in Canada far more successful than he ever imagined. "When I crossed the border with one year of college, I thought I would be lucky to find a job driving a fork lift," he said. "Compared to that, I have been tremendously successful. When I got here people interceded on my behalf and bent the rules. I've been welcomed and encouraged and promoted. Basically, it's been an excellent situation."

Michael married a Canadian woman, and they have four children. He joined the Canadian public service in 1974 and received his Ph.D. in economics in 1977. From 1974 to 1985, he held a variety of positions in central agencies of the government, including the Treasury Board Secretariat, the Department of Finance, and the House of Commons. For a time he worked in the Privy Council Office, examining pension policy, and a few years later in the deputy prime minister's office.

Since 1993, Michael has been the director general of the Institutions and Social Statistics Branch of Statistics Canada, where he is responsible for Canada's statistics on health and education. His work often requires him to travel to the United States to meet with senior American officials and to participate in seminars and conferences at institutions such as Harvard University.

"I am meeting with a disproportionate group of liberal individuals when I go to the United States, so my history with the draft hardly ever comes up," he said. "When it does, the response is always supportive. They say, 'You did the right thing.' I know there are strands of thinking that are contrary to that, especially among paramilitary types, but I tend not to cross their paths. I have a sense there are parts of the South—and blue collar belts—where it would not be wise for me to talk about where I've come from."

7

1974

Patrick Grady: "I Didn't Oppose War in General"

Patrick Grady grew up in Danville, Illinois, at a time when racial segregation was as American as hot apple pie. In that sense, the racial politics of Middle America during the 1950s and early 1960s in states such as Illinois, Indiana, Michigan, Iowa, and Ohio often were different from those of the Deep South in degree only. African Americans were tolerated by polite white society but not fully integrated.

Patrick was born in New York City, but he lived in Danville with his family from the time he was two years old until he graduated from high school in 1965. His father was a pediatrician and his mother was a homemaker. Although his mother had earned a Ph.D. in marketing before getting married, she preferred being a homemaker and never looked for employment after getting married. Patrick had one brother, nine years his junior.

When he was in high school, Patrick, despite being white, joined the local chapter of the NAACP, along with several of his classmates. Racial equality was something he wanted to take a public stand on, and he did in a big way. In 1965, the year he graduated from high school, Martin Luther King led a mass demonstration in Chicago. Patrick hitchhiked to the south side of Chicago to hear him speak.

Years later, Patrick said, "I forget what it was about. But I remember Martin Luther King didn't get there on time. He was about two hours late because he was doing a number of things in the area. I remember being in the crowd and singing. He had an almost hypnotic effect on the crowd. Did you ever see the films of Hitler's Nuremberg rallies? Those large crowds, the way they can be whipped up by people is amazing.

Martin Luther King had the power, but he used it for good. You could see the way they responded, the anticipation, the singing—it was quite a powerful event. I left with a feeling of awe for the power Martin Luther King had over his supporters."

That same year, Canadian Prime Minister Lester Pearson went to Temple University in Philadelphia, Pennsylvania, to deliver a foreign policy speech. He had been awarded the Nobel Prize for Peace in 1957 and was a popular speaker on the subject of world peace. After acknowledging American motives in Vietnam as "honorable—neither mean nor imperialistic," he suggested that the bombing raids ordered by President Lyndon Johnson in the north would probably only harden the resolve of the North Vietnamese to continue the war. Pearson told the college audience that if the United States suspended its bombing raids unilaterally, it might bring the North Vietnamese to the bargaining table. The speech attracted a smattering of media attention, but its biggest impact would not be felt until the following day, when Pearson was invited to Camp David to have lunch with President Johnson.

It was not until 1974 that Canadians were told what happened at that lunch. The speech and the aftermath were generally played down in Canada as well as in the Untied States. Writing about the meeting in the January 1974 issue of *Maclean's*, Charles Ritchie, who was the Canadian ambassador to the United States at the time, described what amounted to a bitter dressing down of the Nobel Prize winner by the president.

Ritchie, who attended the lunch, said that Pearson asked Johnson what he thought of his speech. "Awful," said the president. Then he took Pearson by the arm and led him out onto the terrace. As the conversation grew heated, said Ritchie, he and Johnson aide Mac Bundy left to go for a walk. When they returned, Johnson and Pearson were still at it on the terrace, and their conversation was reaching its climax. Wrote Ritchie in the magazine article, "The President strode up to [Pearson] and seized him by the lapel of his coat—at the same time raising his other arm to the heavens."

Pearson and Johnson parted on good terms later that day, according to Ritchie, but Johnson's unsuccessful attempt to force Pearson into seeing things his way made a lasting impression that probably affected the Canadian open-door policy toward American war resisters in the early years of the war.

The Vietnam War became an issue with Patrick while he was in high school, though at that time, he was not opposed to the war effort. Danville was a conservative community with a population of about 40,000, and most people tended to support the government cause, whatever it happened to be. Patrick carried that attitude off with him to college, but he did not hold onto to it for long. Actually, his position on the war began to take shape the summer before he enrolled in the University of Illinois at Urbana, when he visited the campus and sort of stumbled into an antiwar teach-in. It made a lasting impression.

"I was shocked at the differences in attitudes between Urbana and Danville," he says. "There was very much a strong antiwar sentiment in Urbana. It took me a while before I came around to it. When I did, I became very much interested in the war. I took many courses on Asian politics, including one seminar for honor students on the Vietnam War. I read all the books. The more I read, the more convinced I became that the U.S. foreign policy was way off base and unlikely to yield any tangible benefits to the United States. By my second year of university, I was an adamant opponent of the war."

Patrick went through college in three years instead of four and applied to graduate programs at several universities. He settled on the University of Illinois and began classes in the summer of 1968 on a scholarship, but before the summer was out, he received his draft induction notice. By then, he already had made up his mind about what he would do if drafted; he would go to Canada. His mother was Canadian, born in Hamilton, Ontario, and he had a grandfather who lived in Quebec. Each year, as he was growing up, he spent two weeks in Canada with his grandfather, so it was hardly a foreign country. From an early age, he had considered himself to be half Canadian.

That summer, he married a petite redhead named Jean, who was also a student at the University of Illinois. "She was very much willing to go along with anything I wanted to do," he said. "I never had any opposition from her." Interviewed in 1997, he laughed when he spoke of her willingness to go along with him without question. "Nowadays, she would be more likely to question me."

Patrick decided he had no choice but to go to Canada. "I wasn't really a pacifist the way some people were," he said. "I didn't oppose war in general. That particular war I was opposed to. The vast destruction of a small country—I found it appalling. The thing that always struck me was in World War II, the question was asked, 'Why did the Germans participate?' When governments declare war, if people would just say no, perhaps governments would be less likely to go to war."

Patrick's father was upset when he told him of his plans and tried to talk him out of it, but once he saw that Patrick was determined to go to Canada, he remained supportive of his son. He had served as a medical officer in World War II in the army and was mildly supportive of the Vietnam War at that point, largely because he was a Democrat and felt sympathetic to Lyndon Johnson's efforts to win the war. "My mother was upset for different reasons—and kind of indifferent," said Patrick.

That summer as Patrick and Jean prepared to leave the country, Senator Robert Kennedy was assassinated in California. His death did not have the same impact on Patrick as did the assassination of Martin Luther King earlier that year, but it did seem to provide a sense of urgency to his situation with the draft.

"That year was a roller coaster for all of us," he said. "I was sympathetic to Robert Kennedy to a certain extent because of what he did for the civil rights movement and because of John Kennedy, but I wasn't really involved in his presidential campaign. But I remember the shock of him being killed, the idea that the country was becoming so violent. Then the Democratic Convention [in August 1968], when the police beat the hell out of the demonstrators. I was appalled but not too surprised. Mayor Daley was a funny guy. He was very dictatorial. He liked to run Chicago his way, and he didn't like anything that would disrupt his show."

Patrick and Jean crossed the border in August 1968 at Windsor, Ontario, and went from there to Hamilton, where they spent a couple of days with his grandparents before driving on to Toronto. Patrick had applied to the graduate school at the University of Toronto before leaving Illinois and had been accepted. "I was fortunate," he said. "I never even applied for a scholarship, but they gave me one right out of the blue. They just gave it to me on the spot."

It took nearly two years to complete, but in March 1974 the Watergate grand jury produced its master indictment. Seven of the president's men were named in a fifty-page true bill that charged the men with twenty-four counts of conspiracy, lying, and obstructing justice. Among those charged with crimes were former Attorney General John Mitchell, H. R. Haldeman, John Ehrlichman, and Charles Colson. Three other men were indicted, and eighteen others were named (but not indicted) as participants in the scandal.

President Nixon was not mentioned in the indictment, but sources close to the investigation told reporters that there was evidence he was implicated in the conspiracy. The only reason he was not indicted, suggested the sources, was because of his high office and a belief that Congress, not a grand jury, should be the body to charge a sitting president with crimes. After the new indictments, thirty-five individuals had been charged in the Watergate conspiracy. Not included in that number were individuals involved in other trials, such as the influence-peddling and perjury cases brought by New York prosecutors against Mitchell and former Secretary of Commerce Maurice Stans.

The release of the contents of the White House tapes, the secretly recorded conversations that took place in the Oval Office in the days and weeks after the break-in, backed Nixon into a corner, as talk of impeachment spread throughout the Capitol. The president tried to undo the damage caused by the tapes at a hastily called press conference, but the more he said, the worse he looked. Asked about the taped conversations in which he was discussing hush money for Howard Hunt, a heavily perspiring Nixon admitted to reporters that not everyone hearing the conversation would be persuaded of his innocence. His only defense was a plaintive "I know what I meant."

As the House Judiciary Committee, chaired by New Jersey Representative Peter Rodino, began its investigation of impeachment charges against Nixon, the president hit the road in an attempt to win public support. One of the places he went during that time was Nashville, where he helped open the new home of the Grand Ole Opry. To the nearly 5,000 fans on hand for the opening, he praised country music as a people's art form that "radiates the love of this nation—patriotism." Country singer Roy Acuff presented him with a yo-yo, but Nixon was unable to spin it and ended up looking foolish and hopelessly out of place as he dangled the yo-yo like a limp noodle.

Spokesmen for Nixon said it was unthinkable that the House of Representatives would impeach the president and that it was even more far-fetched that the Senate would convict him, since he had the hardcore support of forty Senators, more than enough to block the twothirds majority needed for conviction. Besides numbers, they argued that they had history on their side. Since ratification of the Constitution in 1789, the impeachment process had been used on only twelve occasions against high federal officials and, of those, only four were convicted. The House Judiciary Committee, not impressed with any of the president's arguments, pushed on with its inquiry.

That March, as the House Judiciary Committee geared up for its impeachment investigation, the Subcommittee on Courts, Civil Liberties, and the Administration of Justice tackled the issue of amnesty with three days of public hearings. Whether it was innocent irony—or a deliberate attempt by political powerbrokers to play one issue against the other—the same group of lawmakers who would decide the fate of the president also were put in the position of passing judgment on the fate of the war exiles in Canada.

Representative Robert Kastenmeier of Wisconsin, the subcommittee chairman, called the hearing to order by saying, "Now that some time has elapsed since the end of our country's direct military involvement in the Vietnam conflict, it ought to be possible to examine rationally the question of whether or not amnesty should be granted to those who refused to serve." The purpose of the hearing, said Kastenmeier, was to examine the amnesty bills currently before Congress and to determine what could—and should—be done to address the issue. Kastenmeier said he was confused by President Nixon's position. He noted that on one occasion he told CBS newsman Dan Rather that he was in favor of amnesty; on other occasions he said he would never support it.

One of the people who went to Washington to testify before the subcommittee was Mrs. Peg Mullen, the state chairman of the Iowa Gold Star families. Her son, Michael, had been killed in 1970 by an artillery shell fired by his own men. He was twenty-five. Mrs. Mullen noted that her son had been killed by "friendly fire" in an incident that was referred to by the military as a "misadventure" and in a war that was undeclared by Congress.

"Gentlemen, the whole Vietnam war was a misadventure," said Mrs. Mullen. "We are all its nonbattle casualties. Only those who have lost sons and husbands and brothers in Vietnam can understand the depth of the anguish and the bitterness my son's death makes me feel. I want to believe—I desperately need to believe—that my son's life was not wasted, that he died for some higher ideal, but what comfort have you given me?"

Mrs. Mullen said she was in favor of an amnesty that did not imply guilt on the part of the war exiles, for she could no more comprehend a war exile who had refused to fight on moral grounds admitting guilt for a moral decision than she could comprehend Congress admitting that it was guilty of committing a crime in allowing the war to continue.

"Forget all the moral and philosophical dilemmas posed by the war in Vietnam, which tore this nation apart for over a dozen years," she said. "Remember only this: The American people have suffered enough because of this war, and we want our children home. . . . If you interpret these young men who refused to serve in Vietnam as having abandoned America in her time of need, then I ask you, 'Did you not, yourselves, as the duly elected representatives subject to the will of the American people, by allowing that war to go on and on and on, abandon us in our time of need?' What difference is there between a government which forces its dissidents to seek exile, and a government which exiles its dissidents? Today, Canada, Sweden, and Europe, the world is filled with a generation of young American Solzhenitsyns. If I am to believe that my son sacrificed his life for some higher ideal, if I am to receive any comfort from my son's death, then let me believe that he died so that some other mother's son, somewhere, might now come home."

Subcommittee member Representative Robert Drinan of Massachusetts thanked Mrs. Mullen for testimony he called the most "moving" and "eloquent" of the day. As the session was being brought to an end by the chairman, Mrs. Mullen interrupted to ask if she could say one thing more. She was given the floor.

The Gold Star mother said she was disturbed by the things that had occurred with the draft. She noted that no senators or representatives had lost sons in Vietnam. On a visit to Washington to discuss the war with Senator Hugh Scott, she said she noticed that many of his aides were draft age. When she asked them why they were not in the service, she said they told her they had received CO exemptions. "Do you know that in the state of Pennsylvania that if you were employed by a large industry, like Bethlehem Steel, Inland Steel, Alleghany, that if you were sweeping the floor, you had an automatic deferment? I think these are the things that you must realize. If you are asking a handful of boys to give two more years to their country, how about the millions of people who knew somebody?"

Mrs. Mullen's comments hit a raw nerve with Representative Henry Smith of New York, who said he had not lost sons in the war because all his children were female. "I appreciate what you have said, but there were some congressmen who lost sons in this war," he said, though he did not provide any names. "There were a lot of congressmen and a lot of senators who had sons in the war."

Testifying in opposition to amnesty was Lieutenant General Leo Benade, the U.S. Army Deputy Assistant Secretary of Defense. "The department agrees with the administration's view that amnesty for draft evaders is not equitable," said Benade. "The alternatives were clear at the time a choice was made and an individual should be required to face the consequences of the choice he made. As in the case of deserters, the Department of Defense is concerned also about the ability of the Selective Service System to function effectively in any future conflict situation which might require induction. Amnesty for draft evaders, either conditional or unconditional, could establish a dangerous precedent which could result in encouraging future draft violations in the expectation of subsequent exoneration. The department is also opposed to the proposals which would provide amnesty on the condition that the draft evader perform some alternate form of service or now serve a period in the Armed Forces."

Addressing the subcommittee on the last day of the hearings was Representative Bella Abzug of New York, who took a pro-amnesty position. "While few critics attempt to justify the war policy itself, they argue that amnesty for war resisters would dishonor the sacrifices made by those Americans who fought in Southeast Asia," she said. "I do not belittle these sacrifices. On the contrary, I mourn them bitterly and deeply because I deem them to have been purposeless, squandered by the government for wrongful ends or no ends at all."

President Nixon kept a low profile on amnesty during the hearings. By May 1974, he had decided to undertake what *Newsweek* called "a desperate gamble for survival." With great ceremony, he went before television cameras to announce that he was handing over to Congress the transcripts of the secret, so-called Watergate tapes. A stack of green, plastic, loose-leaf notebooks loomed in the background as he spoke to the television audience. The notebooks contained, he said, everything that was relevant to the Watergate case. The tapes proved, he said, "that the president has nothing to hide."

Within a week, the verdict was in on his desperate gamble. In a reference to the content of the tapes, the conservative *Chicago Tribune* said, "We have seen the private man, and we are appalled." The *Omaha World-Herald*, which had supported Nixon in three presidential campaigns, suggested that he resign. The *Washington Post* stated, "The question is no longer whether he should be removed from office, but how and when he will go." The tapes were Nixon's last card to play, and when he played them, it was apparent that he had lost everything.

In 1974, Dr. Saul Levine, an associate professor of psychiatry at the University of Toronto, sent the subcommittee of the House Judiciary Committee the results of a study he had conducted on American war exiles two years earlier. It was his view that all the talk about amnesty had an "unsettling" effect on the men.

"In the past few months scores of media men, representing newspapers, radio and TV networks and stations from across the United States and the rest of the world have been conducting interviews here with any expatriates they can find, and questioning them about their feelings about the war, their families, amnesty, their plans, etc.," wrote Levine. "This has led to an exacerbation of personal issues long dormant, and a reawakening of strong feelings."

The majority of war exiles, he reported, had made good adjustments to life in Canada. "It was obvious that there was a marked decrease in the number of 'cries for help' by expatriates in emotional distress over the past couple of years," he wrote. "In other words, by far the majority of exiles were 'making it.' "

Typical of that group "making it" were Patrick and Jean Grady. From 1968 until 1972, Patrick was enrolled at the University of Toronto, from which he received a Ph.D. in economics. Jean took courses at the university until the birth of their daughter Heather in 1970. Two years later a second daughter, Megan, was born; then in 1983 a son, Mark, was born. It was during those four years that the most traumatic events of the Vietnam War took place; but Patrick and Jean had gone to Canada to forge new lives and that meant, for the most part, concentrating on the work at hand and leaving America to the Americans.

"By that point I was getting more removed from the whole thing," Patrick said. "I didn't really feel that [Hubert] Humphrey was any great improvement over Richard Nixon. Both seemed pretty bad. In retrospect, Hubert Humphrey would have been a better president, but at the time he was tainted by his association with LBJ. There was some hope that Nixon would be someone like Eisenhower and end [the war]. He did end it, but not for years. In the spring of 1968, it would have been unbelievable to think it would it would have lasted as long as it did."

The event that attracted his attention the most was the 1969 moon landing. He was surprised that officials at the Toronto City Hall, which, after all, looked like something out of a space-age movie set, installed a giant television screen on the outside of the building so that passers-by could watch the astronauts walk on the moon.

When Patrick left the university in 1972, the job market had been glutted by the influx of Americans, many of whom—like Patrick—had spent the first years of their exile completing the educations that had been interrupted by the war. "Coming out of university was a little difficult," he said. "There were too many Americans in the universities."

Patrick's first job was in the economics department of the Bank of Canada. For the next four years, he and Jean settled into a routine not unlike that of their Canadian-born friends and neighbors. "You hardly ran into anyone who was supportive of U.S. involvement in Vietnam—certainly not at the university," he said. "It wasn't like I was in a strange environment. I pretty much had grown up relating to Canada, so I felt quite comfortable. How would people even know you were an American? They really can't tell the difference."

Only occasionally, did it dawn on Patrick and Jean that, yes, they were Americans. Once they heard from someone who had attended the University of Illinois with them. "He was considering becoming a draft dodger and he looked me up," said Patrick. "He wanted to go see the Toronto Anti-Draft Programme. I said, OK, so we went over there, to an old house just off the University of Toronto campus. I remember going in there and it was a textbook example of what people think draft dodgers are—these guys sitting around with long beards, dressed like hippies. One of them was reading Chairman Mao's little red book. I thought, 'Oh, my God!' "

Patrick worked at the Bank of Canada throughout the Watergate hearings. Some exiles may have been keeping up with American politics, clipping and saving every news story on the subject, but Patrick showed little interest in the proceedings. "There were several people at the bank who watched the thing on television, and they would talk about nothing else, but I really didn't have much interest in it," he said. "The whole thing dragged out so long, just like the O. J. Simpson trial. Some people get into following those things step by step. I would read the newspaper, but I wasn't a Watergate groupie like some people were. I wasn't surprised to see the way Nixon behaved. It was clear he didn't have strong morals. He was unprincipled, really. To hear the whole story, in its appalling detail, was a bit much for me."

Patrick felt the same way about the 1974 amnesty hearings. He barely even noticed that the hearings were taking place. "A lot of the people I knew were draft dodgers, but they kept a low profile and were never identified as such," he said. "I was never one to keep my mouth shut. I wrote the draft board a letter telling them what I was doing and what they could do with it. Periodically, the FBI would talk to my parents. I don't think it phased my father one way or another. It wasn't a threat to him, to his livelihood. My wife's father was contacted, and he found it a little upsetting. They called him at work, and he told them never to do that again. He was working for the U.S. government, an engineer in charge of building Veterans Administration hospitals."

Although the amnesty hearings had an audience in Canada, of more interest to the American expatriates was the politics of Canada. In May 1974, two months after the hearings took place, Prime Minister Trudeau's government was brought down by a vote of no-confidence in the Parliament. That meant that Parliament would have to be dissolved and new elections scheduled. The move did not come as a surprise to Trudeau, who had managed to stay in power for eighteen months with a minority government built on a coalition between his Liberal Party and the New Democratic Party (NPD).

Shortly before the vote took place, Trudeau strolled into the House of Commons one day and gestured toward David Lewis, leader of the New Democratic Party, and said, "So we have . . . 'David the Daisy,' plucking his petals one by one. We will have an election, we will not have an election. Will we? Will we not?"

The next day, all thirty-one members of the New Democratic Party showed up in the Commons wearing daisies in their lapels. Lewis strolled across the floor of the Commons and presented the prime minister with a daisy of his own. Good-naturedly, Trudeau held up the flower and began plucking off its pedals one by one. "Yes, no, yes, no," he said to the delight of the Parliament. The answer, of course, was yes.

Many American expatriates were more supportive of the New Democratic Party than the Liberal Party, but it was the latter that had been in power since the early days of the Vietnam War. The Americans knew no other government but Trudeau's liberals. The thought of a victory by the Conservatives concerned many expatriates, who feared that a Conservative victory could have an adverse impact on their status in Canada.

Going into the elections, Trudeau's Liberal Party seemed to be in trouble. A Gallup Poll showed the Liberals at forty-two percent, the Conservatives at thirty-four percent, and the NDP at eighteen percent. Under the American system, a forty-two percent majority would be enough to be elected president, but under the Canadian parliamentary system, it is the number of seats in the House of Commons, not election votes, that determines the prime minister—a forty-two percent margin, while a majority, was not enough to guarantee a ruling majority for the Liberal Party.

A week before the election, Trudeau told a Windsor, Ontario, audience, "There is a moment in every campaign when it catches fire, and I feel in this campaign it's here tonight." From there he went to Toronto, where the Liberals held a giant rally in Varsity Stadium, featuring not just the area candidates and Trudeau, but a singing group named The Travelers and the Grease Ball Boogie Band.

When the votes were counted, the Liberals won 141 seats to the Conservative's 95 and the NDP's 16. It was an astonishing victory for Trudeau and a miserable defeat for the NDP, which saw David Lewis go down to defeat in his home district. It was the first time since 1926 that a Liberal prime minister had been returned to power after a defeat in the Commons and a low rating in the opinion polls. The election guaranteed Canada five years of stability at a time when the United States seemed to be falling apart.

Most American war exiles had never known any Canadian leader but Trudeau. Whatever their politics, they took comfort in the fact that he would be around for a while longer—at least until the amnesty debate was buried, once and for all.

One week before the House Judiciary Committee was scheduled to vote on articles of impeachment, President Nixon's attorney, James St. Clair, appeared before the committee to argue his client's innocence.

His words were eloquent, though not convincing, and what little good he did for the president was undermined by the efforts of White House press secretary Ron Ziegler, who denounced the committee as a "kangaroo court" and Nixon supporter Rabbi Varuch Korff who flooded the halls of Congress with wild-eyed zealots wearing badges that demanded "Fairness to the Presidency."

St. Clair was no match for the committee's chief counsel John Doar, whose televised report to the lawmakers on the evidence against Richard Nixon was spellbinding. In all, he had gathered twenty-two volumes of evidence. Doar said to the committee, "Reasonable men acting reasonably would find the president guilty."

The first article of impeachment against President Nixon accused him of nine crimes against the people, including lying to law enforcement officials, misuse of the Central Intelligence Agency, obstruction of justice, and "endeavoring to cause prospective defendants, and individuals duly tried and convicted, to expect favored treatment and consideration in return for their silence or false testimony."

When the vote was taken, Article I of the impeachment bill was approved by the committee by a vote of twenty-seven to eleven. Among those voting not to impeach was Republican Representative Henry Smith of New York, who had sparred with the Gold Star mother over the issue of government corruption, and Representative Trent Lott of Mississippi, a Republican who went on to become the majority leader of the Senate. Committee Chairman Peter Rodino was so moved by the vote—and the seriousness of the event—that when he attempted to address his staff members afterward, he choked up and left the room to be alone with his thoughts.

The committee vote was only the first step in the impeachment process. Before President Nixon actually could be removed from office, there would have to be a vote of the full House membership and then a trial in the Senate. But when Nixon's advisors did a head count, they discovered that they did not have the votes to prevail. At that point, Nixon had two choices: he could resign from office, or he could undergo the trauma of impeachment and hope for a miracle. He chose to resign.

Sitting behind his desk in the Oval Office, he gazed into the television cameras and submitted his resignation directly to the American people. "To leave office before my term is completed is opposed to every instinct in my body," he said, delivering a sixteen-minute speech, most of which recapped what he felt had been his accomplishments in office. Despite his achievements, he said, he felt it was "in the interests of America" to step down. Having said that, he walked out of the Oval Office and to a waiting helicopter, thus becoming the first president to ever resign in disgrace.

Vice President Gerald Ford was quickly sworn in by Supreme Court Chief Justice Warren Burger, thus becoming the nation's thirty-eighth president. In a brief speech immediately after the ceremony, Ford said simply, "Our long nightmare is over—our Constitution works." For the remainder of the day, the new president, whom Lyndon Johnson had once joked had "played football too long without his helmet," met with the press corps, his economic advisors, and diplomats from fifty-seven countries. The next morning he met with the Nixon Cabinet and set the wheels of change in motion.

On the following Sunday, President Ford gave his first televised address to the nation. The purpose of the address was to announce that he was granting a "full, free and absolute pardon" to former President Nixon for all crimes committed against the American people. Said Ford: "I feel that Richard Nixon and his loved ones have suffered enough, and will continue to suffer no matter what I do, no matter what we as a great and good nation can do together to make his goal of peace come true."

Nixon responded to the pardon with a written statement, which read in part: "No words can describe the depth of my regret and pain at the anguish my mistakes over Watergate have caused the nation and the Presidency—a nation I so deeply love, and an institution I so greatly respect. I know that many fair-minded people believe that my motivations and actions in the Watergate affair were intentionally self-serving and illegal. I now understand how my own mistakes and misjudgments have contributed to that belief and seemed to support it. This burden is the heaviest one of all to bear."

In his second week of office, President Ford went to Chicago to address a convention of nearly 5,000 Veterans of Foreign Wars. He told the cheering audience that he had nominated a former V.F.W. national commander as administrator of Veterans Affairs. The cheering continued when he said, "Unconditional, blanket amnesty for anyone who illegally evaded or fled military service is wrong."

Then he dropped a bombshell that left the audience sitting in stunned silence. He said he wanted those Americans who had left the country to avoid the draft or had deserted from the armed forces to come home "if they want to work their way back."

"So I am throwing the weight of my presidency into the scales of justice on the side of leniency," he said. "I foresee their earned re-entry into a new atmosphere of hope, hard work and mutual trust. I will act promptly, fairly and firmly in the same spirit that guided Abraham Lincoln and Harry Truman."

On the way back to Washington, Ford explained to the press corps that his decision had been based on the views of his children and of former Secretary of Defense Melvin Laird, who had tried to persuade Nixon to modify his hard-line stand on amnesty. When asked why he had chosen a V.F.W. convention at which to make his announcement, Ford said: "I thought that the right audience would be an audience that might be difficult. It would have been a little cowardice, I think, if I'd picked an audience that was ecstatic."

The next day, the delegates at the V.F.W. convention adopted a resolution that rejected any kind of amnesty for those who had been opposed to the war in Vietnam. That same day, Ford announced his choice for a vice-president—Nelson Rockefeller of New York—and proceeded with plans for his "earned re-entry" amnesty. He ordered Attorney General William Saxbe and Defense Secretary James Schlesinger to begin a case-by-case review of those who had been charged with draft evasion or desertion, and he instructed them to formulate a plan as soon as possible to implement the amnesty.

Congressional reaction to Ford's plan was generally positive. Senate Republican leader Robert Griffin of Michigan said it was a "courageous" move to "heal the wounds." Senator Howard Baker said it was the "very right thing" to do. Senator Edward Kennedy of Massachusetts characterized it as a "fresh breeze from the White House."

John Kerry, the former head of Viet Nam Veterans Against the War, said he felt the war resisters should not have to perform any type of public service, but he welcomed the gesture, since "the purpose of amnesty is to forget the war and heal the wounds." Opposed to any type of amnesty was Senator Barry Goldwater of Arizona, who said it amounted to "throwing mud in the faces of millions of men who have served this country."

A few days after Ford's speech at the V.F.W. convention, Ronald Anderson, a thirty-one-year-old deserter who had been living in Vancouver, British Columbia, for five years, crossed the border into Washington State on family business. When a border guard routinely put his name into the computer and discovered that he was wanted for desertion, he told Anderson to pull over. Anderson was ordered out of his car and escorted inside the customs building, where he was asked for identification. Anderson showed a customs official his British Columbia driver's license. Not satisfied, the customs official asked for his wallet. Anderson told him he had no right to take his wallet. With that, the customs official entered an office, leaving Anderson seated outside alone.

Realizing he was in trouble, Anderson jumped to his feet and dashed for the door. Once outside, he broke into a run and ran for the border with several guards in pursuit. Fifty feet inside Canadian territory, he was tackled by the guards, handcuffed, and carried upside-down back across the border into the United States. He was transported in a Navy Shore Patrol van to Seattle, where he was turned over to the military police. His beard was shaved, and he was told he was being processed for a court-martial hearing that would take place within two weeks.

When the Canadian government learned of the incident, it lodged a complaint and made a formal request for Anderson's return. Seven days later, American officials shamefacedly turned Anderson over to Canadian authorities. According to the *Toronto Star*, a Canadian diplomat told Anderson that Prime Minister Trudeau had personally been involved in the release negotiations. Back in Washington, reporters asked officials at the State Department if the White House had been involved, to which the spokesman replied, "The White House was certainly involved."

On September 16, 1974, President Ford issued an executive order that established a program to carry out his "earned re-entry" for Vietnam War exiles. "This program has been formulated to permit these individuals to return to American society without risking criminal prosecution or incarceration for qualifying offenses if they acknowledge their allegiance to the United States and satisfactorily serve a period of alternate civilian service," said the executive order. "The program is designed to conciliate divergent elements of American society which were polarized by the protracted period of conscription necessary to sustain United States activities in Vietnam."

The White House estimated that 500,000 American soldiers had deserted during the course of the war and, of that number, approximately 12,500 were still in exile. The estimated number of draft resisters eligible for the program was set at 15,000. The number of men who had left the country to avoid the draft was actually ten to fifteen times higher than that, but during the past two years, individual federal prosecutors had declared their own amnesty by dropping charges, thus reducing the number of men still wanted under outstanding warrants. At the time the executive order was issued, the White House said there were approximately 130 men in federal prisons on draft-evasion charges.

Under the terms of the "earned re-entry" program, returning war exiles would agree to perform two years of public service in programs approved by Selective Service officials. The jobs would have to promote the national health or interest and would have to provide a standard of living comparable to the standard of living extended to those in the military. Anyone wishing to participate in the program would be allowed a fifteen-day grace period after entering the country to contact federal prosecutors in the jurisdictions of their draft boards. A deadline of January 31, 1975, was declared for the program. Anyone who failed to enroll in the program before that date would be prosecuted if apprehended and subject to a punishment of five years in a federal prison.

In the first week of the offer, officials received only about 760 telephone inquiries about the offer. In San Francisco, a man turned himself in to authorities, only to be told that the warrant for his arrest had been dropped years ago. At a federal prison in Oklahoma, war resister Steven Bezich was offered a month-long furlough from prison so that his case could be reviewed. He turned it down and stayed in prison. "This is a conditional release," he told a reporter for *Newsweek*. "I accept no conditions of release."

Within the first few weeks, it became apparent that it was a plan with which few people were happy. Opponents of the war said it did not go far enough. Supporters of the war said it went too far. Complicating its implementation were loopholes that let deserters off scott-free if they were willing to accept undesirable discharges and a provision that prohibited war exiles who had taken out citizenship in other countries from participating in the program.

A New York mother told reporters she did not get it. It was the same deal, she said, that had been offered to her son by FBI agents since 1970. It was left to the Reverend Theodore Hesburgh, president of Notre Dame and a member of the clemency board established to carry out the program, to put it in perspective for reporters: "As long as Nixon was in, these guys could rot as far as he was concerned. It's the difference between no chance and some chance."

Patrick and Jean Grady did not bat an eye at President Ford's offer of amnesty. They were raising a family, and Patrick had a good job at the Bank of Canada. Why would they give that up—and uproot their children—to return to the United States so that Patrick could do public service work for two years? It did not make sense to them.

For some war exiles, it did make sense. Not everyone who went to Canada had the same offer to return. Not all federal prosecutors felt the same way. Over the years, some prosecutors notified war exiles that charges against them would be dropped if they returned to perform public service. Others refused to allow exiles to return to perform public service under any circumstances. Basically, it depended on where the exile's home district was located. If he was from the South, where federal prosecutors enjoyed a reputation for right-wing politics, he was simply out of luck. This, of course, detracted from the purpose of Ford's offer: to level the playing field and offer all exiles the same opportunity to return.

One of the first war exiles to return was Myron Ostapchuk, a twenty-eight-year-old Buffalo-born resister who had lived in Canada for seven years. He and his American-born wife, Carol, had fled to Canada in 1967 with ten dollars in their pockets. "I know I'm a test case," he told a reporter for the *Toronto Star*, "and I'm frightened." Carol told reporters she was afraid he was going to be disappointed. She had crossed the border many times to visit her family during the time they were in Canada, and what she saw did not please her. The United States had changed in seven years. It was not the same country Myron had left behind.

Myron rented a van and filled it with books and momentos accumulated during his years of exile and, with Carol at his side—and with a *Toronto Star* reporter and photographer not far behind—struck out for the border crossing at Niagara Falls. "I hope [other exiles] don't hold it against me for going back," he said.

As Myron and Carol crossed the border at the Fort Erie Peace Bridge, Carol clutched his hand and cried. Waiting for them on the American side were twenty-eight television and newspaper reporters, all of whom wanted to know "how it felt" to be back in the United States. Myron naturally said it felt great.

When they arrived in Buffalo, they were greeted by Myron's father, who served up Kielbasa sausages and Ukrainian vodka to celebrate the homecoming. He told his son that they had received many letters and phone calls since the news media had reported he would be returning. Most of the calls and letters had been encouraging, but not all were. One caller threatened to "blow him up" when he arrived. That was the reason his mother was not there to greet him; she had been admitted to a hospital with suspected ulcers.

Amid all the confusion, Myron and Carol announced news of a different sort: Two days before leaving Canada, Carol had learned she was pregnant with their first child. Carol was beaming when she told a *Toronto Star* reporter that Myron had made a slip of the tongue when someone had asked him about his immediate plans. The first order of business, he said, was to drive Carol "home" to Canada to finish up their business there. Carol made much of the fact that he had used the word "home." Clearly, Canada was home to her, despite Myron's decision to return.

On the West coast, two exiles from Vancouver returned to San Francisco with different results. Musician John Barry hired a lawyer and surrendered to the U.S. States Attorney's office and was told he would probably only have to work for six months because he supported his widowed mother.

Twenty-eight-year-old Doug Bitle tried to talk to the same U.S. Attorney's office over the telephone, but they told him they would only talk to him in person. Bitle flew to San Francisco and contacted several lawyers, since he did not want to turn himself in without legal advice, but when he learned that a lawyer would charge him between five hundred to twenty-five hundred dollars to represent him, he took the next flight back to Vancouver. He told reporters that he never would have left the country if he had been given an opportunity to do public service in the beginning.

Very few war exiles followed in their footsteps. Most of those interviewed by the Canadian news media said they planned to boycott President Ford's offer of amnesty. *Amex-Canada* took a hard line and urged everyone to boycott the offer. "It soon became apparent that this was merely a move to set the stage for an early, full pardon for Richard Nixon," said the magazine. "But this cynical attempt to play war resisters off against Nixon as part of a continuing cover-up was doomed to failure from the start. For his very real and very serious crimes, Richard Nixon has received an unconditional amnesty—plus a posh pension."

The Toronto *Globe and Mail*, which bills itself as Canada's "national newspaper," took a position not too far removed from the one taken by *Amex-Canada*. In an editorial entitled "A Tough Choice for Exiles," the newspaper warned that once an exile returned, the American Justice Department would not allow him to come back if he changed his mind. Then, echoing *Amex-Canada*, the newspaper observed: "[The exiles] will also remember that the President of their country offered a better deal to his predecessor who tried to destroy the democratic institutions of their country than he did to them."

Interviewed by the *Toronto Star*, Jim Francis, a Canadian National Railways employee from Chicago, said he had no intention of accepting the offer: "I think the American people are under the impression we're all just dying to come home when in reality most of us have been here long enough to see that Canada is actually a much better place to live." One reason for staying, he said, was a higher standard of living. He cited the Canadian health-care plan as one advantage of life in Canada.

Alfred Clemens, who had lived in Toronto since 1969 with his wife, said the amnesty made him sick, since he did not want to go back to the United States "as a criminal or an outlaw, or even a second-class citizen. I don't think it took a lot of courage to go to the war. I think it took more to give up our way of life, our families, our friends and our jobs." The only amnesty he would accept, he said, would be an unconditional one. Scott Didlake had fled Crystal Springs, Mississippi, because of his views about the war. He did not see any point in returning. "We can't compromise about the truth," he told a reporter for the *Toronto Star*. "We really have to stick it out."

Canadians were interested in how the war exiles would react to the amnesty, for they had invested in the exiles just as the exiles had invested in Canada, but after a flurry of news stories over the first few weeks of the amnesty offer, most lost interest and turned to other matters. The same month of the amnesty, the Canadian government announced a sixty percent price increase for natural gas going across the border into the United States. That did not go over well with American officials, who declared the increase a breach of contract and a breach of the "historic spirit of reliable, amicable and cooperative relations" between the two countries.

Also that month, *Star Week*, the *Toronto Star's* entertainment guide, did a cover story on up-and-coming actress Julie Amato. She was the star of "House of Pride," a thirty-minute prime-time television drama produced by the CBC. In addition to the television show, the glamorous blonde actress had signed a two-year contract to do commercials for Carling's Black Label beer. The commercials would be run in the United States, allowing her to become the newest Mabel in a long line of "Hey Mabel! Black Label!" advertisements. Reporter Anita Latner thought Julie had a resemblance to Hollywood film star Faye Dunaway, "not the fidgety Dunaway of *Bonnie and Clyde*, but the seven-years-older, sleeker and businesslike Dunaway of *Chinatown*."

What made the story interesting was not the glowing account it gave of Julie's success, but the fact that Julie was a draft dodger who had come to Canada with her medical student husband to protest the Vietnam War. Before leaving the country, Julie had entered the Miss New York State contest (which she won) and the Miss America Pageant (in which she was a finalist). The Miss America Pageant earned her a new car, a new wardrobe, and $3,000 in cash—all of which came in useful when she left America and sought exile in Canada.

President Ford's amnesty was not the real story that month. The real story was Julie Amato—and the tens of thousands like her—who had found productive new lives in Canada. Julie ultimately divorced her husband, but kept the country that had extended her a helping hand when she needed it the most.

Of greater interest to Canadians than amnesty was the continuing saga of Pierre and Margaret Trudeau. That month it was revealed that the prime minister's twenty-six-year-old wife had checked into Montreal's Royal Victoria Hospital for a check-up. When the news media pressed Trudeau for an explanation, he went to Montreal to join Margaret for a press conference. Looking pale and stressed out, Margaret told a group of about 100 reporters that she was under psychiatric care for severe emotional stress. Asked by reporters for his prognosis, Trudeau said it was his wife's press conference, and he would have nothing to say. As he was leaving the hospital, he was overheard to say to a hospital official that he felt the press had no business there at such a private moment.

Patrick and Jean Grady stayed put because they felt rooted in Canada. In 1976, Patrick left the Bank of Canada to work for the national government as an economic consultant. He has held several senior positions in the government since that time and has served as an economic advisor to Prime Minister Jean Chretien. In 1992, he published a book entitled *The Economic Consequences of Quebec Sovereignty*, and in 1995, he published a second book about Quebec entitled *Dividing the House*. He has written a novel about his life as a draft dodger but at the time of this printing has not yet found a publisher for it.

"I've done quite well because I was half-Canadian and half-American and could operate in both environments," he said. "In the old days, there was a misconception that the people who came to Canada were all student radicals, left-wing types—very few were, though some were. I knew some students in SDS at the University of Toronto, but most were just ordinary people. Most were opposed to the war, but some, I guess, just didn't want to go into the Army. I don't necessarily think high moral principle guided everyone's decision."

8

1975–1977
Oliver Drerup: "America Lost Its Way"

When Oliver Drerup's parents emigrated to the United States in 1939—his father was a German Catholic and his mother was a German Jew—it was to flee persecution from the Nazis during World War II. Both were from well-to-do families who lost everything they owned when the Nazis came into power. When they arrived in the United States, they were classified as enemy aliens and directed to live in Long Island, New York, for the duration of the war. They were prohibited from traveling, but it was a small price to pay for their freedom. They were deeply grateful to the United States for accepting them during a time of great need, and they enthusiastically embraced the American system of government.

At the end of the war, when they were allowed to leave Long Island, they moved to Littleton, New Hampshire. Oliver's mother was a linguist who spoke seven languages and dreamed of someday working for the United Nations. She would have preferred to remain in New York, where she could have had an opportunity to fulfill her dreams, but her devotion to her husband was a stronger influence. Oliver's father was a painter and a craftsman, and he felt would do better in a more rural setting. In time, he would become one of the best-known enamelists in the world.

Two years after they left Long Island, Oliver was born. "They felt the openness of the American system was a solution to many of the problems they had experienced in Germany, and they were very grateful to America," said Oliver. "They raised me as an American, which is never easy when you are a first generation. I grew up very much in love with the country and very much in love with New Hampshire."

From an early age, Oliver was aware of his mother's unfulfilled ambition to work for the United Nations and of her unyielding devotion to his father. The fact that she chose living with his father over a career in the city made a lasting impression on Oliver. One of his earliest memories is of a dinner conversation that revolved around whether they should purchase a German-made Volkswagen (an automobile designed by Nazi engineers). For seven years, they debated the issue, with his mother and father taking opposing sides. Eventually, they bought the car; it is not clear who won the argument.

"This place where my parents selected to live was a cultural backwater," said Oliver. "Look at any list and you will find that Louisiana and New Hampshire are vying for last place. The public school system in New Hampshire was pretty poor then. I began attending school in a one-room schoolhouse, then later went to a consolidated school. Everyone was trying to do a reasonable job, but the educational requirements, compared to what my parents went through in Europe, were pretty low, and they struggled to send me to a private school."

By the time he entered junior high, his parents were able to send him to the private school. It marked a turning point in his life. "My last year of private high school I lost my appreciation for authority almost entirely," he said. "There were a number of things about the system that I thought stank. As a result of antagonizing the administration, I ended up failing my last year and doing what we euphemistically refer to as a postgraduate year of high school."

When Oliver failed his final year at the private school, his parents placed him back in the public school. To his displeasure, he found himself sitting one row behind students he had started out with in the first grade. "At that point, I recognized the value of an education. I could see how my world view had altered and theirs had not. I decided to dig in and get serious. It was then that I became aware of the problems in Vietnam."

After graduation, he enrolled in a private school called Franconian College. Founded by teachers from Antioch and Baird who were desirous of a more radical educational style than was being offered at mainstream institutions, it found a natural constituency in the exploding baby boom generation.

"It was a pretty wide open college," said Oliver. "It had an enormous impact on me. It served me very well, but it destroyed other people because it was a formless type of education. Beyond the core curriculum, people were encouraged to do their own thing. There were a number of left-wing people there—experiments with drugs and music, the whole nine yards. It was a pretty vibrant experience for me. My third year, I went to Europe to study archeology and spent eighteen months traveling in the Middle East."

That spring before he left for Europe, he was devastated by the assassination of Martin Luther King (a common thread for most war resisters). "We had very few examples of blacks who were tolerant," he said. "Foremost among them were King and Malcom X—and they killed them both. It was terrible."

Oliver was in England when Robert Kennedy was killed. "I was walking out of an underpass and I saw the headlines on a sandwich board. It said, 'Kennedy assassinated.' The earth moved. I didn't know which Kennedy. It just wiped me out. It was dreadful. America has no way to cope with its hatred except by using guns. It's going to be the end of the republic. Unless saner minds prevail, it will tear the country completely apart."

By the time Oliver returned from Europe to complete his final year at Franconian College, his views on Vietnam had solidified. "I spent a lot of time thinking about conscientious objection, and I spent a lot of time thinking about the army and the navy. I researched all the options. I went to talk to all the recruiters, and I went to talk to the people in Boston who were coaching people on how to apply for conscientious-objector status. I found out I was not a conscientious objector. They ask questions such as, if someone was raping your mother, what would you do? Well, I would kill the son of a bitch, so I'm really not a CO even thought I feel strongly that what one does in one's life is to avoid circumstances in which one would have to kill someone. That's what the 'Rifleman' taught me [a popular television drama of the early 1960s]. America was founded on the notion that inappropriate taxation and inappropriate wars were not what we were all about. The notion that there could be a war that was not declared by Congress just beggars the imagination. Somewhere between the Bay of Pigs and the start of the war in Vietnam, America lost its way and still hasn't found its way back."

"I have profited greatly by my experience of listening to my parents. I didn't see war as gallant. I didn't see the opportunity of going there as either heroic or gallant. I saw it as simply leaving oneself open for horror. It wasn't so much that I thought about the Vietnamese as a people, anymore than I thought about any of us as people. I think I would have made a very different decision in the second world war. I believe that I would have done something different, but I don't know that."

For about a year, Oliver talked to his parents about his options. Canada always came up as a possibility, but Oliver was reluctant to give up on his parents (and his country) and continued to look for alternatives. He just could not see himself carrying a gun off to war. Once, to find out what that would be like, he went to his selectman and applied for a permit to carry a concealed weapon. It was approved, and for months, he walked around with a pistol hidden beneath his jacket.

It was his way of finding out if it would be possible for him to go to war. "In the end, I decided that I certainly had no faith that the army or the navy were any of the things they were telling me they were, and I knew I was not a CO and couldn't do that. So, it was an act of logical elimination. I was left with going either to Sweden or Canada—and I didn't speak Swedish."

In July 1969, Oliver loaded up his car will all his possessions and struck out for Canada. "Good Americans fight when they have to, but don't when they don't have to. I'm convinced that Thomas Jefferson, had he been alive, would have been in the car with me." Somewhere along the New York-Canada border (he does not recall the precise point), he crossed over and told Canadian immigration officials that he wanted to apply for landed immigrant status.

"I was so green," he said. "They had a point system and you got a point for speaking English, a point for how much money you had, and so on. They had a huge book that contained all the professions, and they went through the book and ascribed points to the applicant. I had just graduated in archeology and was full of myself because I thought archeology was the bee's knees. When I arrived at the border, the chap was very kind, and he asked me what I did. I said I was an archeologist. He encouraged me to say I could teach, but I said, 'I guess I could, but I'm really an archeologist.' Of course, the number of points Canada ascribed to archeology was zero, unlike teacher. The bottom line was that I could not get in, mostly because I did not have a job. This poor bastard was confronted with the necessity of deporting me, despite the fact that he was sympathetic. He had to fill out a deportation order and send me back to the United States. I contemplated eating that order."

When Oliver returned to the American side of the border, his reception was as bad as he had feared. Customs officials took him into a building and phoned his draft board. "They told them I was leaving the country, and they ought to get right on it," he said. "They trammeled all over my constitutional rights."

Oliver left that border crossing and drove to another one. This time he entered Canada as a tourist and looked for a job (that took about a week). Then he returned to the States and entered Canada again, this time armed with a job offer as a potter and the good sense not to call himself an archeologist when he applied for landed immigrant status. One day after arriving in Canada, he received his induction notice.

For two years after the withdrawal of the last remaining American combat troops in Vietnam, those Americans who had supported the war—and those who had vehemently opposed it—were afforded a respite from the rhetoric of peace and the reality of war. For the first time in over a decade, there had been no television footage of the carnage of war and photographs of terror-struck civilians and teenage American warriors with missing limbs and no hope for tomorrow.

Then, in March 1975, when it appeared that Americans at long last would be able to put the war behind them with a form of collective amnesia, the bubble burst. Without notifying American officials, South Vietnamese President Nguyen Van Thieu abruptly pulled all his troops back to a position that formed a defense perimeter just northeast of Saigon. Without firing a shot, the North Vietnamese army was able to take control of three-quarters of South Vietnam, nearly 30,000 square miles.

President Ford was stunned. Thieu had surrendered everything that 56,400 American soldiers had died defending—and without a fight. The White House put out feelers to test Congress's interest in providing Thieu with three more years of military aid. But there was no chance of that. A law passed the year before barred any president from spending a dime for U.S. combat in Indochina. Democratic Senator Adlai Stevenson III told reporters that three more years would not solve anything. A Republican senator, who asked not to be identified, was even more blunt with a *Newsweek* reporter: "It looks hopeless. Screw it. Let's get out."

Ford got the message loud and clear. As North Vietnamese troops encircled Saigon from the north and the Viet Cong pressed from the south, Ford went to New Orleans to deliver an address to students at Tulane University. Someone had to say it. Someone had to make it official. Rising to the occasion, Ford told the students that "the war is finished as far as America is concerned," but that did not "portend neither the end of the world nor of America's leadership in the world."

With Saigon surrounded, President Thieu sat in his palace and waited for word on what to do next. He was not sure what the message would be or who would deliver it. He just knew a message would come. The message he awaited originated in Paris, where a member of the Viet Cong delegation passed it to an American representative, who dispatched it to Washington. From there, the message was sent to U.S. Ambassador Graham Martin at the American embassy in Saigon.

Martin tried all day without success to reach Thieu by telephone. The following day he got into his black Cadillac limousine and drove the six blocks from the embassy to the presidential palace in an effort to locate the missing president. Thieu was there all right; he was just in no mood to answer the telephone. Martin personally delivered the message: He had forty-eight hours to resign or Saigon would be leveled.

That was not the message Thieu had anticipated. If he had expected the American government to encourage him to "win one for the gipper," he was grimly mistaken. Thieu told Martin he did not want to resign. Martin told him he had no choice. There were no marines on the way to rescue him from the palace. Realizing he had no realistic option but surrender, Thieu resigned and then four days later fled to Taiwan aboard a U.S. military transport. But he did not go quietly. Before leaving, he launched a bitter attack against America for abandoning him in a time of need.

Once Thieu stepped aside, the biggest problem facing American officials was how to extricate the 1,100 Americans still in the city, many of them working out of the embassy. Another problem was how to evacuate the estimated 130,000 South Vietnamese who were eligible for assistance because of marriage or because they had worked for the American government. With the city surrounded, the North Vietnamese and the Viet Cong patiently waited for America to pack up and leave.

Giant U.S. Air Force transport jets flew in and out of Saigon, carrying as many as 5,000 people out in a single day. Some of the Vietnamese went to tent cities on Guam and Wake, and others went to military bases in the United States. Not everyone was happy to see the Vietnamese arrive in America—many were greeted by placard carrying protesters with signs that read "Only Ford wants them."

Ford asked Congress to authorize 327 million dollars for humanitarian aid, but the bill included a provision that would allow the president to send American combat troops to Vietnam to police the evacuation, so it was defeated by a vote of 246 to 162 in the House of Representatives. Reflecting public opinion, Congress wanted no more deals; its members just wanted the nightmare to end.

Once everyone who could be evacuated on the transports was out of Saigon, it was decided to take the remaining 7,000 Americans and Vietnamese out by helicopter. It took eighteen hours for the helicopters to airlift that many people out of the city and onto the decks of forty U.S. warships. Many Vietnamese had to be turned away when they stormed the embassy in desperate attempts to climb into the helicopters. There was a fifteen-foot concrete wall around the embassy, but even that was often not enough to prevent chaos from the street from tumbling over the fence and onto the embassy grounds.

Inside the compound were an assortment of security guards, CIA agents, and State Department volunteers. *Newsweek* correspondent Loren Jenkins showed up at the embassy with his small bag of belongings and was an eyewitness to much of the chaos. In the midst of the insanity, Ambassador Martin tried to drive home to pack his bags and pick up his black poodle, Nitnoy; but his chauffeur was unable to get the car out the gate because of the crowds gathered in the street. Nonplused, Martin got out of the car and walked the three blocks to his house. An hour and a half later, reported Jenkins, Martin returned to the embassy compound, "trailed by his cook, two flack-jacketed security men carrying his suitcase and briefcase and another leading Nitnoy on a leash."

Martin landed safely aboard the USS *Blue Ridge* with his pet poodle, but the evacuation was not without its costs in human lives—four U.S. Marines were killed on the final day, bringing the total number of Americans who died in Vietnam to 56,559—or its cost in national pride as photographs surfaced of Marines smashing the hands of frightened Vietnamese with rifle butts as they fought to climb over the embassy wall in the hope of being airlifted to safety. The last man to leave Vietnam was a U.S. Marine clutching a brown paper bag that contained the American flag that had flown over the embassy.

In the weeks that followed, it became apparent that the evacuation had been botched, and many people had been left behind. Martin came under bitter attack from military officials who felt he had mishandled it. The sight of his poodle being walked about the deck by a handler, while American supporters were being abandoned was more than many of them could stand. One angry foreign service official aboard the *Blue Ridge* told *Time* magazine correspondent William Stewart that he thought it was criminal that so many politicians had made it to safety, "while people who have worked for us for ten years were left behind." Others were disheartened by reports that prostitutes had been given a priority, in some instances, over more established citizens in need of evacuation.

Amid the desperation and chaos, the North Vietnamese and Viet Cong armies stood idly by, not lifting a finger to stop the fleeing Vietnamese and Americans. Not a single helicopter was shot down, and none of the overcrowded barges were sunk. Back in the United States, President Ford expressed disgust that so many Americans were expressing hostility toward the Vietnamese resettlement in the United States. "It just burns me up," he said. "We didn't do that with the Hungarians; we didn't do it with the Cubans. Damn it, we're not going to do it now."

Not helping matters, former South Vietnamese leader Nguyen Cao Ky strode about the tent city at Camp Pendleton, California, still wearing a military uniform with an ascot. He walked about shaking hands, kissing babies, telling small crowds of refugees that they had nothing to be ashamed of. They were in exile because of bad leadership, he said, which was the fault of President Thieu, the "most despicable man in the world." To show that not all Americans were unsympathetic to the Vietnamese exiles, a New York restaurant owner sent Ky a wire offering him a job as a chauffeur.

By mid-May, American news magazines were focusing on the peaceful manner in which the North Vietnamese and the Viet Cong had established order in Saigon. A *Time* headline read: "Saigon: A Calm Week Under Communism." Reporters said there was no indication the bloody reprisals feared by some had taken place. The longest, most divisive war in American history had ended with barely a whimper.

Incredibly, by June, the American news media were no longer even doing stories on Vietnam. The big news was the report issued by Nelson Rockefeller's commission on the illicit domestic operations of the CIA. The inquiry had found the secret agency guilty of all charges: namely, that CIA operatives had committed a series of crimes against American citizens, including illegal wiretaps, burglaries, secret testing of experimental drugs on unsuspecting Americans (LSD was one drug used), and the accumulation of a "veritable mountain" of dossiers on citizens, particularly those in the antiwar and civil rights movements.

The results of the commission proved that those war exiles in Canada who suspected that they and their families were under surveillance were probably right. Hopefully, they were not targets of a larger CIA operation that was found by the Rockefeller commission to have made use of various methods to control human behavior, including "radiation, electric-shock, psychology, psychiatry, sociology and harassment substances." Some of the actions undertaken by the CIA, according to investigators, were deemed too inflammatory to ever be made known to the American public.

That first summer, Oliver Drerup lived in Hadley, Quebec, where he worked for a potter. He wanted to explore his talents as a craftsman to discover if he had his father's creative ability. He discovered he enjoyed working with his hands but he did not have his father's talent. That fall he applied for and got a job as a teaching assistant in the anthropology department at McGill University in Montreal. To make ends meet, he tended bar in the evenings.

"The first days I was here, there was a house in which several guys who were deserters passed through—sort of a safe house operated by social workers," said Oliver. "The few deserters I encountered were in tough shape. I had seen the 'lie' from the outset, my education had made that possible; but the deserters, as a rule, tended to be people with less education and had more pressures on them to join [the army] in the first place and only after the fact realized they had made a dreadful choice. There may have been some FBI activity around them, but I have no proof; it was hearsay at the time."

Soon Oliver was joined by a woman named Elizabeth, an architectural student he had met in England. Her feeling was that if she stayed in Canada, she wanted to build a house, because that was the sort of thing she could not do in England without applying for an endless assortment of building stamps and planning permits. In rural Quebec, all she had to do was purchase a piece of property and get to work. "She and I purchased a piece of property very close to the American border, close to New Hampshire," said Oliver. "I wanted to be close to my parents."

With the house completed, Oliver changed jobs in 1970, taking a job teaching history to seventh and eighth grade students at a private school in Montreal. His enthusiasm for his house—and the high quality of the design and workmanship—infected several of the teachers at the school, so that he and Elizabeth soon had contracts to build houses for two of the teachers at the school. Almost by accident, Oliver discovered an avocation that allowed him to utilize skills that, while perhaps not as artistically creative as those possessed by his father, afforded him the opportunity to be creative with his intellect and, in a sense, his hands.

Once Oliver and Elizabeth completed the houses for the teachers, they realized they were onto something good. Oliver quit teaching and formed a construction company with Elizabeth and a man who had been one of his students at McGill. "At that point, we had become very much involved in solar energy and were building solar houses," said Oliver. "The three of us built houses for the next seven years, until Renee Leveque came into power in Quebec, at which point everyone stopped building immovable property."

When President Ford offered his "earned re-entry" amnesty in the fall of 1974, Oliver gave serious consideration to accepting it. "In the end, I didn't because I didn't feel I owed my country anything," said Oliver. "If anything, they owed me one." All the renewed publicity did make him curious about his file. He hired an attorney who, for a small fee, retrieved a copy of his draft records for him.

"I was amused to learn when my file was opened that I had been interviewed by the FBI while at university," he said. "I don't remember the interview. No one ever identified themselves as my interviewer. Either it was concocted and never took place or the interviewers never identified themselves to me. The conclusions they drew as a result of the interview included that I was a radical and an unsuitable sort of chap. My parents received numerous visits from the FBI, and I have no idea what they might have done. I have no delusions about the importance of my draft evasion. I know the FBI visited my parents and I know it was a waste of taxpayers' money."

By spring 1975, both the American and Canadian news media were focusing on the failure of Ford's amnesty offer. In an editorial in the May–July issue, *Amex-Canada* said that war resisters had been quick to "see through" Ford's offer. "We want reconciliation, but not Ford's brand," said the editorial. "The reconciliation for which we long is with our families, friends, veterans, communities, fellow workers, and last but not least the people of Indochina. We don't want a superficial reconciliation, but one based upon genuine understanding of the nature and meaning of the war. Certainly we don't want to be reconciled with the war planners, profiteers, and generals."

Echoing that sentiment was William Schiller, a thirty-three-year-old draft resister who had sought refuge in Sweden. By the time Ford made the offer, he had found a career as a newspaper reporter. "I'm still an American, and if I had to do it all over again, make the choice of coming over here or fighting in Vietnam, I'd make the same choice," he said in an interview with *Parade* magazine. "I think if the government wants you to go and kill other people in the name of American glory or interests, whether your government is right or wrong, then you've got to make a decision. Is there much difference between United States soldiers massacring innocent women and children at My Lai and Hitler's men massacring the Jews?"

Schiller refused Ford's offer.

Oddly enough, the individuals who seemed to benefit most from the offer were the people who needed it the most—the deserters. A loophole in the amnesty plan allowed deserters to drop out of the program without penalty. They would receive a dishonorable discharge from the armed forces, but they would have their freedom, and to most, that was all that counted. According to figures released by the Selective Service in August 1975, almost half of the 4,503 deserters who joined the program had dropped out or been kicked out. Another 1,000 men processed for work assignments never reported at all. Many of the deserters who reported for work assignments were Vietnam veterans.

Selective Services officials would not release the names of those enrolled in the programs, but they told of a wounded veteran from New York who took a job working with mentally retarded children, and a former marine from a Southern state who entered the program as a jailer's assistant and ended up as a sheriff's deputy.

Albert Gargiulo, a draft resister who took a job for $11,000 per year with the West Palm Beach, Florida, engineer's staff, was fired after residents protested that he was given the job. Gargiulo, who had a master's degree in engineering, had returned to Florida under Ford's plan with his wife and two-year-old son after living for four years in exile in South America. Before he was fired, one county commissioner said, "If he stays, his job and even his life in the community is going to be very unpleasant." The county commissioner told Associated Press that he had received a call from a resident who said, "I lost my son and all I got was a flag; this man hid and now he gets a good-paying job."

When the Pentagon issued its final report on the clemency program, it said that only twenty percent of the 106,472 individuals classified as deserters or draft resisters had applied for clemency. One of the surprises of the report was the disclosure that nine women had been classified as deserters. Another was the fact that nearly twenty percent of those classified as deserters had served in Vietnam.

Nearly a year after the amnesty was declared, only 130 men processed by the clemency board had reported to jobs. The board said it had received applications from over 21,000 men, but had a difficult time explaining the discrepancies in numbers to reporters. Said Selective Service director Byron Pepitone: "Even though we didn't get the numbers we anticipated, President Ford has attained more of his initial goal than lots of people give him credit for."

Obviously there were some war resisters in Canada who benefited from Ford's amnesty, but most were like Oliver Drerup, who was too busy building a business to pay much attention to what was happening politically across the border. After leaving Quebec, he and Elizabeth moved to Toronto in the late 1970s. They found a new partner and incorporated their home-building company. Soon they had a payroll of about thirty employees.

Although the business prospered, Oliver's relationship with Elizabeth did not, and they ceased living together. Oliver ended up marrying Pat, a woman he had met as a student at the University of Wisconsin. She brought a child from a previous marriage into the relationship, and eventually, they added three additional children of their own. When his company received a contract to build a house in Ottawa, Oliver went to supervise the project and ended up moving his entire family there to live.

Oliver has nothing but praise for the Canadian people. "I have found them to be immensely accepting and understanding, and I feel I was welcomed with open arms," he said. "I am very appreciative for what this country has done for me. In 1969, you could go out to dinner on the story. I don't think the Canadian military establishment is very appreciative, but I don't encounter them often."

Not surprisingly, Oliver's view of America is different today than it was when he was growing up in New Hampshire. "America is an incredible place, a very powerful country," he said. "While we were homesteading, we raised horses. Elizabeth loved horses. Horses are very bright about some things, but you can spook them simply by walking into a stable with a bag over your shoulder. They're too large to be that spooky, and I feel the same way about the United States. It is too big and too powerful to be as stupid as it is. America is the last bully on the playground."

Life in Canada was comfortable for most residents in 1976, but the economy was not exactly booming. Inflation had been held at six percent, but an unemployment rate of a little over seven percent created a vague sense of unease. Prime Minister Trudeau, who had been given a free reign to govern until 1979 without another election, seemed a changed man in many respects. At fifty-six, the normally arrogant and combative leader often seemed tired and uncertain of his political decisions. He stunned the Canadian financial community in 1976 by declaring that the free-market system in Canada was dead. He meant that new solutions, possibly government imposed, would have to be imposed to strengthen the economy, but some people interpreted his comments to mean that new, authoritarian measures were being considered.

Later, it was learned that many of Trudeau's mood swings were the result of a faltering marriage; but at the time, the Margaret factor was greatly underrated, despite the news media's constant attention to her adventures. In February 1976, she went to Florida on vacation without Pierre, staying in the home with an Ottawa multimillionaire. Newspapers called it her "freedom trip," while she called it a Valentine present from her husband.

Later, on a trip to California with Pierre, she looked out the hotel window and saw a group of picketers below on the sidewalk protesting something or other. As a joke, she went downstairs without telling Pierre, joined the protesters without identifying herself, and marched in a circle with a picket sign beneath their hotel window. In her own indomitable, individualistic way, she had become the Canadian spiritual equivalent of an American war resister. She was sort of a marriage resister. She could make American war resisters smile in ways no one else could ever understand.

After less than one year on the job—and with the 1976 presidential campaign just beginning—President Gerald Ford decided to throw his hat in the ring for a full term. The latest Gallup poll showed him to be eleven percentage points ahead of his nearest rival for the Republican nomination—Ronald Reagan of California—but two points behind undeclared Democratic candidate Senator Hubert Humphrey.

Seemingly coming out of nowhere was former Georgia governor Jimmy Carter, who shocked political pundits in January by winning the Iowa Democratic caucuses. Polls showed him to be the leading contender in New Hampshire. Suddenly, Carter was the Democrat to beat. Carter had lots of positions on lots of issues, but the one that attracted the most attention was the one on amnesty. Ford's "earned re-entry" program was proving to be a failure, as most war exiles simply ignored it. Once again, amnesty had become the campaign issue that would not go away.

In late January, Carter answered questions on a variety of topics from *Newsweek*'s chief political correspondent Hal Bruno. He said he thought abortion was wrong, capital punishment was right and, to the surprise of many, advocated a new solution to the amnesty question. While expressing opposition to a blanket amnesty, he said he would favor a blanket pardon.

Carter drew a distinction between the two. "Amnesty means what you did was right; pardon means what you did is forgiven," he said. "I cannot equate the actions of those who went to Vietnam thinking it was wrong—many of whom lost their lives—with those who thought it was wrong and defected. But exile for this long a period of time is adequate punishment."

Oddly enough, the more Carter talked about granting pardons to Vietnam War exiles, the more support he seemed to get in the primaries. That was in marked contrast to previous elections, when the very mention of amnesty would have been enough to bury any candidate. But the Vietnam War had changed America in ways that defied understanding.

The war was over, the prisoners of war had been returned, and all that remained was a final disposition on amnesty for those who had opposed the war and put their lives on the line to honor their beliefs. Not until the amnesty issue was resolved would there be any chance of

Americans putting the war behind them. America was clearly ready to move on.

That July, Carter easily won the Democratic nomination and prepared to square off against the winner of the Republican nomination. There was never much question that the nomination was Ford's for the losing—political parties are loathe to say no to an incumbent president—but Ronald Reagan gave him a good race and was obviously a force to be reckoned with in future campaigns.

Americans had a lot to think about that summer. July 4th marked the two hundredth anniversary of the Declaration of Independence. *Newsweek* published a special issue entitled "Our America: A Self-Portrait at 200." Two of the most interesting interviews contained in that issue were with Jack Colhoun, the Toronto army deserter who was a regular writer for *Amex-Canada*, and John Behan, a marine sergeant who lost both legs in Vietnam. Colhoun said he felt he had no choice but to desert. "I had been brought up as an American Patriot . . . [but] Nixon ordered the invasion of Cambodia, and campuses went berserk," he said. "I just decided it was absurd to go to jail—I was trying to light a match in a hurricane." Colhoun said his mother died after he left the country, and he was unable to be with her in her final days. He said he wanted to return to the United States but was not hopeful that would ever happen.

Without ever addressing the issue of amnesty, John Behan expressed a belief in his country—and in its resiliency—that went a long way in explaining why the mood of the country had changed toward war resisters. Behan went to Vietnam because he believed in the war. He regretted losing his legs. He was not bitter about fighting in the war, but he was unhappy about the way it turned out. The best way to deal with that disappointment, he said, was to move on to other things. "Vietnam was a big black eye, and we've been able to stand up and take that punch, and we're going on from there," he said. "We're proceeding ahead with our future."

Immediately after the Democratic convention, polls showed Carter was an astonishing thirty-three percentage points ahead of Ford, but predictably that margin shrank to only ten points after the Republican convention. For his running mate, Carter chose liberal senator Walter Mondale of Minnesota, a Washington insider who was much admired by his colleagues for his civility and progressive views. Ford also chose a senator for his running mate, but his choice—Robert Dole of Kansas—was no fan of progressive views or campaign civility.

The two candidates differed substantially on many issues, but it was Carter's promise of a pardon for Vietnam War exiles that seemed to generate the most spark. Ford was vulnerable on that issue because of his "earned re-entry" amnesty and because of the pardon he issued to former President Nixon. He could hardly be convincing taking positions against pardons. Dole, a veteran of World War II who had lost use of an arm in combat, was chosen as the attack dog on the issue of pardons.

Carter wasted no time bringing the issue to a boil. To remind voters of his position on the issue, he went to Seattle to address a convention of American Legionnaires. Wearing his American Legionnaires cap—he, too, was a veteran of the armed forces, having served in the navy aboard an atomic submarine—he restated his promise of a pardon, saying he disagreed with the tactics of Vietnam era draft-dodgers but felt that issuing a pardon was the right thing to do. He was greeted by cries of "No, no, no" and a wave of hoots and boos as the Legionnaires showed their displeasure.

The following day, Dole appeared before the same convention and denounced Carter's position on pardons. He was roundly applauded by the veterans, the vast majority of whom had served in World War II. Later, most commentators agreed that Carter had been the clear winner in the confrontation. He was praised for his forthrightness and for taking a moral stand before a hostile audience. "Carter beards the Legion: Boos, but a media coup" read a headline in *Newsweek*. By contrast, Dole appeared mean-spirited and out of touch with the feelings of most Americans about the war.

An editorial in the Greenville, Mississippi, *Delta Democrat-Times*, a Pulitzer Prize-winning newspaper owned by Hodding Carter III, said that Jimmy Carter was right to advocate a pardon for Vietnam War exiles—and the Legionnaires were wrong to boo him—because "as it turns out, the draft resisters were more truly patriotic than those Americans who behaved like 'good Germans' and blindly endorsed what their government was doing in that small Southeast Asian nation." The editorial pointed out the obvious: Polls showed that most Americans supported the idea of a general amnesty. "They want the war to be over, finally and totally, and that means bringing home the exiles who fled rather than fight in an unjust war and pardoning those who remained at home and went to jail."

Not in agreement was the Memphis-based Holiday Inn Corporation, which allowed a motel manager in Greenville to put the following message on its marquee: "Mr. Carter should give peanuts, not amnesty or pardons." Said the manager, a retired Air Force veteran: "They deserted to Canada and other countries—let 'em stay there!"

By the time election day arrived, Carter and Ford were running neck-to-neck. Ford described the outcome as a "horse race," but said he was confident of victory. Less willing to make predictions was Carter, who, instead, focused on what he would accomplish during his first one hundred days: First, he wanted to reorganize two thousand federal agencies; second, he wanted to grant a pardon to Vietnam War draft resisters. Despite advice from some advisors that he should not keep the pardon issue so high on his list, Carter stuck to his guns in the final days of the campaign.

When the dust had settled on election day, Jimmy Carter had been chosen the thirty-ninth president of the United States. His instincts on the pardon issue had been right on target. Clearly, American voters did not want to quibble over pardons; most were like Vietnam veteran John Behan, who, more than anything else, just wanted to move on and explore new frontiers.

Six hours after being swore in, President Carter retired to the Oval Office and summoned a group of his closest advisors, including attorney-general designate Griffin Bell. To their surprise, he told them he was ready to issue an unconditional pardon to virtually all men who had peacefully resisted the draft during the Vietnam War. His advisors were stunned. They knew he planned to issue the pardon but to make it his first act as president caught them completely off guard.

As with Ford's amnesty, few people directly involved with the issue were pleased with Carter's pardon, except those who wanted to close the books on Vietnam. American exiles in Canada and Sweden were unhappy that deserters were not included. Senator Barry Goldwater called it "the most disgraceful thing a president has ever done." Rightwing veterans organizations said it would undermine military discipline.

David Blakeney, adjutant of the Mississippi American Legion, surprised some when he said that veterans had been impressed with Carter at their Seattle convention. "He knew what he was in for when he got up and said he was for the blanket pardon," he told United Press International. "We booed the blanket pardon question, but we applauded the man. It took a lot to get in front of a group as he did." Hollis Smith, commander of the Veterans of Foreign Wars in Mississippi, told reporters he was not bitter about the pardon. Said Smith: "We opposed the pardon, we expressed our displeasure, and now we're moving on to other things."

So went the rest of the nation. The debate over the war would continue for decades to come, but with one stroke of his pen, President Carter had effectively ended, once and for all, the amnesty-and-pardon debate.

"I am very confident that I was one of the first people to cross the border after [President] Carter's pardon," said Oliver Drerup. "Twenty-four hours after he announced it, I was back there because my mother was dying of cancer. She passed away that spring. It was a tremendous thing for me to be with her, and I will thank Carter for that forever. I think history is going to be very good to Carter, and I think he deserves it.

"What America needs are presidents who don't need second terms to justify themselves. Presidents who don't behave in such a way that they will be re-elected, but rather have the strength of character to do what needs to be done. We haven't seen anyone like that since John F. Kennedy, except for Carter."

Once Carter signed the pardon, it took the focus off of the war resisters. There was no bureaucracy to process their repatriation. It was there for them to take if they wanted it. Of course, the deserters were left high and dry since it did not apply to them. Although Carter was himself a veteran—and said all along he did not think deserters should receive the same treatment as resisters—his decision to exclude them was more practical than ideological, since he was convinced that the loophole in President Ford's amnesty already had allowed the return of any deserters who wanted to be repatriated.

With the war resisters fading out of the news in 1977, there arrived a new Indochina news connection as supporters of the old Vietnamese, Laotian, and Cambodian regimes found themselves unwanted by the new Communist rulers. *Newsweek* reported that refugees from the three countries were pouring out at a rate of seventeen hundred per month. The magazine said there were eighty thousand men, women, and children in refugee camps in Thailand and aboard the leaky, overcrowded vessels in international waters. The problem was that no one wanted them.

Since the fall of Vietnam, the United States had taken in about 145,000 Asians at a cost of $522 million, but individual congressmen declared that there was a limit to American generosity.

Apart from the continuing plight of the refugees, the big news in 1977 was Francis Ford Coppola's movie *Apocalypse Now*, the Vietnam epic he had begun filming in June 1976 in the Philippines. The script had been written in 1967 by John Milius, an unrepentant hawk, but by the time filming had begun, the script had become something else entirely in the hands of Coppola. Entertainment value aside, the movie is important historically because it marks the beginning of America's peculiar penchant, one which continues to this day, of only discussing the war in allegorical terms. Coppola took reality and transformed it into art. Americans took Coppola's art and embraced it as reality. It was a way to discuss the war and its aftermath without actually dealing with the reality of it.

Throughout the 1970s and 1980s, Oliver continued building houses, making the American dream of home ownership come true for hundreds of Canadians, proving that the American Dream was alive and well—if only in Canada. In 1997, he sold his construction firm to take a position as manager of products and services for Canada Mortgage and Housing Corporation, an agency that is similar to America's Department of Housing and Urban Development (HUD). Part of his job is to build demonstration homes and to assist Canadian firms to export their products to other countries. He has traveled to Russia, Japan, and Australia to lecture on home building.

"I probably have been exporting more building services than any other person in the country," he said. Sometimes his work has taken him to the United States, where he has consulted with utility companies and homebuilders. Once he went to Alaska to help establish something called the Alaskan Craftsman Home Program, a clone of a successful Canadian program.

Just as Oliver's career has undergone changes in recent years, so has his personal life. In 1994, Oliver and Pat divorced, after a marriage of fifteen years. Pat is now working on her Ph.D. in feminist studies at a university in Ottawa.

Even after all these years—it is still hard for him to believe that his journey began nearly thirty years ago—he continues to be amazed by the Canadian experience. "I am stunned by what it means to be a Canadian. It is an astonishing undertaking. Viewed from the United States, Canadians appear to be kinder, gentler Americans—and nothing could be further from the truth. I still learn things every day. The differences are so subtle . . . that a tourist could never get it right.

"For example, in Ontario there is strict control of the sale of liquor and beer. It's different in Quebec, where you can go to the local grocery store and buy a bottle anywhere. In Ontario, we have a beer commission that is similar to the liquor commission. The community I live in is so small, we don't have a liquor store, but we do have a beer store. It is so small it does not take back the empty bottles. It contracts with the local grocery for the return of the bottles. The grocery owner runs his business with high school kids. So one day this young girl hands me this piece of paper, Xeroxed, that asks me to write down the number of empties I am returning, my name, and my phone number. I said, 'Excuse me, but the bottles are right here and you are welcome to count them, but I am not going to sign this paper.' I said, 'Forget it, piss off,' which is a very American thing to do. 'You have the contract, not me. You fill it out.' That kind of thing goes on all the time. I am amazed at how my American upbringing predisposes me to see things that my Canadian-born friends do not."

Oliver has never regretted going to Canada, and has, in fact, become a Canadian citizen. "In the beginning, when I couldn't return, I never regretted it but I found it very burdensome, and I am grateful that I can travel there and not be cut off from my aging father. Americans are the most highly motivated people in the world. I have a tremendous respect and love for that. Had it turned out differently, were I not be able to travel there, it would be a source of regret to me. The fact that I can return has created an environment in which I have no reason to have any regrets. If I had to do it again, I would.

"Forgive me for being self-righteous, but I think what I did was right and I think what I did was American, and I think most Americans would agree with that. If we are going to war, we should want to win it. The fact that a bunch of guys in black pajamas beat the shit out of the U.S. Army . . . if we had been in the war for real, I would have wanted to win it, not lose it. We should have dropped the bomb if what those people did was so evil. The fact that we did not is an indication of how wrong it was. It should never have gotten to the point that it did. America has a wide conservative stripe through it. Americans in their hearts are a very righteous people, and that always tends to make them dangerous.

"I was in New Hampshire recently rock climbing. While I was there, three police officers were shot. That has got to stop. The only way it can is to take guns away from people. It is a huge problem. America is just barely a civil society these days."

9

The Aftermath

The irony of it still impresses Patrick Grady.

In August 1995, he was sent to Hanoi by the Asian Development Bank in Manila, Philippines, to conduct an economic study of Vietnam's transition from a central economy to a market socialist economy. He was there about a month.

"What struck me the most was that if you had told the American government [in 1975] what Vietnam would look like in twenty years, with the movement of the market, they would not have believed you," he said. "The Communist Party is still in power, but there is a great fondness for anything American in Hanoi, which is strange. The extent to which the Vietnamese people love America is amazing. They sell T-shirts that say "Good Morning America" and they sell New York Yankees hats. What was the American government trying to stop? They went in there and killed a million and a half people,* lost fifty thousand Americans, to prevent something that would have been an acceptable outcome from the beginning."

Patrick had traveled in Africa in years past, but his trip to Vietnam was his first to an Asian country. He found the cultural differences quite striking. The first thing that caught his attention was the frenetic level of activity that exists in the streets on an everyday basis. "They don't have as many cars and trucks, so they travel by bicycle. People transport things on bicycles instead of trucks. You see five-hundred-pound pigs being moved around on bicycles, and chickens and snakes in baskets

*New figures released in 1997 put the Vietnamese death toll at three million.

that are being taken to restaurants. There's chaos and no traffic regulations."

Despite its poverty—and it is probably among the ten poorest countries in the world—Vietnam remains one of the most advanced countries in Southeast Asia. He said, "Because of being cut off from the world economy for fifteen years, they had to start from scratch. They are trying to make a life for themselves. It is a country with rich resources, but it is a bit of an ecological disaster because of the defoliants and pesticides that were used [by American troops] during the war. They still have lots of birth defects."

While he was in Hanoi, he noticed a steady stream of tourists. Many of the visitors are former American soldiers who want to see what it was like. "That missing in action thing, the way they tied that to policy for years—that was ridiculous. What would anyone have to gain by holding American prisoners for so long?" No one asked Patrick if he was American or Canadian, he said, but he got the feeling they assumed he was American. Patrick was so impressed by the trip that he wrote a novel about the experience when he returned to Canada.

Just as Vietnam has changed in the twenty-five years since the last of the American troops were pulled out, so has America and Canada changed. By 1998, America had Bill Clinton, a president who was himself a draft dodger during the Vietnam War, proving once again that justice is a revolving door that does not know when to quit.

The presidents who fought the war—John F. Kennedy, Lyndon Johnson, and Richard Nixon—are all dead, their presidencies marred by scandal and criminal wrongdoing. Of those three, only the reputation of Kennedy made it unscathed into the 1990s, though new revelations about sex scandals and allegations of ties to organized crime threaten the historical significance of the Kennedy administration.

In 1982, on the tenth anniversary of the Watergate break-in, *Newsweek* magazine published the results of a poll taken to assess the attitudes of Americans toward the scandal. Although fifty-two percent of those questioned said they felt that Watergate was a very serious matter because it revealed corruption in the Nixon administration, an astonishing forty-five percent said they felt it was just politics as usual. Asked if they thought that similar abuses of presidential power could ever happen again, fifty-three percent answered yes.

By the 1990s, politically correct liberals in America began to speak generously of President Nixon's foreign policy "contributions." By that, they meant he should be congratulated for opening the door to Communist China, a longtime favorite liberal cause—at least until tanks ran down political dissidents. War resisters cannot do that. They cannot give Nixon an inch. To them, he will always have blood on his hands.

Nixon apparently did not profit financially to any great extent by the war, but it was power, after all, not money, that was his addiction. To obtain that power, a powerful narcotic in his later years, he traded the lives of fifty thousand American men and nearly three million Vietnamese. The defense industry rewarded him with campaign contributions, a currency he easily converted into power.

"I didn't like anything about that guy," said war resister Andrew Collins. "He was a transparently evil person. I couldn't understand why people couldn't see that. For him to be elected president was confirmation of all my worst suspicions [about America]. It was mind-boggling."

Of the world leaders who had an impact on the lives of American war resisters, only Canadian Prime Minister Pierre Trudeau emerged from the era with his political reputation unscathed. He served as prime minister from 1968 until 1984, except for a seven-month period in 1979 when the Conservative Party held power under the ill-fated leadership of Joe Clark. But Trudeau was not as lucky in love as he was in politics, and his tempestuous marriage to Margaret resulted in a separation in 1977, shortly after she ran off to New York with the Rolling Stones. Asked about their newest groupie, Mick Jagger told the *Evening Standard* that Margaret was "a very sick girl in search of something."

Despite their official separation, Pierre and Margaret stayed in touch, largely for the children's sake, and Margaret did not file for divorce until 1984. With his rating in the polls at rock bottom that year, Trudeau decided the time had come for him retire from public life. He was a remarkable leader, not just because of the astute political skills he possessed in abundance, but because of the moral leadership he provided to a nation—and an influx of disillusioned American war exiles—during an era in which moral leadership was in short supply in the White House.

Exactly how many Americans went to Canada to oppose the war in Vietnam may never be known. From 1964 through 1973, 191,522 American men and women legally emigrated to Canada, according to figures released by Immigration Statistics Canada. In 1981, when those figures were updated, there remained 94,500 American-born men and women in Canada. Of that number, 45,200 were men. Not included in those figures are the thousands of war resisters and deserters who went to Canada and found jobs and blended into the system without ever applying for landed immigrant status or, in later years, citizenship.

So, while we do not know how many war exiles still live in Canada, we can be reasonably confident that—at the very minimum—fifty thousand ultimately chose Canada over the United States. The actual number is probably twice that. In a paper he prepared for Congress on the subject of amnesty, former Attorney General Ramsey Clark estimated that the official figures on legal immigration probably represented only half the number of men actually living in exile.

Easier to measure, perhaps, is the impact the war resisters had on Canada. As the interviews in this book indicate, the resisters have made a solid contribution to Canadian society, becoming influential journalists, advisors to prime ministers, business executives, teachers, and leaders in the communities in which they live. Not included in this book are scores of other high-profile resisters, including national television and radio anchors, university professors, media consultants, and television producers.

As the author was writing this book, he received a letter from Whitman Strong, a Canadian who had been greatly affected and influenced by the American war resisters who passed through his home. The letter writer had spotted the author's name and address in a letter-to-the-editor published in the *Ottawa Citizen*. When Whitman was a child, his father had opened up his home to war resisters, providing them with a safe haven.

"I can still remember some of the faces of those who passed through our home," he wrote. "Often our home was their first Canadian contact once they had left the United States. More often than not, they would arrive without notice. There was always a place at the table and a bed ready for them. We offered them a home until they made contact with friends or other receptive households across Canada. . . . It is with great pride that I recall these events. My father was a man of deep principle and conviction, someone who was not afraid to stand up for what he believed in. Opening our home to these young men who, for reasons of conscience, could no longer remain in the United States was a great lesson to me in compassion and justice. While I have no idea where they are now or what they have made of their lives, I often think of these many young men and at the same time silently thank my father for his living example of love and care offered to total strangers."

In his 1996 book, *Yankee Go Home? Canadians and Anti-Americanism*, Canadian J. L. Granatstein wrote that the exiles had "assimilated into Canadian society, taking citizenship, marrying, raising hockey-playing kids, and reading Canadian newspapers. All that betrayed their American origins was a different accent and, perhaps, a warier eye on the United States than that of their native-born compatriots."

Statistically, Americans in Canada are employed in higher than average percentages than the general population in professional and executive occupations. According to government figures, over twenty-six percent of the Americans in Canada are employed in professional positions (that compares to little over thirteen percent for the general population), with twelve percent working in executive positions (compared to nine percent for the general population).

"I have no way of empirically proving this, but I suspect Canada has been good to most draft dodgers," said war resister, Richard Deaton. "By virtue of their education, middle-class backgrounds, political commitments, and articulateness, dodgers became 'big fish in a small pond.' From a career perspective, most probably achieved greater career mobility than they would have if they had stayed in the United States. The United States lost an entire generation of the 'best and the brightest.' "

Each generation produces its own set of "best and brightest." Clearly, one segment of the best and brightest that America had to offer during the war years found its way to Canada and stayed there, helping to make Canada a better place in which to live. "To the best of my knowledge there's no organization of dodgers or resisters in Canada," said Richard. "We're so well integrated into Canada that we wouldn't recognize each other in any event. We don't advertise ourselves or our background. Interestingly, about one-third of the faculty at the University of Ottawa school of law have American degrees. But we don't sit around talking about the 'good ole days.' "

The biggest misconception Americans have about war resisters is that they were cowards, said Richard. "The more analytical perception is that they were highly committed ideologies. I've had people say that to me [that war resisters were cowards] and I've reacted angrily to it. This argument that has been thrown up, after the fact, strikes me as very spurious. At the time, I never even thought of it. I can't ever remember anyone ever saying anything like that. Maybe they thought it, but none of my close friends ever did. In many ways, it is something I suspect that Americans don't appreciate.

"It took a fair amount of gumption to jump into the unknown. It was a matter of putting one's ass on the line. The people who got used in Vietnam just got used. It was just terrible conditions they came back to—the lack of benefits, educational opportunities—they were tainted with that label of being baby killers, and so on. There is a lot of truth that in our hubris we weren't sufficiently generous in understanding those who went to Vietnam. In terms of antiwar politics, it was tactically inappropriate. American society swept those people [the veterans] under the rug because they wanted to forget the war and how divisive it was."

The first time Richard went back to the United States was to visit his uncle in New York City. While there, he went to Staten Island for old times sake. Afterward, he returned to the city on the ferry and caught a subway back to his uncle's house. On the subway, he sat next to someone he recognized. It was his old high school track coach.

"He didn't recognize me, but I recognized him," said Richard. "I was going to ask him how he was and then I remembered something. When I went to Wisconsin, his son enlisted in the Marine Corps. I didn't want him to turn around on me and get into a confrontation about the politics of the war, and I didn't want to know whether his son was or was not killed in Vietnam. I never acknowledged his existence, and he never knew who I was."

"Canada is what America should aspire to be," said Diane Francis. "Canada has all the economic opportunities that the United States offers. It has had a little too much socialism in its system, but that is getting out. The underclass is housed and fed. The middle class is not impoverished if they get ill. Our cities work. People live downtown. Our crime rate is a fraction of what it is in the United States. Racism is still pervasive in Canada, but there is so much more tolerance here.

"If Canada has a failing, it is a tyranny of tolerance. The opposition in Quebec is allowed to talk in treasonous terms. The union movement is allowed to go a little too far. Canada is sometimes too tolerant. America's problem is that it doesn't look outward enough. People carry an American personality everywhere they go. Canadians are a different people. They are more circumspect, more reasonable.

"Say Russia to a Canadian, and they think hockey. Say Russia to an American, and they think Evil Empire. Those are some of the sociological differences. You have a deference to authority in Canada. It is more authoritarian, but better organized. This is a Roman Catholic country. There have only been two Protestant prime ministers in its history. People are more polite, and it makes for a more peaceful place."

Diane reels off more of Canada's good points, then laughs when she catches herself sounding a bit like a minister of tourism without portfolio. Her enthusiasm for her adopted country is not unusual. Most American war exiles feel the same way. "This sounds like a commercial for Canada," she said good-naturedly. "But I've lived in both places. American individualism is great, but its big problem is its continuing racism and that has ruined the cities of America in my estimation. The middle class has left the cities. There is no tax base. The whole thing is falling apart." She pauses, intellectually toying with her thoughts in the manner of a satisfied convert: "*Our* cities are wonderful."

"I'm sure I paid a considerable price [for my convictions]," said Andrew Collins. "I was fast-tracking my career as an art historian, and I think it would have been a lucrative and satisfying lifestyle. But I'm glad that carrot did not seduce me. The American way of life will overwhelm you with its material possibilities. I think it compromises the hell out of everyone. I never think about any of it anymore. I'm more worried about my child's vaccination's reactions. Or this stock I'm holding that got creamed. I don't think at all about the sixties."

Often people say to Andrew, "You're American, aren't you?" He'll nod, and they'll ask, "Why are you here?" "Vietnam," he'll say—one word and nothing more. "Oh, yeah," they'll say, and move on to other things.

"It [the war] never comes up with other Americans," said Andrew. "Anyone who has been here as long as I have, you become acclimated to the culture. It's like your childhood. You just don't bring it up. Today I don't know anyone who was a draft dodger or deserter—and I used to know lots. People in America probably think we were a bunch of cowards, but I was very proud of my decision. I was not the least bit ashamed of it. After my children, I am proudest of that.

"Everyone I knew back then was arrogantly confident—and history, so far, has proved us correct." Andrew paused to laugh. "Maybe we'll be the goats again. Who knows? I'm really not interested in rehashing it. The people who ask me about it are my contemporaries because they remember it. My position was the only tenable position to have. People who are young enough not to have a clue [about the war], usually don't have an interest in hearing about it."

Andrew's hometown of Memphis seldom crosses his mind these days. He has lost touch with his childhood friend Jesse Winchester and has not heard much about him in recent years. In 1977, a few months after President Carter's pardon, Jesse returned to Memphis for a visit. A reporter for *Rolling Stone* magazine asked him about it. "I noticed little things," he said. "The street names have been changed—there's an Elvis Presley Boulevard now. . . . I was amazed at the things I'd forgotten. I'd forgotten how beautiful a town it was. I was amazed at how Canadian I'd become, too."

If there is a common thread that runs among war resisters, it is a lack of regret for the decisions they made. Andrew is no different. "I almost feel grateful that I was a little bit precocious," said Andrew. "I was not a political animal, but there was not even a flicker of a doubt in my mind about the wrongness of the war. I thought the White House was full of crooks—and it was. I thought the Vietnam War was a quagmire—and it was."

A couple of years ago, Oliver Drerup went to Florida on vacation and found himself in a cab with a driver who had served as a Navy SEAL in Vietnam. He had lost his leg in service to his country and now all he had to show for it was a cabbies' license. That chance encounter made a lasting impression on Oliver.

"Psychologically, he was in dicey condition," he said. "He is the tragedy. I'm not the tragedy. Those guys who went there and then came back without so much as a 'thank you,' to be cast adrift in that absurd medical system and be forced to drive cabs so they can afford medical bills. That guy's story was just unbelievable. It was disgusting, yet it goes on. My life is a cake walk compared to those missing arms and legs and suffering from the aftermath of Agent Orange."

On another trip south, this time to his home state of New Hampshire, Oliver stopped off in Lincoln and visited a memorial that had been erected to honor his former high school classmates who had served in the armed forces. To his astonishment, there was a listing for those who served in Grenada.

"Hello!" Oliver said, his voice rising, showing true emotion. "A guy goes for a forty-eight hour tip to Grenada and his name is up there with the first and second World War vets. Excuse me! I just don't get it. I'm not saying they shouldn't say thank you to the ones who went to Grenada, but it's just not the same."

The biggest misconception about Vietnam-era war resisters, said Oliver, is that they were bad Americans. "I don't believe that for a minute," he said. "What I did was very American. Thomas Jefferson would have counseled me to do exactly as I did. If Thomas Jefferson thought the United States could fight an undeclared war, he would turn over in his grave. The story that comes to mind is the one of Emerson going to see Thoreau in jail. He says, 'What are you doing in there?' And Thoreau says, 'What are you doing out there?' Right on, pal. A whole lot more people should have stood up and been counted over Vietnam."

Michael Wolfson's sister married and subsequently divorced a Vietnam veteran.

"I think there is a terrible irony now because he is in worse shape in terms of mainstream opinion than I am," Michael said. "It is now conventional wisdom that the war was a mistake. That wasn't so twenty years ago. When the draft comes up now, if I'm in the States, people say,

"Oh, you made the right decision." On the other hand, this fellow, my ex-brother-in-law, is basically in a mental institution. . . . He killed a lot of people when he was in Vietnam. Now, when a car backfires on the street, he leaps out of bed and hits the floor. I didn't know him beforehand, but now his life is totally destroyed. He was exposed to Agent Orange and was told to kill people. I'm not sure those people [the veterans] are being looked after very well."

After his return from Canada, Charles Sudduth again took up residence in Mississippi, where he worked first as a tree surgeon, then later started his own land excavation business. Today, his memory of his experiences during the Vietnam War years possess an almost dreamlike quality.

Sometimes he wonders what his life would have been like if he had remained in Canada. He stood for civil rights and was against the war, and although he was on the right side, morally, of both issues, his opinions cost him dearly.

The fact that the government dropped charges against him before the war ended was of little consequence in view of its decision to cover up its reasons for doing so. The government could not take action against draft boards involved in illegal operations without assisting the war resisters who challenged the board's authority. Rather than help the resisters, the government kept quiet and looked the other way.

Whether Mississippi was an exception—or the rule—in allowing state agencies and subversive, right-wing organizations to influence decisions made by local draft boards may never be known because of the destruction of so many government records from that era.

In addition to Charles, Patrolman Pierce and others conspired against a second Mississippi war resister, whom Pierce had literally stalked for years, but the conspiracy was thwarted in 1975 by a courageous newspaper editor, Hodding Carter III, who interceded on the resister's behalf. In 1946, Carter's father had been awarded a Pulitzer Prize for editorials that called for racial tolerance and were critical of the federal government's policy of interring Japanese Americans in prison camps during World War II, so Carter had grown up in a household in which government abuses of power were frequent topics of conversation. A former marine, the younger Carter, like his father, had an appreciation of the military, but he did not like to see innocent people pushed around by abusive government officials.

By the mid-1990s Pierce was dead of cancer, possibly forever closing the door on full disclosure of the government's involvement in a wide range of illegal activities against political dissidents. As late as 1996 and

1997, the Justice Department was still refusing to comply with Freedom of Information requests for information on the Mississippi draft board member's activities, and the FBI was still blacking out Pierce's name on confidential FBI reports, even though both men were government officials, public figures, and deceased.

"You just look at them and wonder, how could any group of people be so ignorant and shortsighted," said Charles of his experiences with state and federal officials in Mississippi. "They lived like they were pioneers in the wilderness, with no knowledge of history, no knowledge of literature, no knowledge of political science—people who were dragged out of the forest and put in charge of the whole state."

In Canada, the draft issue seldom comes up anymore, said Jim Thomas. But when he goes to the States, he frequently encounters people who offer the same gratuitous comments. "We don't blame you," they say, then they move on to other things. "I've never had anyone in the United States speak to me in anger, though I can imagine some mother who lost her son might be angry," he said. "When I'm down there, it is a mixture of people putting it under the rug and false bravado on the part of those who served. Some are really ashamed of what they did.

"Not long ago, we bid on some tickets to go to Washington, D.C., and won," said Jim. "People said, 'Why don't you go see the Vietnam wall?' But I can't go. I know people who died there. In the neighborhood where I grew up, there was a boy on the block from one of the houses next to us who was in the Marine Corps. He was killed by one of those bamboo sticks. A boy I was in Boy Scouts with stepped on a land mine. When he was a young lad, I remember teaching him how to tie knots. The last time I saw him, he spilled coffee all over himself because of a muscle twitch in his one good hand. What a waste!"

The fact that one was a draft dodger is not something that is easily outgrown or discarded or packed into a box and placed on the top shelf of a closet. Nor will the pain and grief, referred to by former Attorney General Ramsey Clark, ever fully be assuaged. When the last surviving soldier of the Civil War died in a Texas hospital in 1959, the Mississippi legislature passed a resolution honoring his service to the Confederacy. The lawmakers still had not gotten around to ratifying the Nineteenth Amendment guaranteeing women the right to vote, but they had time to honor the last Confederate soldier. Old memories die hard.

When the time comes for the last surviving war resister to pass away, it is unlikely his passing will be duly noted by a legislature intent on honoring the memory of the past. Nor is it likely the last surviving Vietnam War veteran will be recognized by a legislative body when he passes over to the other side.

The success stories included in this book should not be taken as incontrovertible proof that all American war exiles found successful lives in Canada. Nor should it be assumed that all those who returned to the United States walked into warm receptions and successful careers. "However we feel about their actions, we should not assume their course has been easy for them, their family, or their friends," Ramsey Clark said in 1974, before President Ford's amnesty had been issued. "They have borne a full measure of grief, hardship, and suffering. It continues until this moment and—even if assuaged by amnesty—will continue until death. The war is the single most significant fact in their lives."

In the final analysis, all that the war resisters and the veterans of Vietnam will ever have to show for their grief is each other. The luck of the draw has bound them together, inextricably, for all eternity, by an ungrateful nation that has moved on to other concerns.

For most Americans, the memory of the war resisters and the veterans is best forgotten, for it is a memory of the nation's darkest and most shameful hour. But for the thousands of men and women who refused to serve in Vietnam—and the thousands who did serve—it is more than just the defining moment of their lives: It is the defining moment of America.

Author's Note

In May 1968, with the backseat of my Mustang convertible filled with all my possessions, I emigrated to Canada—along with my wife, Ina—in opposition to the Vietnam War. I was twenty-one; my wife of less than one year was nineteen. We were just kids, really, fresh out of the University of Mississippi, where I had received a degree in psychology and an intimate understanding of the vagaries of rock 'n' roll as a member of the hottest band on campus.

Ina and I were of the same mind about Vietnam, though we arrived there from different directions. She was the daughter of Charles Taylor, a World War II fighter pilot who served in the notorious Black Sheep Squadron. Taylor was captured by the Japanese and held in a prisoner of war camp until the end of hostilities, an experience that, no doubt, deeply affected the antiwar feelings of his daughter. Simply put, she had seen the effects of war on her father and wanted to be done with war as an issue in her life.

My father served in the Army Air Forces in World War II; I have a paternal uncle who lost his arm aboard a battleship, and a maternal uncle who died of diseases contracted in the South Pacific and another who served in the navy in China; but my views about war—and the Vietnam War in particular—were derived more from a generational knowledge of politics than any preconceived notions I had about the military. My family was promilitary and had a long history of public service.

My great-grandfather, Steven Turner, was a delegate to the Mississippi Constitutional Convention of 1890 and helped write the constitution that is now in effect. Ironically, it was his participation in that undertaking that sowed the seeds of my opposition to the war in Vietnam. Disgusted by the determination of some delegates to turn the convention into an inquisition against blacks, he left the yearlong assembly in a huff.

"I went to Jackson to write law, not to talk about Negroes," he confided to a family member. He had been involved in local politics for most of his life and was offended that the convention was dominated by people who preferred to debate racial politics at the expense of constitutional law. Later, after he had cooled off, he returned to the convention and completed work on the constitution. Sometimes you have to vote with your feet.

It has always been a source of pride to me that a member of my family who was born sixteen years before the end of the Civil War—and who had a brother, James, killed by Union troops on Peachtree Road in Atlanta on July 29, 1864—would have the courage in 1890 to put that war out of his mind long enough to stand up for his convictions.

My cousin, Hilton Waits—I called him Uncle Hilton since he was old enough to be my father—was a longtime member of the Mississippi House of Representatives and served for a time as speaker *pro tempore* of the House. He was an educated, erudite man who had a passion for politics and a lifelong devotion to tax reform. He drafted the legislation for Mississippi's first sales tax and, for many years, was regarded as one of the nation's leading authorities on tax reform.

After my father died in a boating accident (I was eight at the time and witnessed the tragedy), Uncle Hilton took me under his wing, as did several other male family members, and endeavored to educate me on the ways of the world. He took me to Jackson with him to serve as a page in the Mississippi legislature, and he answered my many questions about politics and government. He was a man of uncommon integrity and devotion to duty, and he had a major impact on my life.

A third family member, who shall remain unnamed, was employed by the notorious E. H. "Boss" Crump of Memphis. From the 1920s up until the time he died in 1954—he passed away at approximately the same moment that Elvis Presley walked out on stage for his first appearance at the Louisiana Hayride—Crump controlled the politics of the South, and at times the entire nation, with an iron fist. My illustrious relative was Crump's go-between with bosses of a similar disposition in New Orleans.

Growing up in Mississippi, I metamorphosed into a pre-teen activist who wrote letters to state agencies and newspaper editors protesting the dumping of untreated sewage into the creek that meandered through my hometown. Once I inquired about the safety of local water supplies after I stumbled across a confidential government report that said my town's water supply contained unacceptable levels of harmful bacteria. Elected officials had tried to keep the report a secret. Looking at those letters today, I am not convinced that the agency heads and editors were fully aware of the fact that I was only a kid, for they took my inquiries quite seriously.

On top of my politically obnoxious ways, my mother had raised me to value human life and to be respectful of the rights of others, particularly the many African Americans who lived in our small community. Basically, I was raised to stand up for what I thought was right—and I thought the war in Vietnam was dead wrong.

Ina and I lived in Canada for seven years. I held the same job the entire time, working for the Canadian government to find families for homeless children. In 1975, we returned to the United States, and I worked for the State of Mississippi for two years, fulfilling my public service obligation to the Selective Service System, before embarking on a long and satisfying career as an author and journalist (thanks, in part, to the gumption of world-class journalist and former State Department spokesman Hodding Carter III, who gave me my first newspaper job).

Ina and I are now divorced, but I will always be grateful to her for the support she offered me at a time when I needed it the most. Not only is she the mother of my only son, she is a living testament to what I wrote in the introduction about the role of women in the Great American Exodus to Canada.

For years I have wondered about my fellow resisters who remained in Canada. Who are they? How have they changed? What contributions have they made to Canadian society? How do they look back on their decision to refuse service in Vietnam? Do any of them have regrets?

North to Canada has allowed me to answer those questions, at least to my own satisfaction.

Notes

INTRODUCTION

Information on the draft was derived from a number of sources, including the House Judiciary Committee, the Justice Department, various news reports, and Loren Baritz's book *Backfire: Vietnam—The Myths That Made Us Fight* (New York: Ballatine, 1985).

Information on American emigration to Canada was derived from Immigration Statistics Canada.

Information about American migration was taken from *Americans Abroad: A Comparative Study of Emigrants from the United States* by Arnold Dashefsky, Jan DeAmicis, Bernard Lazerwitz, and Ephraim Tabory (New York: Plenum Press, 1992).

CHAPTER 1

Diane Francis was interviewed by the author in 1997.

Most of the news stories referred to in this chapter were obtained from *Newsweek*, the *New Republic*, and *Time* magazine. Historical information relating to Vietnam prior to 1967 was obtained from a variety of sources, including Bernard Fall's *Viet-Nam Witness* (New York: Praeger, 1966) and the book he co-edited with Marcus G. Raskin, *The Viet-Nam Reader* (New York: Vintage Books, 1965). Also very useful was the Foreign Policy Association's publication, "Vietnam: Vital Issues in the Great Debate."

Information in this chapter and in subsequent chapters about surveillance of American citizens by the military, the FBI, and the CIA was obtained from a variety of sources, but mostly from the *Final Report of the Select Committee to Study Governmental Operations* (U.S. Senate; Washington, D.C.: U.S. Government Printing Office, 1976) and Christopher H. Pyle's book, *Military Surveillance of Civilian Politics* (New York: Garland Publishing, 1986).

Coverage of Queen Elizabeth's visit to Canada can be found in *Time* (July 7, 1967).

Additional information about Abe Fortas's relationship with President Lyndon Johnson can be found in James Dickerson, *Dixie's Dirty Secret* (M. E. Sharpe, 1998).

White House aide Fred Panzer's memo to President Johnson can be found at the Lyndon B. Johnson Library in file JL 3/King. The account of Los Angeles police officers being trained as snipers by the marines at Camp Pendleton came from *Newsweek* (October 7, 1968). Information about Captain Dale Noyd was obtained from Roger Neville Williams, *The New Exiles: American War Resisters in Canada* (New York: Liveright Publishers, 1971).

Unsigned articles in the *New Republic* included: "Kill for Peace" (August 5, 1967); "Talking While Fighting" (April 20, 1968); "Nixon's Choice" (November 16, 1968); and "If Not LBJ, What?" (February 24, 1968). Unsigned articles in *Time* included: "The Draft: Thanks, but No Thanks" (March 3, 1967). Unsigned articles in *Newsweek* included: "Bobby's Last, Longest Day" (June 17, 1968); "The President: Order of Battle" (April 22, 1968); "The Battle of Chicago" (September 9, 1968); "Chicago: Verdict on the Violence" (December 9, 1968); "The Other Shoe" (May 6, 1968); "Seven Days in April" and "The First Steps Toward Peace?" (April 15, 1968); "Paris—And a War of Words" (May 13, 1968); "Ky Notes" (April 29, 1968); "Can South Vietnam Stand Alone?" (December 16, 1968); "November Song: LBJ Looks Back" (November 25, 1968); "Antiwar 'U.S. Military Week'" (August 26, 1968); and "Finally, Nixon's the One" (November 11, 1968).

Prime Minister Trudeau's comments about war resisters were published in the September 1968 issue of the *United Church Observer*. He was interviewed by the magazine's editor, Rev. A. C. Forrest.

CHAPTER 2

Andrew Collins was interviewed by the author in 1997.

Information about Jesse Winchester was obtained from a variety of sources, including an interview with the author in the mid-1980s, Roger Neville Williams' *The New Exiles: American War Resisters in Canada* (New York: Liveright Publishers, 1971), and the *Encyclopedia of Folk, Country & Western Music* by Irwin Stambler and Grelun Landon (New York: St. Martin's, 1969).

Battlefield casualties were published in *Newsweek* (March 31, 1969).

The story of Christopher and Molly Youngs was told in the Toronto *Globe and Mail* (undated).

The border crossing incident involving the buses was reported by the Toronto *Globe and Mail* and the *Toronto Star*. John Osborne offers a descriptive account of the meeting between President Richard Nixon and President Thieu of South Vietnam in his article, "Back from Midway," the *New Republic* (June 21, 1969).

Unsigned articles in *Newsweek* included: "It Can't Happen Here—Can It?" (May 5, 1969); "With Lowered Voice, Enter Mr. Nixon" and "Saigon Attitudes" (February 3, 1969); "Scoring Points" (January 6, 1969); "The War: Nixon's Big Test" (March 31, 1969); "Beginning of the End?" (July 21, 1969); "Green Berets to Trial" and "On the Horns of a Dilemma" (September 29, 1969); "The Meaning of the Moratorium" and "Oct. 15: A Day to Remember"

(October 27, 1969); "The President: Withdrawal Pains (September 1, 1969); "Nixon and the Moratorium" (October 20, 1969); "The Periscope: Vietnamization (Continued)" (May 19, 1969); "Vietnam: What's Going on Here?" (September 22, 1969); "The Killings at Song My" and "The War Crime Issue: Some Nagging Questions" (December 8, 1969).

Unsigned articles in the *New Republic* included: "Draft Reform" (May 31, 1969); "Graduate Student Draft" (February 15, 1969); "Nixon's Inch" (May 24, 1969); "Green Berets and the CIA," for information about General Creighton Abrams's decision to arrest Colonel Robert Rheault (August 23, 1969). Unsigned articles in the Memphis *The Commercial Appeal* included: "Court Sets Restrictions on Evader's Movement" (January 9, 1976) and "1970 Draftee Comes Home to Face Trial" (January 8, 1976). Unsigned article in the Memphis *Press-Scimitar*: "Plea Entered in Draft Case" (January 7, 1976). Unsigned article in *Common Sense, The Catholic Weekly* (January 18, 1976).

CHAPTER 3

Charles Sudduth was interviewed by the author in 1996.

When the author went to the federal court clerk's office in Greenville, Mississippi, in 1996 and asked to see the records from the Jenkins case, he was told the records had been destroyed. When the author requested information from the National Headquarters of the Selective Service about Mississippi draft board accords under the Freedom of Information Act, he was told those files, too, had been destroyed. Freedom of Information requests to the U.S. attorney's office have gone unanswered.

Although all trace of the Mississippi draft board member's twenty-five year tenure had been destroyed, the Selective Service office did supply the author with records of his contact with the local board as a registrant in 1941. His name is one of thirty-two on a tally sheet that lists everyone's classification from initial notification to induction. Revealing of the board's activity at that time is the fact that only six of the thirty-two men on the list were white—and all of those receiving 1-A status (the most eligible for the draft) were black.

Information about the Jackson State killings was obtained from a variety of news sources, secret files of the Mississippi State Sovereignty Commission, and Tim Spofford's *Lynch Street: The May 1970 Slayings of Jackson State College* (Kent, OH: Kent State University Press, 1988). Information about the Kent State killings was obtained from news sources and I. F. Stone, *The Killings at Kent State: How Murder Went Unpunished* (New York: New York Review Book, 1971).

President Richard Nixon's visit to the Middle East and his visit with Pope Paul was reported on by *Newsweek*.

Rick Abraham was interviewed by the author in 1996. He was present in the courtroom when the Leland, Mississippi, police officer testified about the board member's involvement in the Ku Klux Klan. When the author requested the files of that case from the federal court clerk in Greenville, Mississippi, he was told they had been destroyed. He asked the U.S. attorney's office for information but was referred to Justice Department headquarters in Washington. The Justice Department did not respond to the author's request for information. William Burnley did not respond to requests for an interview.

Unsigned articles in *Newsweek* included: "The Campus: Bring Us Together" (October 5, 1970); "A President's Progress" (October 12, 1970); "Canada: The Answer Was Murder" (October 26, 1970); "Vietnamization Is Not Peace" (November 23, 1970); "Nixon's Gamble: Operation Total Victory?" (May 11, 1970); "Cambodia: Caught in a Cross Fire" (May 4, 1970); "The Rebellion of the Campus" and "Mr. Nixon's Home Front" (May 18, 1970); "More About Song My" (January 19, 1970); "A Duel Over the Power to Make War" (May 25, 1970); "A New Bombing Policy" (December 21, 1970); "The FBI: Happy Birthday" (January 12, 1970); and "Why the Death Toll?" (August 31, 1970).

Unsigned articles in *Time* included: "Kent State: Martyrdom That Shook the Country" (May 15, 1970). Unsigned articles in the *New Republic* included: "Love It or Leave It" (August 1, 1970) and "Staying Alive Until 1973" (May 16, 1970). Unsigned article on Kent State killings in *Life* (May 15, 1970). Information about Canada's contribution to the Vietnam War effort in *Maclean's* (March 1970) and Jim Kunen and Laura Jacknick (*Maclean's*, February 1970).

The story of the Florida cemetery's refusal to bury a black soldier was reported by Associated Press and published in the *New York Times* (August 23, 1970). Reports of Senator George McGovern opening a campaign office was reported in *Newsweek* (September 21, 1970). Information about conduct of the RCMP during the Quebec crisis was obtained in *Maclean's* (October 1970).

CHAPTER 4

Richard Deaton was interviewed by the author in 1997 and 1998.

Information about Prime Minister Pierre Trudeau's marriage to Margaret Sinclair was derived from many magazine and newspaper sources and Felicity Cochrane's book, *Margaret Trudeau: The Prime Minister's Runaway Wife* (New York: Signet, 1978).

Information about the My Lai massacre was derived from various magazine and newspaper articles and Seymour M. Hersh's *My Lai 4: A Report on the Massacre and Its Aftermath* (New York: Random House, 1970).

Unsigned articles in *Newsweek* included: "Canada's Other U.S. Emigrants" (May 24, 1971); "Let's Get Out," for an account of Colonel Hackworth's resignation from the U.S. Army (July 5, 1971); "The Periscope: Humphrey Makes His Move" (November 8, 1971); "Congress: The Draft Gap" (July 12, 1971); "Pentagon Papers: Ellsberg Today" (December 6, 1971); "A Profile of the New Voter" (October 25, 1971); "The Last Big Push—Or a Wider War?" (February 15, 1971); "Operation Steel Tiger" (January 18, 1971); "Widening the War to Wind It Down?" (February 8, 1971); "Once More a Time for Protest" (May 3, 1971); "Military Justice: Countdown for Calley" (August 30, 1971); "Demonstrations: Spring Offensive" (April 26, 1971); "Judgment at Fort Benning" and "Who Else Is Guilty?" (April 12, 1971); "Courts Martial: With Calley at My Lai" (January 25, 1971); "Debate Over Cambodia" (February 1, 1971); "The Periscope: The Boys We'll Leave Behind" (June 21, 1971); and "The Periscope: Snoop vs. Countersnoop" and "Armed Forces: Guilty—Sort of," for an account of the trial of Capt. Thomas Culver (July 26, 1971).

Unsigned articles in the *New Republic* included: "The Veterans' March to Boston" (June 12, 1971); "Nixon's Chance to End the War" (July 17, 1971); and "In the Draft" (October 9, 1971).

CHAPTER 5

Jim Thomas was interviewed by the author in 1997.

Information about Bill Clinton was obtained from a variety of sources, including *Newsweek*, *The Commercial Appeal* (Memphis, Tennessee), the *Washington Post*, and the *New York Times*.

Unsigned articles in *Newsweek* included: "The Spies Who Came in from the Heat" (September 18, 1972); "Nixon's Great Triumph" (November 13, 1972); "Peace Is at Hand" and "The Vietnam Deal: Why Now?" (November 6, 1972); "The New Majority," "Democrats: Hard Labor," and "Bad News" (September 4, 1972); "The Battle for Quang Tri" (July 17, 1972); "Marking Time" (July 31, 1972); "The Battle of the POWs" (October 9, 1972); "The Watergate Trail" (August 14, 1972); "Operation Watergate" (July 3, 1972); "Is It an Era—Or Only an Hour?" (July 24, 1972); "Periscope: The Rear Guard in Vietnam" and "Portents of Peace" (June 26, 1972); "Nixon's Vietnam Gamble" (May 22, 1972); "Vietnam: The Specter of Defeat" (May 15, 1972); "Watergate: Very Offensive Security" (October 23, 1972); "McGovern Tries Giving 'em Hell" (October 16, 1972); "Newsmakers," for account of birth of Justin Trudeau (January 10, 1972); "Now, It's a New Democratic Race" (May 8, 1972); "Vietnam: An Issue That Won't Go Away" (February 14, 1972); "Vietnam: An Issue in '72" (January 24, 1972); and "Vietnam: War of Attrition" (June 12, 1972).

Unsigned articles in the *New Republic* included "The Dismal Election" (November 18, 1972). "Draft Dodger Amnesty," the editorial that appeared in *The Recorder & Times*, was in the June 24, 1972, issue.

CHAPTER 6

Michael Wolfson was interviewed by the author in 1997and 1998.

The author's descriptions of Toronto and Yonge Street are based on his own recollections and on news stories.

Dee Charles Knight's letter to the author was dated January 10, 1973.

Martin O'Malley wrote about Thomas Lee York for the *Globe and Mail* (December 15, 1973) and Bill Lewis wrote about him for the *Toronto Star*.

Newsweek published excerpts from the POW briefing in its February 5, 1973, edition.

The *Amex-Canada* articles on amnesty were in its May–June 1973 issue.

Unsigned articles in *Newsweek* included: "Watergate: Now It's a Federal Case" (September 25, 1972); "On the Rebound?" (September 3, 1973); "The President's Best Defense" (September 17, 1973); "They Had a Little List" (July 9, 1973); "The Fall of Mr. Law and Order" (October 22, 1973); "The Bombing Stops, the Wait Begins" (August 27, 1973); "Canada: 'Non' to Separatism" (November 12, 1973); "The Nixon Tapes" (July 30, 1973); "Mr. Nixon Comes Out Fighting" (November 26, 1973); "Watergate: Drip, Drip, Drip" (December 24, 1973); "Watergate: The Dam Bursts" and "Twisting Arms to Heal the Peace" (April 30, 1973); "A Government in Turmoil" and "A Wintry Springtime in Paris" (May 7, 1973); "Indochina: To Bomb or Not to Bomb" (May 14, 1973); "Back to Paris for Another Try" and "At War Over the War" (January 15, 1973); "POW Showdown: Hanoi Gives In" (March 12, 1973); "Nixon Acts—America Watches" and "Indochina: A Lot to Be Done" (June 25, 1973); "They're Coming Home At Last" and "Congress Throws the Gauntlet" (February 19, 1973); "Exposing the Big Cover-Up" (May 28, 1973); "And the Mess Goes On" and "Ellsberg: Case Dismissed" (May 21, 1973); "Mr. Nixon States His Case" and "Blueprint for a Super Secret Police" (June 4, 1973); "For Whom the Bells Toll" (February 5, 1973); "What Went Wrong?" (January 1, 1973); "How Solid a Peace?" and "When the POW's Come Home Again" (January 29, 1973); "Time Out for Image-Polishing" [about President Nguyen Van Thieu] (April 9, 1973); "POW's: The Peace Committee" (April 2, 1973).

Unsigned articles on amnesty included: "Amnesty: A Peace Not at Hand" (February 12, 1973) in *Newsweek* and "Never, Never for Amnesty?" (February 17, 1973) in the *New Republic*. Shana Alexander's article on amnesty was in *Newsweek* (March 19, 1973).

Canada's involvement in the Vietnam cease-fire was reported on in an unsigned article in *Time-Canada* entitled "Shaky Start in Viet Nam" (February 12, 1973).

Canada's political climate was reported on by *Time-Canada* in an unsigned article entitled "The Remaking of Pierre Trudeau" (May 14, 1973) and "The Trouble with the Tories" (July 16, 1973). Claude Lemelin wrote about Finance Minister John Turner in the April 1973 issue of *Maclean's*. In an article entitled "Please Grit Your Teeth, Mr. Stanfield," Peter C. Newman wrote about Conservative Party leader Robert Stanfield and the state of the Liberal Party under Pierre Trudeau's leadership.

Irving Penn's photographs and commentary on Big Brother and the Holding Company and the Grateful Dead appeared in the January 9, 1968, issue of *Look* magazine.

The April 16, 1968, edition of *Look* magazine contains several articles of interest: "Showdown for Non-Violence" by Dr. Martin Luther King, Jr.; "An Interview with a Vietcong Terrorist" by Oriana Fallaci; and "Bobby's Decision," an article by Warren Rogers on Robert Kennedy's decision to enter the presidential campaign.

David Lewis's letter to the editor on amnesty was in the July 9, 1973, issue of the *Toronto Star*; Alex Scala's reply was published in the July 17, 1973, issue of the newspaper.

Len Grannemann's story was told by Associated Press writer Richard E. Meyer and was published in the June 12, 1973, edition of the Brockville, Ontario, *The Recorder and Times*.

CHAPTER 7

Patrick Grady was interviewed by the author in 1997 and 1998.

Unsigned articles on amnesty included: "Amnesty at Last" in *Newsweek* (September 30, 1974); "Justice: The Amnesty Issue" in *Time* (September 9, 1974); "Next, A Vietnam Amnesty" in *Newsweek* (September 16, 1974); "Amnesty: Limited Program, Limited Response," *Time-Canada* (September 30, 1974); "Outlook for Amnesty" in *Newsweek* (September 2, 1974); "A Tough Choice for Exiles," *The Globe and Mail* (September 17, 1974); "War Resisters Reject Amnesty—It's Punishment" in *The Toronto Star* (September 17, 1974); and "Clemency Plan for American Draft-Evaders" in *The Globe and Mail* (September 17, 1974).

An unsigned article on President Gerald Ford's pardon of former President Richard Nixon, "Was Justice Done?," was published in *Newsweek* (September

16, 1974). The text of the pardon was published in *Newsweek* (September 16, 1974).

Coverage of President Gerald Ford's swearing in was provided by *Newsweek* (August 19, 1974) and of his first week in office, "The Sun Is Shining Again" (August 26, 1974).

Unsigned articles on the 1974 Canadian election included: "Still Waiting for the Election Fire" in *Time-Canada* (July 1, 1974); "The Liberals: Back in Strength" in *Time-Canada* (July 22, 1974); "Canada: Unlucky Pierre" in *Newsweek* (May 20, 1974); "Once More with Feeling" in *Time-Canada* (May 20, 1974); and "Equal Time" in *Time-Canada* (September 2, 1974).

Ronald Anderson's ordeal was reported in *Newsweek*, "Amnesty: Hot Pursuit" (September 9, 1974); in *The Toronto Star* on September 7, 1974, in an article written by Paul King; and "U.S. Will Hand Over Deserter Arrested on Canadian Soil" by Ross Munro in the *Globe and Mail*.

Prime Minister Trudeau's visit with Margaret in Montreal Royal Victoria Hospital was reported on by *Time-Canada* (September 30, 1974).

Unsigned articles on Watergate and impeachment included: "A Flight from Reality?" in *Newsweek* (June 17, 1974); "All About Impeachment" in *Newsweek* (March 25, 1974); "Ehrlichman's Story: I Was Had" in *Newsweek* (December 23, 1974); "How Good a Case?" in *Newsweek* (July 29, 1974); "The Fateful Vote" in *Newsweek* (August 5, 1974); "Are the Articles Sound?" in *Newsweek* (August 12, 1974); "I Know What I Meant" in *Newsweek* (March 18, 1974); and "The President's Strategy for Survival" in *Time* (March 25, 1974). *Newsweek* published an entire issue on Watergate on May 13, 1974.

Newsweek published the text of the first article of impeachment in its August 5, 1974, issue.

An unsigned article on the misuse of power by Internal Revenue Service, "Politics and the IRS," was published in *Newsweek* (July 29, 1974).

Julie Amato was profiled by Anita Latner in the November 2, 1974, issue of *Star Week*.

Amex-Canada published extensive commentary on President Gerald Ford's amnesty plan in its October and November–December 1974 issues.

CHAPTER 8

Oliver Drerup was interviewed by the author in 1997.

Unsigned articles on the last days of the war in Vietnam included: "Vietnam's Last Battle" in *Newsweek* (April 28, 1975); "Next, the Struggle for Saigon" in *Time* (April 28, 1975); "The Great Retreat" and "A Pathway of Blood" in *Newsweek* (March 31, 1975); "Saigon: A Calm Week Under Communism" and "Bitter Debate on Who Got Out," which included information about Ambassador Graham Martin's poodle, in *Time* (May 19, 1975); "Hail from the Chief" in *Newsweek* (May 19, 1975); "The End of an Era" in *Newsweek* (May 5, 1975).

Details of the fall of Saigon can be found in "Last Exit from Saigon," written by Milton Benjamin, Loren Jenkins, Ron Moreau, Bernard Krisher, and William Cook in *Newsweek* (May 5, 1975); "We Beat the Americans" by Tom Mathews, Harry Rolnick and Lloyd Norman in *Newsweek* (May 5, 1975); "From Vietnam to What?" by Richard Steele, Henry Hubbard, and Tom Joyce in *Newsweek* (May 12, 1975); "The Long Day of the Copters" by Milton Benjamin, Loren Jenkins, Nicholas Proffitt, Ron Moreau, and Lloyd Norman in *Newsweek* (May 12, 1975); "Spectacle of Defeat" by Tom Mathews, Mel Elfin, Thomas DeFrank, and Loren Jenkins in *Newsweek* (April 14, 1975); "The Yanks Are Coming" by Elizabeth Peer, Nicholas Proffitt, and Jeff Copeland in *Newsweek* (April 14, 1975); and a series of unsigned articles in the May 5, 1975, issue of *Time*.

The Vietnamese exodus was reported on in "Hail from the Chief" by David Alpern, Philip Cook, Tom Joyce, Sunde Smith, and Martin Kasindorf in *Newsweek* (May 19, 1975); in "True Tales of the Exodus" by James Gaines, Sunde Smith, and Elaine Sciolino in *Newsweek* (May 19, 1975); and "A Baby Kisser in Tent City," an account of Nguyen Cao Ky's experiences in a refugee camp, by David Alpern and Sunde Smith in *Newsweek* (May 19, 1975).

Abuses of power by the CIA were detailed in "The Cloak Comes Off" by Peter Goldman, Anthony Marro, Evert Clark, and Thomas DeFrank in *Newsweek* (June 23, 1975).

The visit to the Veterans of Foreign Wars convention in Seattle by Jimmy Carter and Bob Dole was reported on by Tom Mathews and Elaine Shannon in "On to the Great Debates" in *Newsweek* (September 6, 1976). Carter's position on pardons for Vietnam War resisters was explained in "Carter Meets the Questions" in *Newsweek* (February 2, 1976). Jimmy Carter's victory at the Democratic Convention was reported on in "The Jimmycrats" in *Newsweek* (July 26, 1976).

The stories of John Behan, the Vietnam amputee, and Jack Colhoun, the deserter, were published in the July 4, 1976, issue of *Newsweek*. The aftermath of President Jimmy Carter's pardon of war resisters was reported on by Susan Fraker, Jon Lowell, Eleanor Clift, and Mary Lord in *Newsweek* (January 31, 1977).

William Schiller's story was told in the July 18, 1976, issue of *Parade*.

In an August 23, 1975, dispatch, "Two-Thirds of Deserters in Ford Program 'Beating Rap,' " Associated Press writer Jerry Baulch wrote about the failure of the amnesty program. The story of Holiday Inn's marquee campaign was reported on in the January 13, 1977, edition of the *Delta Democrat-Times*.

The "Carter Is Right" editorial in the *Delta Democrat-Times* was published in the August 27, 1976, issue.

Amex-Canada published extensive articles on amnesty in the May–July 1975 and October–November 1975 issues.

CHAPTER 9

The *Newsweek* poll on public attitudes on the tenth anniversary of Watergate was published in the June 14, 1982, issue.

Canadian immigration figures can be found in *Americans Abroad: A Comparative Study of Emigrants from the United States* by Arnold Dashefsky, Jan DeAmicis, Bernard Lazerwitz, and Ephraim Tabory (New York: Plenum Press, 1992).

Facts and figures on Canadian elections were derived from a number of sources, including *Canada Today*, an informational booklet published by the Canadian government for American journalists, the Associated Press, the *New York Times*, the Toronto *Globe and Mail*, the *Toronto Star*, *Maclean's*, *Saturday Night*, *Newsweek*, and *Time*. Information about Prime Minister Pierre Trudeau and his wife, Margaret, was obtained from most of those same sources.

Bibliography

BOOKS

Baritz, Loren. *Backfire: Vietnam—The Myths That Made Us Fight*. New York: Ballantine, 1985.

Beschloss, Michael R. *Taking Charge: The Johnson White House Tapes, 1963–1964*. New York: Simon & Schuster, 1997.

Cochrane, Felicity. *Margaret Trudeau: The Prime Minister's Runaway Wife*. New York: Signet, 1978.

Dashefsky, Arnold, Jan DeAmicis, Bernard Lazerwitz, and Ephraim Tabory. *Americans Abroad: A Comparative Study of Emigrants from the United States*. New York: Plenum Press, 1992.

Fall, Bernard B. *Viet-Nam Witness*. New York: Praeger, 1966.

Finn, James, ed. *A Conflict of Loyalties: The Case for Conscientious Objection*. New York: Pegasus, 1968.

Granatstein, J. L. *Yankee Go Home? Canadians and Anti-Americanism*. Toronto: HarperCollins, 1996.

Hersh, Seymour M. *My Lai 4: A Report on the Massacre and Its Aftermath*. New York: Random House, 1970.

Kahin, George McTurnan. *Governments and Politics of Southeast Asia*. Ithaca, NY: Cornell University Press, 1964.

Kennedy, Robert F. *To Seek a Newer World*. New York: Bantam, 1968.

Killmer, Richard L., Robert S. Lecky, and Debrah S. Wiley. *They Can't Go Home Again*. Philadelphia, PA: Pilgrim Press, 1971.

Mailer, Norman. *St. George and the Godfather*. New York: New American Library, 1972.

Morgan, Allen. *Dropping Out in 3/4 Time*. New York: Seabury Press, 1972.

Morgenthau, Hans J. *Politics Among Nations*. New York: Alfred A. Knopf, 1967.

Polner, Murray. *When Can I Come Home?* Garden City, NY: Anchor Books, 1972.

Pyle, Christopher H. *Military Surveillance of Civilian Politics (1967–1970).* New York: Garland Publishing, 1986.

Raskin, Marcus G., and Bernard B. Fall. *The Viet-Nam Reader.* New York: Vintage Books, 1965.

Russell, Bertrand. *Has Man a Future?* London, England: Penguin Books, 1961.

———. *War Crimes in Vietnam.* New York: Monthly Review Press, 1967.

Sheehan, Neil, Hedrick Smith, E. W. Kenworthy, and Fox Butterfield. *The Pentagon Papers.* New York: Bantam, 1971.

Spofford, Tim. *Lynch Street: The May 1970 Slayings at Jackson State College.* Kent, OH: Kent State University Press, 1988.

Stone, I. F. *The Killings at Kent State: How Murder Went Unpunished.* New York: A New York Review Book, 1971.

Story, Norah. *The Oxford Companion to Canadian History and Literature.* New York: Oxford University Press, 1967.

Thompson, Hunter S. *Fear and Loathing: On the Campaign Trail '72.* New York: Popular Library, 1973.

Wall, Byron, ed. *Manual for Draft-Age Immigrants to Canada.* Toronto: House of Anansi, 1968.

The Washington Post, comp. *The Presidential Transcripts.* New York: Dell, 1974.

Williams, Roger Neville. *The New Exiles: American War Resisters in Canada.* New York: Liveright Publishers, 1971.

Woodward, Bob, and Carl Bernstein. *The Final Days.* New York: Simon & Schuster, 1976.

GOVERNMENT PUBLICATIONS

U.S. Department of Justice. *Task Force to Review the FBI Martin Luther King, Jr., Security and Assassination Investigations.* Washington, D.C.: U.S. Government Printing Office, 1977.

U.S. House of Representatives, Committee on the Judiciary. *Amnesty—Hearings Before the Subcommittee on Courts, Civil Liberties, and the Administration of Justice.* Washington, D.C.: U.S. Government Printing Office, 1974.

U.S. Senate. *Final Report of the Select Committee to Study Governmental Operations with Respect to Intelligence Activities.* Washington, D.C.: U.S. Government Printing Office, 1976.

MAGAZINE AND NEWSPAPER ARTICLES

Alexander, Shana. "Amnesty, Agony and Responsibility." *Newsweek* (March 19, 1973).

Andrews, Bernadette. "Young U.S. Exiles and Their Wives Reject Ford's Amnesty Offer." *The Toronto Star* (September 18, 1974).

Bickel, Alexander M. "Will the Democrats Survive Miami?" *New Republic* (July 15, 1972).

Bingham, Jonathan B. "Replacing the Draft." *New Republic* (January 16, 1971).

Black, Kay Pittman. "Accused Draft Evader May Be Allowed to Return to Canada." *The Press-Scimitar* (January 8, 1976).

————. "Draft Board Violation Draws Probation." *The Press-Scimitar* (undated).

Bundy, William P. "Exporting Political Trouble." *Newsweek* (September 13, 1971).

Chriss, Nicholas C. "Amnesty Critics Infuriate McGovern." *Los Angeles Times* (September 20, 1972).

Church, George J. "Is Bill Clinton for Real?" *Time* (January 27, 1992).

Crawford, Kenneth. "Song My's Shock Wave." *Newsweek* (December 15, 1969).

Donovan, Brian. "The Man Who Beat the Army." *New Republic* (January 31, 1970).

Eayrs, James. "Dilettante in Power: The First Three Years of P. E. Trudeau." *Saturday Night* (April 1971).

————. "The Stupidity of Power." *Saturday Night* (December 1969).

Francis, Diane. "McNamara's Tale Is a 'Self-Serving and Defensive Memoir.' " *The Financial Post* (July 18, 1995).

Frayne, Trent. "U.S. Amnesty: Would Johnny Go Marching Home?" *Toronto Star* (February 19, 1972).

Fulford, Robert. "Our Newest Minority. . . . " *Saturday Night* (November 1968).

Gooding, Richard. "An Exile in My Own Country." *Look* (February 24, 1970).

Gordon, Walter. "Last Chance for Canada." *Maclean's* (September 1972).

Gray, John. "The View from Ottawa." *Maclean's* (January 1972).

Haggart, Ron, and Aubrey Golden. "War Measures." *Maclean's* (February 1971).

Handelman, Stephen. "Draft Dodger Going Home, Admits He's Afraid." *Toronto Star* (September 19, 1974).

Kahin, George. "Negotiations: The View from Hanoi." *New Republic* (November 6, 1971).

Lollar, Michael. "5-Year Probation Given in Draft Board Case." *The Commercial Appeal* (undated).

Mailer, Norman. "The Evil in the Room." *Life* (July 28, 1972).

Margulies, Martin B. "Draft Exiles Who Can Come Home." *Parade* (April 30, 1972).

Mathews, Tom. "Pierre Trudeau Superstar." *Newsweek* (November 6, 1972).

Meryman, Richard. "The Infighting Was Ferocious." *Life* (July 21, 1972).

Montgomery, Charlotte. "Draft Dodgers Fear U.S. Won't Open Door." *Toronto Star* (March 14, 1974).

Morgenthau, Hans J. "What Price Victory?" *New Republic* (February 20, 1971).

Newman, Christina. "Our Heroes on the Russian Front." *Maclean's* (August 1971).

Osborne, John. "Back from Midway." *New Republic* (June 21, 1969).

Parker, Maynard. "The Illusion of Vietnamization." *Newsweek* (September 29, 1969).

Pekkanen, John. "Tragedy at Kent State." *Life* (May 15, 1970).

Poirier, Mormand. "An American Atrocity." *Esquire* (August 1969).

Reston, James, Jr. "Universal Amnesty." *New Republic* (February 5, 1972).

Sallot, Lynne. "Autobiography of a Kent State Survivor." *Toronto Star* (August 8, 1972).

Schlesinger, Arthur, Jr. "Case for George McGovern." *New Republic* (February 26, 1972).

Segal, Clancy. "Harry Pincus: A Tribute." *Amex-Canada* (September 1, 1972).

Spencer, William. "Why They Won't Fight." *Weekend Magazine* (February 7, 1970).

Stewart, Walter. "All Canada Wants for Christmas Is Itself." *Maclean's* (December 1971).

Thomas, William. "Journey into Exile." *The Commercial Appeal* (February 23, 1969).

Wicker, Tom. "Nixon's First Year." *New Republic* (January 24, 1970).

Williams, Roger Neville. "Strong-Arm Rule in Canada." *New Republic* (January 30, 1971).

Index

About the Author

JAMES DICKERSON is a veteran journalist who has written for numerous magazines and newspapers. He is the author of seven books, including *Goin' Back to Memphis* and *Women on Top*.